GAME MISCONDUCT

GAME MISCONDUCT

Alan Eagleson and the Corruption of Hockey

RUSS CONWAY

MACFARLANE WALTER & ROSS

TORONTO

Macfarlane Walter & Ross
37A Hazelton Avenue
Toronto, Canada M5R 2E3

CANADIAN CATALOGUING IN PUBLICATION DATA
AVAILABLE ON REQUEST

The publisher gratefully acknowledges the support
of the Canada Council and the Ontario Arts Council

Printed and bound in the United States

This book is dedicated to two great men:
Irving E. Rogers Jr. and Paul S. Conway Jr.

CONTENTS

	Acknowledgments	xi
1	The Boys Are Back in Town	1
2	The Roots of Revolt	18
3	Inadvertent Damage	43
4	The Walking Wounded	57
5	Simple Acts of Friendship	88
6	Best-Laid Plans	106
7	Betrayal	129
8	In Whose Interest?	151
9	The Million-Dollar Carrot	168
10	Everybody's Banker	181
11	Fast and Loose	198
12	Foreign Exchange	213
13	Nowhere to Hide	229
14	The Wheels of Justice	243
	Epilogue	265
	Photo Credits	271
	Index	273

ACKNOWLEDGMENTS

Long ago, I learned I was working for special people at the *Eagle-Tribune* of Lawrence, Massachusetts, the suburban Boston newspaper that has employed me since 1967. Irving E. Rogers Jr., the publisher, and the Rogers family — which has owned the paper since its inception in 1867 — have been more like family to me than employers. Without their support, and that of Dan Warner, the paper's editor, whose compassion has made me a better reporter over the years, the investigative series from which this book has grown would never have been written.

I'm indebted to many other people at the *Eagle-Tribune*. Thanks to John O'Neil, Bill Burt, Joe Murphy, Mike Muldoon, Hector Longo, Max Bishop, Dave Dyer, Mark Juba, John McLaughlin, Roger Thibodeau, Rodney Thibodeau, Roger Aziz, and Joe Cotton. *Eagle-Tribune* City Editor Al White is the best there is. He guided me through some demanding work.

Thanks also to Gerry Molina, Greg Lang, Fran Sangermano, Brad Goldstein, Ron Pollina, Carl Russo, Marc McGeehan, Chip Rogers, Bill Lucey, Ellen Howard, Laurie D'Amore, Leigh Higginbottom, Melissa Aumais, Corrine Pelletier, Josie Mangano, Anne Sherlock, Paul Calzetta, and *Eagle-Tribune* lawyer Peter Caruso and his staff. Veteran Bruins photographer Al

Ruelle was also a big help.

I can never fully convey the gratitude I feel to my father, and my mother, for an upbringing that stressed honesty, integrity, responsibility, and appreciation. The saddest part of chasing this story down was that it robbed me of time with my dad, Paul S. Conway Jr., who encouraged and supported me from the beginning until he died of cancer at age seventy on November 2, 1993. My brother, Mark, and his family were a godsend during my father's final days, as was my fiancée at the time, Debbie Cassidy, who had the patience of Job. More recently, Sabrina Vigrabs has been patient through the final months of this project, as has Louise Nissel while looking after my ill mother.

Retired Maple Leaf defenseman Carl Brewer and his companion, Sue Foster, went out of their way to help, any time, any place. They provided invaluable information and saved me legwork all over Ontario. To Bruce Dowbiggin, a Toronto CBC-TV sportscaster, I also owe a great debt. Gordie Howe and his wife, Colleen, supplied many documents, as did lawyer Mark Zigler. And I can never thank Bobby Orr enough for his support, or his wife, Peggy, for her uplifting spirit. I applaud the leadership of Andy Moog and many of the executive board members who brought the National Hockey League Players' Association into a new era under the astute leadership of Bob Goodenow. I also applaud the new NHL administration under Commissioner Gary Bettman. I thank them all for their cooperation.

Hundreds of people aided in the collection of information, documents, and interviews over more than five years, and this book could not have been done without their assistance. By their own wishes, six remain confidential. They know who they are, and I am deeply grateful for their help.

My sincere thanks to the following former or current pro hockey players: Fred Ahern, Earl Anderson, Lou Angotti, Don Awrey, Ralph Backstrom, Garnet "Ace" Bailey, Dave Barr, Jamie Bateman, Andy Bathgate, Mike Baumgartner, Bobby Beers, Roger Belanger, Red Berenson, Nick Beverley, Henry Boucha, Ray Bourque, Rick Bowness, Andy Brickley, Ross Brooks, Johnny Bucyk, Gordie Buynak, Lyndon Byers, Guy Carbonneau, Wayne Cashman, Blair Chapman, Gerry Cheevers, Dave Christian, Bill Clement, Geoff Courtnall, Terry Crisp, Gary Croteau, Bruce Crowder, Bob Dailey, Cleon Daskalakis,

John Davidson, Marcel Dionne, Gary Doak, Jim Dorey, Ken Dryden, Woody Dumart, Ron Ellis, Phil Esposito, Tony Esposito, Ferny Flaman, Dave Forbes, Dwight Foster, Jim Fox, Robbie Ftorek, Bob Gainey, Danny Gare, John Garrett, Mike Gartner, Rod Gilbert, Mike Gillis, Butch Goring, Ted Green, Wayne Gretzky, Billy Harris, Jim Harrison, Paul Henderson, Ken Hodge, Ken Hodge Jr., Randy Holt, Gordie Howe, Mark Howe, Harry Howell, Willie Huber, Bobby Hull, Brent Hull, Dave Hynes, Don Jackson, Craig Janney, Stan Jonathan, Trevor Johansen, Mark Johnson, Eddie Johnston, Steve Kasper, Eddie Kea, Doug Keans, Red Kelly, Dave Keon, Gordie Kluzak, Jim Korn, Skip Krake, Tom Kurvers, Dick Lamby, Dave Langevin, Claude Larose, Pierre Larouche, Jeff Lazaro, Reggie Leach, Steve Leach, Reggie Lemelin, Mario Lemieux, Rick Ley, Trevor Linden, Eric Lindros, Ken Linseman, Jim Lorentz, Jack Lynch, Fleming Mackell, Craig MacTavish, Dan Mandich, Frank Mahovlich, Don Marcotte, Nevin Markwart, Rick Martin, Keith McCreary, Brad McCrimmon, Don McKenney, Johnny McKenzie, Peter McNab, Marty McSorley, Rick Middleton, Mike Milbury, Bobby Miller, Doug Mohns, Joey Mullen, Craig Muni, Ron Murphy, Vaclav Nedomansky, Cam Neely, Mike O'Connell, Terry O'Reilly, Bobby Orr, Rosaire Paiement, Wilf Paiement, Brad Park, Al Pedersen, Barry Pederson, Jim Peplinski, Larry Pleau, Dave Poulin, Denis Potvin, Pat Quinn, Craig Ramsay, Jean Ratelle, Mickey Redmond, Dave Reid, Henri Richard, Gordie Roberts, Luc Robitaille, Mike Robitaille, Dale Rolfe, Bobby Rousseau, Tom Rowe, Rocky Saganiuk, Dollard St. Laurent, Derek Sanderson, Eddie Sandford, Jim Sandlak, André Savard, Bobby Schmautz, Milt Schmidt, Norm Schmidt, Al Secord, Eddie Shack, Glen Sharpley, Gregg Sheppard, Dave Silk, Charlie Simmer, Frank Simonetti, Louis Sleigher, Brad Smith, Dallas Smith, Rick Smith, Tom Songin, Fred Stanfield, Allan Stanley, Pat Stapleton, Vic Stasiuk, Scott Stevens, Bob Sweeney, Don Sweeney, Dale Tallon, Marc Tardif, Michael Thelven, Cliff Thompson, Esa Tikkanen, Walter Tkaczuk, Mario Tremblay, Bryan Trottier, Ian Turnbull, Norm Ullman, Rogie Vachon, Carol Vadnais, Pat Verbeek, Ryan Walter, Glen Wesley, Eddie Westfall, Bill White, Doug Wilson, and Murray Wilson.

Thanks also to these former and current hockey officials: Weston Adams Jr., John Ashley, Marcel Aubut, Howard Baldwin, Brian Burke, Munson Campbell, Ron Caron, Don Cherry, Gordie Clark, Murray Costello,

John Dionne, Emile Francis, Len Frizoli, Lloyd Gilmour, Michael Gobuty, Larry Gordon, Richard Gordon, Bob Goodenow, Wally Harris, Heidi Holland, Derek Holmes, Bruce Hood, Harley Hotchkiss, Jeremy Jacobs, Don Johnson, Tom Johnson, Eddie Johnston, Bucky Kane, Mike Keenan, Dr. Louis Kolb, Lou Lamoriello, Ted Lindsay, Ian Macdonald, Bruce McNall, Don Meehan, Paul Mooney, John Muckler, Dennis Murphy, Bryan Murray, Lou Nanne, Will Norris, Brian O'Neill, Jeff Pash, Craig Patrick, Arthur Pincus, Bob Plager, Peter Pocklington, Sam Pollock, Ian Pulver, Bill Putnam, Larry Regan, Gordon Renwick, Ron Roberts, Ron Ryan, Glen Sather, Mike Shanahan, Sam Simpson, Harry Sinden, Neil Smith, Gilbert Stein, Bill Torrey, Frank Udvari, and John Ziegler.

I received invaluable help from experts in various fields, especially pensions, insurance, mortgages, and the law in Canada and the United States. I am grateful to Bob Allan, Chet Arnold, Isabel A. Balon, Mike Barnett, Steve Bartlett, RCMP Staff Sgt. John K. Beer, Mark Belanger, Rick Betterley, Leonard Bloom, Al Bond, Robert Bradshaw, Irv Brewda, Dennis Bykowski, Allan Checkoway, Rick Curran, Charles Curtis, Charles Dettrey, Ted Dipple, George Donaldson, Jim Edgeworth, Lynda Ellis, David Ezekiel, Larry Falconer, Steve Freyer, Ed Garvey, Tony Giovinazzo, Jane Hansen, Robin Ingle, Helen LaPorte, Floyd Laughren, John Leeson, Diane Lusk, James I. McCartney, Robert MacMillan, Sam Meisner, Paul Morris, Bob Murray, Lou Oppenheim, Dennis Paquette, Mark Perrone, Ron Pollina, Larry Rauch, Ron Salcer, Michael Sergi, William H. Shaheen, Rod Stamler, Bob Tierney, Rollie Thompson, Adam Vine, Jim Warlock, and Rich Winter. And a special thanks to Lorraine Mahoney for her expertise.

Many lawyers were consulted along the way, and I thank them for their contributions: Neil Abbott, John Agro, Richard Ben-Veneste, Bill Bittner, David Brown, Bob Caporale, Paul Cavalluzzo, David Dempster, Bill Dermody, Alan Dick, Jean-Paul Doile, Ken Felter, Ed Ferren, Fred Freeman, Michelle Gordon, Keith Hanzel, Michael Healey, Robert Keefe, Larry Latto, Thomas J. Lockwood, Bill McFarland, Richard Park, Martin Oberman, Jim Quinn, Frank Rapp, Louise Hélène Senecal, Brian Smith, Robert Vedatsky, Russ Waddell, Rich Winter, and Mark Zigler. Special thanks to Peter Jacobsen for his thoroughness and professionalism.

Other people who contributed to this project and deserve acknowledgement include: Ian Adams, Marty Alsemgeest, Jane Antonacci, Regina Arthur, Kim Atwood, Roger Baikie, David Baker Sr., Edward Budzban, Elizabeth Carter, Graeme Clark, Rick Curran, Senator Keith Davey, David Dingwall, Marie Hélène Donaldson, Margaret Dougherty, Bill Dovey, John Earle, Victor Fanikos, Bill Fox, Malcolm Gray, George Gross, Bob Haggert, General Alexander Haig, Jane Hansen, Judge Richard Holland, Ron Jakelis, Peter Karmanos Jr., Shane Kelford, Bob Kilger, Timothy J. Lemay, Lloyd Ludwig, Ian McClelland, Dr. Tom McKeam, Roy McMurtry, Stu McLeod, Dennis Mills, Hugh Murphy, Cam Natale, Arnie Patterson, Pat Reid, Senator Louis Robichaud, Ron Robison, Jim Rutherford, Kim Stedman, John Tait, Martin Tauber, Judy Ungerman, Randy Vataha, Patty Walker, Bernard J. Warren, Bill Watters, and Flora Wendling.

Canadian journalists who particularly helped me were Roy MacGregor and Kathryn May of the *Ottawa Citizen*; Mary Ormsby of the *Toronto Star*; author Stevie Cameron; Mike Simpson of the *Toronto Sun*; and Steve Dryden of *The Hockey News*. Thanks all. Many other media colleagues on both sides of the border also offered assistance, for which I'm grateful: Tony Allen, Dave Anderson, Vic Batchelder, Michael Bates, Sandy Bergin, Christie Blatchford, Clark Booth, David Cruise, Kevin Paul Dupont, Bob Edwell, Stan Fischler, Red Fisher, Joe Fitzgerald, Brad Goldstein, Charlie Greenwell, Alison Griffiths, John Gunn, Karen Guregian, Steve Harris, Tom Henshaw, Jim Kelley, Joe Lapointe, Mike Loftus, Will McDonough, Bob McKenzie, Bob McKeown, D. Leo Monahan, Scott Morrison, Mark Mulvoy, Lester Munson, Paul Palango, Bert Raymond, Fran Rosa, Randy Starkman, Al Strachan, Gary A. Uberstine, Mike Ulmer, and Lee Zeidman.

Special thanks to Liz Harrison, Judy Hayes, Colleen Howe, Jennifer Kea, Wendy Muni, and the folks at La Bec Rouge in Hampton Beach, New Hampshire, and Fours in Boston. Thanks to Wendy Thomas for her copy editing and proofreading, and to Liba Berry for the index.

Last but certainly not least, there is the craft of boiling down five years of my life, sorting out all the intertwined stories and characters and incidents and turning them into a book. I am fortunate and appreciative to have worked with the Bobby Orr of editors, Gary Ross, and the unique Toronto publishing company of which he's a partner, Macfarlane Walter & Ross.

1

THE BOYS ARE BACK IN TOWN

"I've had trouble over the years figuring out which side Eagleson's on, the players' or the owners'. He wears so many hats I think even he gets screwed up sometimes."
KEN LINSEMAN

I T WAS HARD TO BELIEVE that twenty years had passed. The faces of the 1970 Boston Bruins hadn't changed much, but some of the waistlines had. Several former players — such as Ken Hodge and a snow-white Johnny McKenzie — showed more than a touch of gray. Dallas Smith was completely bald, but then he'd been nearly bald when he played. So had Wayne Carleton, who caused more than a few double takes when he showed up at the reunion with a full toupee.

It was June 1, 1990, twenty years after Bobby Orr, in midair, had snapped a shot past Glenn Hall in sudden-death overtime, giving the Bruins a four-game sweep of St. Louis and their first Stanley Cup in twenty-nine years. Here they were, back in Boston exactly two decades later, nearly everybody from that championship team except Billy Speer, who had died a few years earlier when his snowmobile plunged through thin ice near Bobcaygeon, Ontario.

Orr had been the driving force behind the reunion, as he had been behind the team, lining up sponsorships, overseeing airline tickets, arranging accommodation. He'd done all this despite being hobbled a month earlier by yet another knee operation, his tenth since 1968. It hadn't gone well, but he'd put off the follow-up arthroscopic surgery until after the reunion. I'd become friends with Orr while covering the Bruins for my paper, the Lawrence *Eagle-Tribune*, in the early 1970s, and we'd remained friendly after his retirement. He'd asked if I'd help him locate some of the sportswriters and broadcasters who had covered the 1970 Bruins.

For the Sunday afternoon of the reunion, Gerry Cheevers had organized an outing to Rockingham Park, a thoroughbred track in Salem, New Hampshire. Phil Esposito, chomping a big cigar, studied *The Racing Form* with Ken Hodge. Ace Bailey and Teddy Green hammed it up, swashbucklers to the end. Chili had been served in crock pots, and the conversation turned to laughter when Bailey and Green put the empty pots on their heads, handles under their chins, like German helmets.

Eddie Johnston, who with Cheevers had backstopped the Bruins to two Stanley Cups in three years — 1970 and 1972 — reminisced with Wayne Cashman about a long-ago night in Chicago. After a few brews, emphasizing a point during a friendly argument, "E.J. kept pounding his hand on the table," Cashman recalled. "Next morning, we're getting ready to go for our morning skate and I spot him over in one corner of the lobby. I say, 'Good morning. Your head okay this morning?' E.J. shakes his head. He's wearing this big fur coat. He opens the front a little and whispers, 'Look at my hand.' His catching hand was puffed out twice its size. He says, 'Shuuussh! Don't say anything.' We took the bus to the Stadium, dressed, and got on the ice as fast as we could. Remember, Eddie?"

Johnston smiled sheepishly.

Dallas Smith picked up the story. "Bobby lobs a shot and Eddie goes down screaming, 'Oh, my hand! My hand!' He skates off to the dressing room. The reporters show up for practice and get a story: 'Johnston hit by Orr shot in practice. Breaks hand. Out for a month!'"

Laughter echoed through the tent and continued all afternoon. Phil Esposito recalled the time at Massachusetts General Hospital when, recovering from knee surgery, he'd been wheeled out by five teammates wearing masks and surgical garb. They pushed him, wheelchair and all, to a local bar, where they stayed for several hours until nurses and doctors noticed he was missing.

"They couldn't get me through the swinging door, so Dallas broke off a piece of aluminum," Esposito remembered. "Harry Sinden sent me the bill two months later. I had to pay it, too, Smitty. Eight hundred bucks!"

Munching an ear of corn, Don Awrey spotted Dallas Smith and me studying *The Racing Form* and waved us over. "Let's team up and pick a winner," he suggested, which nearly made Esposito gag on his cigar.

"Now there's the trifecta of all time. You three guys couldn't pick your noses."

"Aw, come on," said Awrey. "I'm not like you, Espo. I need the money. I'm out of work."

"What do you mean?" I asked Awrey. "What are you doing these days?"

"Nothing," said Awrey. "Need anybody at the paper? Right now things are tight, real tight. There's no work."

I'd known Awrey since covering the 1970 championship team, and liked him. He'd attended several car races I'd been involved with, a hobby and part-time business of mine during the 1970s and 1980s.

"Isn't there something in hockey you can do? Can't somebody help you get into scouting or coaching?"

"Nothing so far. It's starting to get to me. I've got a pension coming, thirteen or fourteen grand, but I can't live off that. It's in Canadian money."

I was again surprised by the paltriness of NHL pensions. A major-league pension paid only $14,000 Canadian, maybe $10,000 U.S., to a player who'd spent sixteen years in the NHL?

"And I contributed extra," said Awrey. "Most players don't even get that."

I suggested he call the union, the NHL Players' Association, for help.

"You kidding me?" said Awrey. "Alan Eagleson help me get a job? He won't even talk to me. He only helps players he represented — the ones who kept him in to run the association, or the ones he was an agent for."

Awrey pointed to ex-players like Bobby Clarke and Tony Esposito, both former presidents of the NHLPA. He felt they had landed good NHL jobs in part because of Eagleson's influence. He pointed out that Bob Pulford, the Chicago general manager whom Eagleson represented, had been well taken care of, and that Mike Keenan, also an Eagleson client, had wound up coaching Team Canada in 1987.

"Al wasn't my agent." Awrey shrugged. "He wouldn't pick up the phone for me."

But Eagleson was the head of the union, I said. When Awrey was playing, Eagleson had negotiated the collective agreements that included benefits — such as pensions — affecting Awrey and the other players for the rest of their lives.

"Eagle kept our salaries down because nobody really knew what the other guy was making. Free agency? That was a joke, too. We got screwed. We're talking about Alan Eagleson, pensions, how he didn't help us over the years," Awrey told Dallas Smith.

Smith, I knew, was not an Eagleson fan. He had said many of the same things to me as far back as 1976. In the summer of 1976, Orr, an Eagleson client, had been allowed to leave the Bruins and sign with Chicago as a free agent, with no compensation to Boston. Bruins president Paul Mooney had filed suit in U.S. federal court, seeking compensation from Chicago, but a Chicago judge had dismissed the suit when Chicago agreed to give the Bruins "future considerations." NHL records do not indicate that any compensation was ever made. "We didn't get anything that I remember," recalled Boston president Harry Sinden, "except a lot of grief."

Dallas Smith had also been having contract trouble with the Bruins and wanted to test the open market. As he pointed out then and reiterated at the reunion, he couldn't sign with another team unless Boston was compensated with either players or draft choices.

"Eagleson was Bobby's agent," said Smith, "and it was okay for Bobby to leave the Bruins for Chicago with nothing in return. But if I got a better offer from another club, the other club was going to have to give up players to sign me. I was ready to sue Eagleson, sue the Players' Association, sue the league for restraint of trade. Damn, I should have done it! There were two sets of rules, one for Eagleson and one for the rest of us."

Smith reminded me that we had talked one night while he was holding out. He had hinted that he and his agent, Mike Carroll, were going to file suit, an echo of the Curt Flood case. Flood had successfully challenged major-league baseball's restrictive free-agency rules in 1970.

"Mike called Eagleson," Smith recalled, "and Eagle told him, 'No way can

4

Dallas sign somewhere else. He's not a free agent without compensation.' Why could Orr go free and not me? Remember?"

I recalled the incident well, because Orr had phoned me not long afterward. "He's going to sue us, isn't he?" Orr kept asking. I said that Smith certainly wasn't going to sue him, but suing Eagleson was a possibility. Orr's association with Eagleson was so close in those days that he spoke of "we" or "us." Orr asked me to pass a message to Smith: it would take years to settle such a suit, so he'd better be prepared to sit out a long while.

"Bobby was ticked off," Smith recalled. "He was my friend. I got to second-guessing myself." Smith gave in, changed his mind about the suit, and signed with the Bruins.

Strange, I thought, that afternoon at the racetrack. Here these same players were, retired now, all these years later, still talking about free agency. Nothing had changed.

NOT THREE WEEKS before the reunion, Ray Bourque and Andy Moog, members of the 1990 Bruins, had raised the same subject with me. I'd known Bourque, the Bruins captain, since he came to Boston in 1979 and lived with Dwight Foster, Al Secord, and Brad McCrimmon in an apartment complex not far from my office. During the 1990 Stanley Cup finals he'd agreed to keep a diary for the *Eagle-Tribune*, and we got together for daily tape-recording sessions. Bourque talked about everything from his pre-game meal to the Bruins' game plan for Edmonton. Each day the paper had published an installment.

One day we ended up talking about free agency. Bourque was happy in Boston and wanted to finish his career with the Bruins, but he couldn't understand why hockey wasn't like baseball, where a player with six years' experience could become an unrestricted free agent, able to sign with any team. Hockey players get only so many years in the NHL — on average, fewer than five — and Bourque wondered why, when a player's contract expired, he shouldn't be able to go to the team willing to offer the best salary. As the NHL's finest defenseman — he had just won the Norris Trophy for the second year in succession — Bourque faced a dilemma in testing the free-agent market under current compensation rules. What team would risk giving up five first-round draft picks, the mandated compensation at the time, or a marquee player of its own, to sign a player of his caliber?

"There's no other business like ours," said Bourque. "If you decided to leave your newspaper because another paper gave you a better deal, would your new paper have to give your old paper five sportswriters? I don't think it's fair. It should have been corrected years ago."

Andy Moog, too, openly questioned the system. The spunky goaltender had left Edmonton after the 1986–87 season, opting to play for Canada in the 1988 Olympics. One of his complaints with the union had to do with salary disclosure, or rather lack of it. He ended up being dealt to Boston in March of 1988.

"For years the NHL kept us in the dark when it came to salaries," Moog had told me before the Bruins reunion. "In order to establish a market by value, we wanted player salary disclosure. Eagleson kept telling us it wasn't a good idea, that what a player made wasn't another player's business. We told each other from time to time, but I always thought if salaries were disclosed, we'd have more competition among the teams trying to sign players. It took forever to get salaries made public because the owners knew we'd have something to compare ourselves to."

GERRY CHEEVERS BREEZED by and asked Awrey and me how we'd done on the last race.

"We're talking about Eagleson, your buddy," Awrey said.

"My buddy?" said Cheevers. "He did a contract for me once and got me something like a fifteen-hundred-dollar raise. Then he sent me the bill. I think it was for three grand. Whatever it was, I lost money on the deal."

Yet another Eagleson story. In the years since Dallas Smith's complaint, I realized, many players had voiced their displeasure with Eagleson. As far back as 1977, Terry O'Reilly, a former Bruins captain, had told me that the owners had Eagleson in their pocket. The feisty O'Reilly claimed that Eagleson had sold out the players in 1977 by agreeing to a one-third buy-out clause in their contracts. The year before, Eagleson had assured the players that their official NHL-NHLPA owner-player contracts guaranteed full pay over the duration of the agreement. Now a team could cut a player and pay him only a third of his

contracted pay. O'Reilly felt Eagleson should have fought to keep the co-
tracts at their full value and challenged him about it at a player rep meeting.

"Eagleson said, 'If you weren't running off getting married, you wouldn't
be asking stupid questions!'" O'Reilly recalled. "I snapped. I said, 'I'm not
supposed to ask a question? Since when are you the Father, the Son, and the
Holy Ghost? I'm not going to put up with this crap!'" O'Reilly walked out.
"He was so sarcastic, so arrogant. He'd talk down to anybody asking a question. Who the hell did he think he was? I quit as player rep then and there.
Mike Milbury was a pretty good friend and I told him, 'You take the job. I
can't put up with somebody who's supposedly representing our best interests
but won't explain why he agrees to a one-third buy-out.'

"From then on," said O'Reilly, "when Eagleson made the rounds at the
beginning of the season for his little pep speech in the dressing room, I
always walked out. I didn't trust him."

Milbury himself later expressed concern about Eagleson. At a bar in the
Queen Elizabeth Hotel in Montreal, on an off-day during the 1979 playoffs,
Milbury told me he was going to openly challenge Eagleson's union leadership. Why, he asked, was Eagleson allowed so many obvious conflicts of
interest? He ran the players' union, but as an agent, he also represented
about 150 NHL players. How could he represent the players properly when
he needed approval from the owners to use players in a Canada Cup tournament? How could he represent players and at the same time represent
coaches and general managers?

Milbury, who had joined the Bruins after graduating from Colgate
University, got more and more worked up. How could Eagleson run the
Canada Cup while doing all these other things? What accounting methods
did he use? What was he doing to help players in need? Why were their
salaries so low compared to salaries in other sports? Why had Eagleson over-
seen an NHL-WHA merger when it killed competition for players?

For the most part, Milbury's questions fell on deaf ears, and his mini-
revolt eventually fizzled. But it wasn't long before other players picked up
the theme. During the 1980–81 season Brad Park, one of the all-time-great
Bruins defensemen, told me he didn't like the way Eagleson ran the NHLPA.
A union vice president, Park felt outmanned by player reps he believed were

, rubber-stamping whatever Eagleson wanted them to.
deck, said Park, hand-picking the president and vice
o formal election by the membership: "It was run by
...en for Eagleson."

...c Milbury, Park pointed to Eagleson's many conflicts of interest. How could one man serve as executive director of the union, run an agent business that represented some (but not all) of the union members, and run the Canada Cup tournament as well? Park felt the NHLPA job should have been full-time and questioned how much time the ubiquitous Eagleson actually spent on union business.

During the 1980–81 season, Phil Esposito, another of the great Bruins, retired as a player. That summer I ended up in a foursome with him at a charity golf tournament at Andover Country Club, north of Boston. The conversation got around to Johnny Bucyk, a former Bruin who, after the 1971–72 season, had turned down a better offer from the rival World Hockey Association. Bucyk opted to stay in Boston, unlike his teammates Derek Sanderson, Johnny McKenzie, and Gerry Cheevers, all of whom signed fat contracts with WHA teams. Esposito shook his head at the memory. He was making a good salary in Boston at the time, he said, but Bucyk should have taken the money and run.

Esposito had been president of the NHL Players' Association when the NHL-WHA merger took place in 1979. Eagleson had come to him at the summer meetings in Nassau, he said, and done some arm-twisting to get him to support the merger. Eagleson promised that player pensions would be increased by league owners if the players voted for the merger. Esposito wasn't convinced the merger was a good idea, he said, but he took a long walk on the beach the night before the vote. In the end, he urged the other players to support the merger.

Esposito said he asked Eagleson exactly what the players were getting out of it but never did get a clear answer. His understanding was that a lump sum from the expansion fees collected by NHL owners from the new teams would go directly to the players' pension fund. But he never followed up. "I still don't know what we got out of it," Esposito said on the golf course.

At Eagleson's urging, Esposito had helped the NHL owners drive a stake through the heart of the competition while they collected $24 million from Edmonton, Hartford, Quebec, and Winnipeg, the four WHA teams admitted to the NHL. The NHL players had supported the merger, yet not even their union's president understood what they received in return.

A year later, I spoke at length with Gregg Sheppard about Eagleson. Sheppard had been a talented Bruins center in the 1970s and a friend who lived during the season in Boxford, north of Boston. Before the 1978–79 season, he was part of a three-way swap that landed him in Pittsburgh. When his career ended, after the 1981–82 season, he spoke blisteringly of the way Eagleson operated. He claimed that NHL careers had been shortened because of the WHA merger, that NHLPA information on the union's operation was vague at best, and that it was time things changed. He thought somebody should look into Eagleson's business practices. What actually happened to Canada Cup money? Nobody seemed to know. Why was Eagleson so friendly with NHL owners, Sheppard wondered, and with league president John Ziegler?

ROSAIRE PAIEMENT GOT TALKING about some of the same things when I visited him in Florida in 1984. I'd first met Paiement after a Boston-Vancouver game in 1971, when he fought Bobby Orr twice. It was the only time I ever saw Orr get the tar beaten out of him; in the second fight, Paiement burst the stitches over Orr's eye that were the result of their earlier scrap. "He came looking for a fight," Paiement said afterward in the dressing room. "I'm not going to back down, whether it's Bobby or another player. It's part of my job. No big deal."

Years later, after his own career ended with an eye injury suffered in a fight with Dave Semenko, Paiement bought the Coral Plaza Motel in Fort Lauderdale. He put in a sports bar, The Penalty Box, and it was there, one night in 1984, that we talked about Eagleson. Paiement, too, wondered about Eagleson's role in the demise of the WHA, which eliminated competition for players. He also told me that his brother's money had been used in various loans orchestrated by Eagleson.

Wilf Paiement, ten years younger than Rosaire, had been the second overall NHL draft pick in 1974. Eagleson had been his agent, although Bill Watters, an Eagleson employee at the time, did much of the work. Paiement insisted that some of his brother's money had been loaned to Bobby Orr in the mid-1970s for the Orr–Walton Sports Camp in Orillia. Eagleson, said Paiement, also invested some of Wilf's money in the Cleveland Barons NHL team before the team folded in 1977.

"Wait a minute," I said. "Your brother was playing for one NHL team while he had money invested in another? Even Eagleson wouldn't pull a stunt like that. And Wilf made a loan to Bobby Orr?"

Suppose Shaquille O'Neal of the Orlando Magic had money invested in the Phoenix Suns, or made a loan to Charles Barkley for a basketball camp, when the two men were opponents on the court. This would be a clear-cut conflict, not permitted, I believe, in any other major sport. Was Paiement certain of his facts? He said he was and predicted that Eagleson would end up president of the NHL. He pointed again to the NHL-WHA merger, which, he said, had saved the owners a ton of money.

A few months after my visit with Paiement, in the summer of 1984, *Sports Illustrated* published a piece that centered on Eagleson's conflicts of interest. Entitled "The Man Who Rules Hockey," the article, by John Papanek and Bill Brubaker, dealt with the central issue the players had spoken about: Eagleson's simultaneous roles as union boss, player agent, international hockey czar, and friend of NHL management. Though the article was highly critical and prompted threats of legal action, Eagleson escaped unscathed.

The collective agreement that he had negotiated on behalf of the NHLPA in 1981 expired in 1986. The players were keen on securing free agency in the new agreement, so that they could shop their services when their contracts expired. Under Eagleson's leadership, however, they settled instead for an improved pension plan. By the terms of the agreement, skaters with 400 NHL career games, and goaltenders with about half that many, would receive a lump-sum $250,000 cash pension at age fifty-five.

Not long after the new deal was struck, I got talking with Tom Johnson in his Bruins office. A Hall of Fame defenseman and the Bruins assistant general manager at the time, Johnson was a fan of Eagleson's. "How can you help but like the guy?" he once said. "Particularly you writers. No matter what he does, he's always good for a story, right?"

I asked him about the collective agreement. Johnson, wearing his customary bow tie, leaned back in his office chair. "That's a helluva deal they got," he said. "Imagine, a pension of 250 grand for playing 400 games."

Indeed, on the face of it, it wasn't a bad deal for the players. Mike Milbury even came out of retirement just to qualify for the so-called senior player benefit. But the more I thought about it, the less sense it made. Why would any player, in his mid-twenties, say, agree to a $250,000 pension thirty years down the line rather than pushing for free agency? If he was making $100,000 in 1986 and had a crack at doubling his pay if teams were free to compete for his services, why wouldn't he take the dollars earlier in life, before inflation had eroded their value? Besides, what was the real cost of a team's pension contribution for a player who wouldn't collect for thirty years? Not much. The pension seemed a cheap price for the owners to pay to avoid free agency.

I raised the question one day with Ken Linseman, who had been traded to the Bruins by Edmonton in 1984. Linseman, a speedy center nicknamed The Rat, was financially astute; he may be the only Boston player I've ever seen, after practice, turning to the financial pages ahead of the sports page.

"We would have been better off sticking to free agency," Linseman said. "But what do you expect from Eagleson? He pushed the deal through. I've had trouble over the years figuring out which side he's on, the players' or the owners'. He wears so many hats I think even he gets screwed up sometimes."

In 1988, an unexpected voice joined the chorus of disapproval of Eagleson's methods. The Stanley Cup finals that year featured the Bruins, coached by Terry O'Reilly, against the defending-champion Edmonton Oilers. The annual Stanley Cup Final luncheon was held in Boston on the off-day between Games 3 and 4 of the series. Walking out of the hotel after the luncheon, I heard somebody shout my name. There in a white stretch limo was Ace Bailey, the former Bruin who was now an Edmonton scout.

"Hey, Russ! Want a ride? Hop in."

Bailey asked where I was headed. I told him my car was parked in its usual place near the Garden. He said traffic was tied up — why not go for a beer at Champions? "Ninety-nine already took off," Bailey said. "We'll grab him by the ears."

Wayne Gretzky had just had his wavy locks trimmed to a near crew cut, which gave him a jug-eared look. "There he is," said Bailey. "Looks like the Comanches got hold of him." Gretzky, amazingly, was able to walk down a busy street in downtown Boston during the Stanley Cup finals unrecognized — his haircut probably had the desired effect. As the limo pulled alongside, Bailey leaned out the window and, in a high-pitched voice, said, "Hey, Blondie! Wanna go for a ride?" Gretzky smiled and hopped in.

Bailey introduced me as a writer friend who went back to the Bruins' Stanley Cup years in the early 1970s. We slipped into a back room at Champions, a sports bar in the Copley Marriott Hotel, and for the next couple of hours swapped stories. The conversation got around to Bobby Orr. Reference was made to Orr's departure from Boston to Chicago in 1976, and the fact that he failed to finish his playing career in Boston because Bruins owner Jeremy Jacobs didn't want to pay to keep him — or so everyone believed at the time.

Gretzky compared Orr's situation back then to his own with Edmonton owner Peter Pocklington. He said he thought this would be his final season in Edmonton; he understood that a trade was being discussed because Pocklington wanted to unload his salary. This irked Gretzky no end because he had given everything to help make Edmonton a great team — the Oilers had won three Stanley Cups in four years — and he'd made Pocklington a bundle in the process.

I wondered aloud how much money Pocklington had made because of Gretzky. Gretzky shrugged. Bailey said it was like the Canada Cup — nobody really knew what the numbers were. Gretzky laughed. "Talk about cooking the books. God only knows what Al's done there."

I asked what he meant. Gretzky said that the players didn't get much information about the Canada Cup tournaments. Detailed accounting of income and expenses wasn't made available to the NHLPA. Eagleson ran the show. The players weren't informed about TV rights, gate receipts, and advertising. Gretzky said he almost didn't play in the 1987 Canada Cup tournament but was talked into it by Glen Sather, the Edmonton coach and general manager, a pal of Eagleson's, and a Team Canada general manager that year. Gretzky said he had never complained about Eagleson's stranglehold on the Canada Cup because he didn't want to look like a troublemaker. People might take it the wrong way. After all, during international tournaments he was playing for his country, and supposedly for all other NHL players; Eagleson claimed that Canada Cup proceeds fattened the pension fund.

The conversation at Champions ended when Janet Jones, Gretzky's fiancée, showed up to join him for dinner at the Bailey home in Lynnfield, north of Boston.

Next morning, before Edmonton's game-day skate, I encountered Gretzky in the corridor near the Oilers' dressing room. Again I asked him, "You really think Eagleson plays games with the Canada Cup books?"

Gretzky flashed his white teeth. "He doesn't run it for nothing, believe me."

The Oilers went on to sweep the Bruins and win the Stanley Cup again. Gretzky, as he'd predicted, was traded that summer. Los Angeles owner Bruce McNall sent Martin Gelinas, Jimmy Carson, three first-round draft picks, and $15 million to the Oilers, a story that dominated the hockey world.

Meanwhile, more rumors were swirling about Eagleson. More players were questioning his business dealings and his stewardship of the NHLPA. Steve Kasper, a teammate of Gretzky's in Los Angeles after being traded by the Bruins in early 1989, told me that Eagleson was under scrutiny by two player agents, Rich Winter and Ron Salcer. Kasper said that a move was afoot to replace Eagleson. The agents had evidently done some checking into him. Kasper said things were going to come to a head at the annual NHLPA meetings that spring in Florida. He said he expected that the union would wind up with a new executive director.

At the 1989 meetings in Palm Beach, the players had learned about loans Eagleson made from NHLPA funds to his own friends and associates. Millions of dollars had been loaned out, apparently, yet not one player said he knew about it. The players also learned that the $250,000 lump-sum pension, negotiated by Eagleson in 1986, was actually coming out of a pension surplus, not from new contributions. Kasper was furious. "My mind's made up," he told me. "I don't feel comfortable with Eagleson at all. He's been in there way too long and we need a new director."

Kasper said the players were forming a search committee to replace him. Another meeting had been scheduled for July to resolve the matter. But that meeting, it turned out, was postponed, and Kasper was unable to make the rescheduled meeting, at which Eagleson was returned to power. The players were led to believe that an audit report had endorsed his handling of NHLPA funds, and they voted 29–0 to keep him on as executive director.

THE FOLLOWING SEASON, 1989–90, during a game at the Boston Garden, I wound up sitting beside Gordie Howe in the press box. Between periods we got chatting. Howe was working for the Hartford Whalers. He made a remark about "us retired players" having to work "because we sure can't live off the pensions we get." I asked how much his pension was. "Oh, I'm too embarrassed to tell you," he said sheepishly. Fifty thousand? "I wish," Howe laughed. "Nothing like that."

Howe had played until he was fifty-two years old. He'd put in an astonishing thirty-two pro seasons, twenty-six in the NHL. "Your pension's got to be up there, after all those years," I said, "with the extra pension money from the Canada Cup and NHL-Soviet exhibition games."

"That's Eagleson's propaganda," said Howe. "Those games didn't mean diddly-squat to us retired players. We got a little increase a couple of years ago, but not much." His pension, he said, was "somewhere around thirteen or fourteen thousand, mostly in Canadian money. My wife knows about those things better than I do, but it's not much, I can tell you that. I'm not complaining. I've had a great life in hockey. I learned a long time ago if you can't say something good about somebody, don't bother talking about them. But the man who was supposedly looking after our interests, running the Players' Association, it turns out he didn't do such a good job." If he'd spent twenty-six years on an assembly line, Howe said, or digging ditches for the city, he'd have had a better pension.

Late that season another of the great players expressed similar sentiments. Jean Béliveau shook his head and called the NHL pension "a damned disgrace." "Look at what happened to Doug Harvey," he said of his former teammate, a Hall of Fame defenseman who died a pauper in 1989. Béliveau said he thought the NHLPA and the league should upgrade the pensions of retired players as well as current players in the new collective bargaining agreements. He was one of the fortunate ones, he said, having been taken on by the Canadiens' front office. But many players who helped build the game, he said, had fallen through the cracks.

At the reunion of the 1970 Boston team that summer, then, the grumbling about Eagleson came as no surprise. What did surprise me was Don Awrey's claim that Eagleson wouldn't even help him find a job. The night after the racetrack outing, the former players all gathered at Guest Quarters Suites Hotel. Fred Stanfield, Rick Smith, John Adams, and Jim Lorentz were chatting when the subject of Eagleson came up. They all felt he had been too cozy with management and agreed that the players had been almost afraid of him.

Phil Esposito joined in. He made the point that Eagleson's modus operandi was to embarrass or bully anybody who questioned him. "I asked him a simple question one time at a players' meeting, and he took my head off in front of everybody! He'd call you every name in the book, make you feel dumb. He'd say, 'You stupid or what? You're the one who plays hockey. We're doing it this way.'" Esposito said he quickly learned to keep his mouth shut. If Eagleson could talk that way to a veteran star like Esposito, younger players weren't going to risk looking foolish in front of their peers.

Esposito did a little skit, pretending in one voice to be a player asking a question, and in another to be Eagleson replying, illustrating Eagleson's way of intimidating men who didn't think twice about dropping their gloves during a game but didn't have the nerve to stand up for themselves in a meeting. Esposito said he had to be careful what he said because he soon hoped to be "part of management," heading up a group planning to put an expansion team in Tampa. He mentioned that he thought Eagleson was involved in a competing group.

"What's that?" I said. "Eagleson's going to be an owner, too?"

Esposito shrugged it off — just something he'd heard through the grapevine. Rumors were rampant at the time about who was lobbying league officials or trying to arrange financing for possible expansion teams.

Driving home that night, my feelings were mixed. The reunion had been great; it was a treat to be included. Overall, the 1970 Bruin team members had done well. Orr was firmly established again, having moved from Chicago back to Boston. Esposito had bounced back after being jettisoned as general manager of the Rangers. Wayne Cashman was an assistant coach with the New York Rangers. Eddie Westfall, Derek Sanderson, Gerry Cheevers, Johnny Bucyk, and Jimmy Lorentz were all hockey broadcasters. Eddie Johnston was again an NHL general manager, with Hartford. Fred Stanfield had a furniture business in Buffalo. Johnny McKenzie worked for a bank.

But what about Ron Murphy, who hadn't made it to the reunion because, I gathered, he was down and out, working occasionally as a carpenter in Hagersville, Ontario? And what about Awrey, for sixteen years the embodiment of the selfless, journeyman NHL defenseman? It didn't seem right that he had nobody to turn to at the NHLPA, and no faith in an executive director who was supposedly looking out for the best interests of NHL players past and present.

Why, I wondered, were the pensions so low? Why hadn't the players ever taken control of their own association? Why did no one seem to know the financial details of the Canada Cup tournaments? How had Eagleson managed to finesse the NHL-WHA merger? What had happened between his threatened ouster in 1989 and his unanimous re-election as executive director? What about his rumored work for a prospective new franchise? Why did current players like Ray Bourque and Andy Moog sound so much like the retired Bruins? Twenty years had passed, but little seemed to have changed.

Driving home after the reunion break-up party, I had a flashback of Don Awrey's bloodied face, mashed against the glass, during a game against the Rangers. Awrey epitomized a whole generation of hockey players that today's young fan wouldn't recognize but that I grew up admiring: blue-collar guys who gave their all, played hurt, sacrificed themselves for the team and the game they loved, but who were discarded the moment their usefulness ended.

Dan Warner, my editor at the paper, used to hammer away about the lackadaisical approach of most sportswriters. Every time an Eagleson story had come up in the past, I realized, I'd been guilty of sportswriter's syndrome, caring more about who won and lost than about the sport's underpinnings. Reporting game results was easier than digging into more complex issues. But Awrey's words at the reunion stayed with me, and I promised myself I'd look into it further.

2

THE ROOTS OF REVOLT

"What we found can only be described as a scandal."

ED GARVEY

THE 1989 PALM BEACH meetings seemed a good place to start. By then, a couple of hundred NHL players unhappy with Eagleson had hired Ed Garvey to produce an assessment of their union's leadership. Garvey, a labor lawyer and former head of the NFL Players' Association, worked closely with the agents who had long been suspicious of Eagleson's methods, Rich Winter and Ron Salcer, as well as three Ontario lawyers, John Agro, Bill Dermody, and David Dempster. They produced a fifty-five-page document, "Confidential Report to NHLPA Members." The copy I obtained made for fascinating reading.

"If any other union leader did what Alan Eagleson has done over the past 22 years, the news media would be screaming for an investigation," Garvey informed the players. "The conflicts of interests are shocking, but even more shocking is a pattern of sweetheart agreements with the NHL over all these years." The report stated that "no benefits of any significance were achieved in the entire decade of the 80's through collective bargaining.

"Alan Eagleson may well be the most overpaid executive in the labor movement in North America. Not even the president of the two million member Teamsters union comes close to Alan in wages, benefits, pension and expense accounts." Eagleson never submitted "his new contract to the members for a vote or review of any kind," Garvey reported, nor had the full NHLPA membership "ever been allowed to vote for the president of the Association or for the executive director." As Brad Park had told me years earlier, the union officers were indeed "appointed, not elected."

"Alan Eagleson refused to provide information that is required by law to be made available to all union members," Garvey told the players. "The deliberate decision to avoid United States Labor Law requirements regarding the filing of financial disclosure statements is a major error in judgment." Garvey believed there was "a legitimate question whether there is, in fact, a 'players' association.' For the most part, it seems that Alan runs the Association as his private preserve rather than a union for players."

If many players were troubled by Eagleson's ties to the NHL owners and president, Garvey was appalled. "[Eagleson] admits that John Ziegler is one of his best friends and Bill Wirtz [owner of the Chicago Blackhawks], who lives near him in Florida, is an extremely close friend despite the fact that Wirtz is the chief negotiator for the NHL. [Eagleson] does not take bargaining seriously because he is comfortable with the cozy relationship that has been so good for him." Indeed, Garvey suggested that the Eagleson-Ziegler-Wirtz relationship made negotiations a "charade."

Just before the 1986 collective bargaining talks were to begin in Florida, Larry Latto, a lawyer paid by the players, had dramatically announced that Eagleson would resign without a new contract for himself. Stunned, the players had asked what they could do. Latto told them Eagleson would give them five minutes to decide if they wanted him to stay. To remain, Eagleson demanded a six-year contract in writing. With collective bargaining due to begin that afternoon, the players, also concerned that Eagleson might go to work for the NHL, agreed to give him what he later called "a guaranteed, no-cut, no-trade deal with a lifetime pension."

This gun-to-the-head contract, Garvey reported, called for Eagleson to "devote approximately 60-65% of his working time annually to Association matters. He is his own boss...and there are no rules governing Eagleson's conduct or conflicts." Eagleson's contract included the car of his choice, and the NHLPA, Garvey noted, had been charged expenses of "$43,269 for the past two years. One suspects a fleet of cars could be leased for $21,000 per year."

As for Eagleson's pension, Garvey called it "the most generous in the history of the National Hockey League...$50,000 (U.S.) for life. And it is guaranteed." He compared Eagleson's pension to the players'. "Your pension plan, according to the Trust document adopted in 1987 says: 'After June 30, 1986, all amounts contributed for players for service in any category are no longer guaranteed.' Think about that. Your contributions are not guaranteed as of the last collective bargaining agreement but Alan's are because they are putting aside money every year for his pension." What's more, NHL player pensions were to be paid in Canadian dollars, Eagleson's in U.S. currency. Eagleson's contract also specified that any dispute "be settled by arbitration in accordance with the rules of the American Arbitration Association." Yet the contract Eagleson negotiated for the players made NHL president John Ziegler — the owners' puppet — the arbitrator in most player disputes.

Garvey also looked at Eagleson's role in international hockey. In a March 13, 1989, letter to players, Eagleson had insisted he received no benefit from any international hockey event. Garvey revealed that, in fact, Eagleson received a $25,000 bonus from each Canada Cup tournament or Soviet tour if the Players' Association generated a $600,000 profit from it. "We have asked Hockey Canada to tell us how much money goes to Alan, his law firm, holding companies he controls, family members or other legal entities. The result of our investigation is a big goose egg. The Hockey Canada spokesman, Ron Robinson [Robison] told me: 'We cannot tell you how much money went to Eagleson without Alan's permission, but he has the information if he wants to share it with you.'...And, the man with the information, Alan Eagleson, won't give us the answer.

"While [Eagleson] has always maintained that he 'doesn't make a dime from international hockey,' former employees dispute that and now he admits that Hockey Canada pays some 'overhead.' How much overhead? He won't say. Does he get money from promoting International Hockey; from rink-board advertising as one player assured us he does?"

The report quoted the 1984 *Sports Illustrated* article: "A general manager was quoted by SI as follows: 'Al delivers us the players and we give him international hockey. It's that simple.' ... Alan wants to head international hockey. He can only do so if the NHL owners and Ziegler agree. Therefore, he must not do things at the bargaining table to antagonize them too much or they will dump him — simple as that."

Eagleson had always persuaded players to participate in international hockey events like the Canada Cup by telling them that they were bolstering player pensions. "Unquestioning players have participated for years in international hockey to help the pension fund," Garvey wrote. "Only now do we understand that the money goes to reduce the club's contribution to the pension plan.

"For years Alan Eagleson has bragged that International Hockey brings 'millions of dollars into the player pension fund.' What he forgot to say... is that the money earned by the Association goes to offset the contribution from the NHL Clubs!...[Eagleson] has refused to show us how any additional pension benefits have been gained as a result of these efforts by countless players over the past 13 years. In clear violation of federal law, players have not been provided pension documents so they know what is in their pension....By law, pension plans must send a summary description of the plan to all plan participants, active and retired. You have never received one."

And there was this revelation about the lump-sum pension for players with 400 or more games, part of the 1986 agreement: "The $250,000 benefit did not cost management one dime. The money was reallocated within the pension plan....Instead of improving your pension benefits, or those of retired players, they took the money and put it into a new benefit to make a five year [agreement] more attractive."

Garvey also delved into Eagleson's apparent conflicts, including his representation of individual players. "This flagrant conflict of interest continues under the contract your lawyer gave Alan in 1986, despite a ruling in the United States that it is not permissible for an agent to also head a union." The star players in Eagleson's private business, said Garvey, had "different concerns than the player on a two-way contract struggling to stay up in the NHL." Eagleson earned much more as an agent than he did representing the union. How could union members not personally represented by Eagleson have their best interests looked after by him?

Eagleson's clients included players, coaches, general managers, "and other corporations having involvement with hockey." "When I hire a lawyer to represent me in court," Garvey wrote, "I want his undivided loyalty.... I don't even like my lawyer to be friendly with his opposing lawyers....I have been in all kinds of bargaining situations and I have never had any doubt which side I was on, and the people across the table had no doubt either....When you head a union, you are in a special position of trust. Your actions will change the lives of the people you represent, for good or ill. That is a heavy responsibility. If you agree with management that freedom of contract is bad for the game because owners will lose money, you can't give 100% effort to the players who say they want free agency."

Another area of conflict centered on Eagleson's building on Maitland Street in Toronto. Among expenses paid by the players was $49,000 in rent. "Alan bought a building in Toronto called Maitland House. Soon thereafter, he moved the NHLPA into the building. He says he got independent appraisals on the building but nevertheless, he was bargaining with himself....How does he decide who fixes the plumbing? I would want the executive director driving a hard bargain with the landlord."

Garvey also raised questions about $829,062 in Players' Association expenses "without any supporting documentation for our inspection." According to the report, Eagleson spent more money for meetings, promotions, office expenses, international hockey, car, and donations "than the players pay in dues in one year!"

"Alan Eagleson has helped the NHL," Garvey wrote, "by paving the way for, (a) elimination of a competitive league; and, (b) elimination of competition for players within the NHL monopoly. We will now see how he handles the third element important to control — keeping you in the dark. Monopolies operate best in secrecy. Remember, you are the game, and if they can control your salaries, profit is guaranteed.

"He put down the WHA and he helped bring about the merger without providing any protection for players, and he agreed to the 1/3 buy-out provision" — just as Terry O'Reilly had insisted when he quit as the Bruins player rep in the late 1970s. "He led the first sports union to accept, in negotiations, the equalization rule....He worked with management to keep potential free agents in the web of restrictions....At the Florida meeting, he failed to produce even one document to support his claim that the NHL pays 45% of gross to players. He had to admit, under questioning, that his estimate of millions for the pension fund were false....

"Alan Eagleson has been a vital part of the NHL establishment," Garvey concluded. "He has contributed greatly to keeping salaries down, profits up. He has helped maintain monopoly status, he keeps players tied up, he allows the League to control through non-impartial arbitration; he eliminates freedom whenever it raises its head; and he keeps you in the dark about the economics of the League while singing management's song about the 'fragile' NHL....Our conclusion is that Alan has never fully disclosed the extent of his conflicts to the members of the NHLPA."

Strong stuff. With Garvey's report in hand, I couldn't imagine why the players kept Eagleson. Nor could I understand why the report had been largely pooh-poohed by the sportswriting media, even considering Eagleson's power and his generally good relationships with them. The report was a goldmine, revealing half a dozen seams worth following. I figured there was enough there to keep me going for the next six months.

I was off by about five years.

BACK IN THE DAYS when I promoted auto races in New England, I'd found a useful book called *Law of Professional and Amateur Sports*. It had also been a help when legal issues came up in my work at the *Eagle-Tribune*. I dug out my copy and discovered a chapter called "National Hockey League Contract Negotiations." The chapter was written by John Chapman and Arthur M. Gans, both members of the Law Society of Upper Canada; Gans was chairman of the Civil Litigation Subsection of the Canadian Bar Association between 1981 and 1983.

This passage on NHL pensions caught my eye: "The plan is funded by the teams and by revenues from international hockey series in which NHL players participate. During the course of the negotiations of the last CBA [collective bargaining agreement] the club owners also agreed, subject to regulatory approval, to transfer to the NHLPA a substantial portion of the surplus that had accrued under the previous plan. This plan is to be adminis-tered by the NHLPA."

If this was true, Eagleson was overseeing surplus money from the pen-sion plan. Where did this money go? As I soon learned, Carl Brewer, the former Maple Leaf defenseman, had by then been asking the same question of the National Hockey League Pension Society, operated by league officials, for nearly a year, with no satisfactory answer.

The restrictive free agency in pro hockey was compared to free agency in the NBA, NFL, and major-league baseball. "Only hockey significantly varies from the pattern," the law book noted. "Critics of the NHLPA assert this is proof that the association has not vigorously guarded the players' best inter-ests. Whatever the reasons and the consequences, the hockey negotiating pattern has been one of accommodation between labor and management."

The NHL owners had put down Ted Lindsay's attempt at organizing the players in 1957. There was no players' union until Eagleson formed one in 1967. Hockey did not have a collective bargaining agreement until 1976. The authors noted, "Despite expectations that substantial divisiveness might sur-face, the 1986 negotiations moved rapidly and smoothly. A new agreement was reached well in advance of the season." They observed: "Professional hockey has avoided player strikes, which is not surprising in light of the league's negotiation history."

Reviewing that negotiation history, I wondered if it was mere coinci-dence that Eagleson had signed the first collective agreement in May 1976, just four months before the first Canada Cup series. Or that the NHL-WHA merger immediately preceded the 1980 Olympics, when Eagleson ran Hockey Canada's international committee. Was it coincidence that a new agreement was struck in 1981, another Canada Cup year, and included provision for a 1984 Canada Cup? Or that the latest agreement, in 1986, immediately pre-ceded the 1987 Canada Cup tournament?

If the NHL board of governors refused to give Eagleson permission to use NHL players, there would have been no real Canada Cup. There may have been a tournament, but without bona fide NHL stars it would have been a second-rate affair and a hard sell to sponsors. As Ed Garvey had pointed out, Eagleson needed the owners' cooperation.

The law book talked about an agent's fiduciary duties, his "obligation not to have any undisclosed conflicts of interest." The Eagleson-Wirtz-Orr deal, when Orr left Boston, seemed rife with conflict. As chairman of the NHL board of governors, Bill Wirtz was the most powerful owner. In delivering Orr to Chicago, Eagleson had seemingly put his own interests ahead of his responsibility, as executive director of the Players' Association, to all NHL players, including Orr's teammate Dallas Smith.

The law book addressed free agency, the core issue after Orr's move: "NHL contracts have always contained clauses limiting a player's right to sign with another club at the expiration of his contract. Obvious antitrust implications arise as to the enforceability of such provisions...." As Dallas Smith had suggested, the free-agency rules — which had been unilaterally changed after Orr's move to Chicago, requiring compensation from a player's new team to his old one — were highly restrictive. Eagleson had seen the competitive advantages of free agency when he sought offers at the end of Orr's Bruins contract. Why, three years later, would he push the NHLPA to approve the NHL-WHA merger, thereby reducing competition and allowing the NHL to bring back punitive compensation rules that discouraged the signing of free agents?

"NHL player salaries rapidly escalated in the 1970s at the time of the WHA," wrote the authors, "to the extent that many clubs suffered severe financial losses. Since the demise of the WHA, a major subject of negotiation between the NHLPA and the member clubs has been the content of free-agency rules. The free-agency rules have often been criticized by agents as being slanted heavily in favor of the clubs. The rejoinder of the executive of the NHLPA has been that it negotiates on a great number of issues with the clubs and that one contractual provision cannot be viewed in isolation from the entire package of rights given to the players pursuant to the CBA."

But that one provision — free agency — was the key to salaries. And what was the major issue for players, whose careers lasted, on average, only four and a half seasons? Salaries, most would answer. Eagleson had let free agency, and its escalating effect on salaries, slip away during a golden opportunity to get something in return for approving the NHL-WHA merger.

Another section of the book dealt with the NHL entry draft. Ken Linseman, the former Bruin, had earlier gone to court over the league's draft rules. As an outstanding junior with Kingston in the Ontario Hockey Association, Linseman had scored 114 goals in two seasons. In 1977 he signed to play with Birmingham of the WHA. Though he really wanted to play in the NHL, the league effectively practiced age discrimination, preventing anyone under twenty from doing so. Linseman took the NHL to court, where the drafting arrangement between the NHL and WHA was found to violate antitrust rules. The NHL was compelled to make eighteen-year-old players eligible for the draft.

Linseman did this with no help from Eagleson and the NHL Players' Association. In fact, he said, Eagleson was abrasive and uncooperative. "It was a right-to-work issue," Linseman recalled. "I had a right to go out and earn the best income I could, and they were trying to stop me. Eagleson wouldn't give us the right time of day."

IN EARLY JULY, 1990, I called Eagleson's home in the Rosedale section of Toronto. I'd prepared a list of questions growing out of the Garvey report. I reached him on the first try. He was his usual salty-tongued self.

"Russ Conway? Haven't heard from you in ages. What the fuck you been up to? You still at the newspaper?" I said I was. "Making lots of fuckin' money, I hope. What's up?"

I told him I was working on a story for the *Eagle-Tribune* and wanted to ask him about NHL pensions, his involvement in international hockey, and Ed Garvey's report.

So much for the long-lost-friend tone. He'd "gone through that shit already," he said, been cleared of mismanagement, and wasn't going to waste his time.

"Just a few minutes?"

"Nope. Good luck to you. Bye."

The next day I phoned his office. When I said I was calling from Boston, I was put through promptly. This time I barely got out "Hello" before he jumped on me. He'd already said no interview. Who did I think I was?

I'd always been on pretty good terms with Eagleson. Back when Orr played for Boston, Eagleson had been a pipeline. Our paper broke the story when Orr left the Bruins, and Eagleson gave me another exclusive on the eve of the NHL-WHA merger. His icy tone during these two brief phone conversations made me think that Ed Garvey had been on the mark.

I WAS AT MY DESK at the paper one night when the phone rang. It was Terry O'Reilly.

"Russ, this you? I've got to see you right away. It's an emergency."

"What happened?"

O'Reilly, a rough-and-tumble, give-it-all player with Boston, and subsequently the team's fiery coach, was just as emotional away from the rink. I'd known him since he broke into pro hockey as a rookie with the old Boston Braves, a Bruins' minor-league team. Over the years we'd become good friends. He's an intensely loyal man, deeply sensitive, with a big heart. These days he manages his commercial real estate in Massachusetts and New Hampshire.

"It's about Evan."

Terry's younger son had battled a liver disease since birth. Doctors had advised for years that Evan would need a transplant. We agreed to meet at a restaurant where we had often watched hockey or shot pool. On the drive over, I thought perhaps Evan had taken a bad turn and needed the transplant right away. Doctors had said that the longer he went without one under the proper medication, the better the chance the transplant would ultimately be successful. No wonder Terry would be upset.

He was waiting in the parking lot. I'd seen that wide-eyed, tight-lipped, red-faced expression many times — on the ice, behind the bench, in the dressing room. We found a quiet corner of the restaurant.

"You know what they're trying to do now? Those bastards!"

"Who?"

"The NHL, the Players' Association, whoever handles the insurance. I got a letter in the mail from the league saying there's a change in my insurance. Because of Evan's condition, the first $100,000 will be deductible if I want to continue coverage. Can you believe it?" O'Reilly's voice cracked. "What's going to happen to my kid, my family? It's either pay up or take a hike. Twenty-four grand! That's what it's going to cost me to cover the deductible. My kid's going to need a liver transplant some day. I've busted my ass all these years for the Bruins, the NHL, and now I get this shit in the mail!"

People looked our way. O'Reilly stopped a moment, composing himself. I asked what kind of coverage he'd had before.

"My family's always been covered. I was covered as a player, covered as a coach. I still do some things for the Bruins. Now I get this letter. Real class, eh? 'We know your kid is sick, so we're going to change your coverage.'"

I suggested he call Harry Sinden at the Bruins' office, call the league office, and call the Players' Association in Toronto.

"You know, Parkie keeps saying the NHL owns its own insurance company."

"Run that by me again?"

Brad Park, who also has a son requiring specialized medical care, had told O'Reilly that the league owned and operated its own insurance company.

The next day I called Park, who played for the Bruins, Rangers, and Red Wings. He now lives in Lynnfield and owns and operates a family-amusement center in Amesbury. I told him about my meeting with O'Reilly. Park said he was learning the hard way that retired NHL player insurance plans were a failure. "As players and coaches, we were always led to believe by Alan Eagleson that we had the best insurance coverage in all of sports. I thought the insurance would always be available. If the league does have an insurance company, I wish they'd take care of Robby with it, take care of Evan, and all other players' kids who need the coverage."

Robby Park is one of five children in Brad and Gerri Park's family. Born with cerebral palsy, he later developed epilepsy. He's confined to a wheelchair. Brad and Gerri dress him, put him on the toilet, look after him as best they can. Park is highly sensitive to the needs of the handicapped and, wherever he goes, keeps an eye out for ramps and proper facilities. Robby is his pride and joy.

"In a way, I guess Terry's lucky," Park said. "At least they're going to keep some of Evan's insurance in place for a deductible. In Robby's case, we're hung out to dry. Have you ever tried to get health insurance for somebody with cerebral palsy and epilepsy?"

I asked if the NHL wouldn't do something.

"I even tried calling John Ziegler," said Park. "He said there was nothing the league could do until I knew the cost for a cerebral palsy victim, said the league's insurance carrier didn't include certain coverages, told me to seek help from charitable organizations. The runaround."

Park said that former New York Islander Bob Bourne also had a handicapped child. The league wouldn't help him, Park said, and Bourne moved back to Canada to get help from Canada's universal health-care system.

Even though Park had kept up his NHL medical insurance after retiring as a player and, later, as a Red Wings coach, the insurance would expire in June 1991. "I notified Mr. Ziegler that with cerebral palsy, it depends on the severity of the case. If you have a person with a mild case, there's basically no cost. With a severe case, they could actually be institutionalized and the cost would be enormous. Robby, being a moderate case, could range anywhere from $2,000 a year to $24,000 depending on what he would need — electric wheelchair, things like that."

Along the way, seeking help for his son, Park had heard that the NHL was self-indemnifying — that it operated its own insurance company. "I don't think many players know about it," said Park. "I never did. Supposedly it's an insurance company called Ice, something like that. I don't know if it's true or not."

Over the next couple of weeks I asked many of that year's Bruins — Moog, Bourque, Cam Neely, Glen Wesley, Lyndon Byers, Dave Poulin, Reggie Lemelin, Craig Janney, Bob Sweeney, Don Sweeney, Dave Christian, Ken Hodge Jr. — whether they knew of an insurance company owned by the NHL or a company called Ice. None did. I asked Bobby Orr. He'd never heard of it. Neither had Mike Milbury, the Bruins' coach, or Gordie Clark or Ted Sator, his assistants.

Terry O'Reilly, meanwhile, had called Sam Simpson, the NHLPA director of operations, in Toronto to find out why his coverage was changing. He had also questioned Harry Sinden about it. I told O'Reilly I'd raise it with Sinden as well.

"Why not wait and see what he does," said O'Reilly. "You may hurt my chances of Harry helping me."

I certainly didn't want to do that, but I planned to do a story and I needed to learn more about this phantom company. At Boston Garden, just before Christmas, I asked Sinden how things were going. The Bruins were playing well and he was in an upbeat mood.

"Great, how about you?"

I asked if he'd done all his Christmas shopping. He said he still had some things to pick up.

"Me too," I said. "Trouble is, I had to pay the insurance on my Corvette, which is up around eighteen hundred bucks. Think that Ice insurance company would take car insurance?"

"No," Sinden laughed. "It's not that kind of insurance. Besides, it's run out of Bermuda somewhere."

Bingo!

"How long has the National Hockey League owned Ice?"

He paused. "It's been a while, but I don't know much about it. We didn't want to be a part of it to begin with but it saves the league some money. Like your car insurance, the cost of the NHL's insurance got crazy, so the league...."

Sinden stopped in mid-sentence, saying he had to go.

Driving home I wondered why, if the NHL owned its own insurance company, the players didn't know about it. I had no doubt Eagleson knew about it. If the executive director of the union knew, why didn't the members?

IN THE COURSE OF ASKING former players about their pensions, I'd learned that Carl Brewer was doing the same thing in Toronto, so I gave him a call. After the players received a small pension increase in late 1988, Brewer had sought detailed information from the NHL Pension Society about the pension surplus. His questions had been ignored. The NHL, John Ziegler, and Alan Eagleson all agreed that the NHL's pension surplus belonged to the league. By late 1990 Brewer had sought out Toronto lawyer Mark Zigler, a pension specialist, and organized a meeting to discuss whether the old-timers had grounds for a lawsuit against the NHL. At that meeting, in the Ramada Inn near the airport in Toronto, it was agreed that the retired players would take their case to the current players, Alan Eagleson, and the NHL president. The logical place to do this was Chicago, where the hockey world was about to gather for the 1991 NHL All-Star Game.

While some retired players went to Chicago, others headed to Fort Lauderdale, Florida. I saw a chance to combine work and a holiday with my father, who was battling prostate cancer. Terry O'Reilly had the same idea: he took little Evan, who was pale and had a yellowish tinge to his skin. O'Reilly made the trip as a father-son getaway, savoring the good times, not knowing how many were left — like me and my father.

In Florida, I asked many more players about Ice and got more blank looks. I also collected more Eagleson stories. Wilf Paiement confirmed, as his brother had told me, that his money had indeed been loaned to Bobby Orr's hockey camp and to the Cleveland Barons. Ron Murphy, the former Bruin who hadn't made it to the reunion, said that financially he was in tough shape: "My pension wouldn't get me by for three months in a year." Tom Songin said he hadn't been in the NHL long enough to worry about pensions, but he never understood how Eagleson could be an agent, run the union, and promote the Canada Cup.

Ferny Flaman, the Hall of Fame Boston defenseman, told me his pension wouldn't make the poverty requirement in the United States, which I later found to be literally true. Reggie Leach, whom I had covered when he was a Bruin, before he went on to an outstanding career with the Flyers, was highly critical of the "horrible" pensions. Leach, now in the landscaping business near Philadelphia, also questioned Eagleson's close relationship with owners.

Long-time NHL referee Bruce Hood said the entire NHL-NHLPA relationship "has been a total joke for years. Eagleson puts his own people on the board as officers, the ones who won't question him about anything." Hood said that the officials and players had once been in the same pension plan; that had changed, but he was uncertain how and why.

Denis Herron, the former Montreal and Pittsburgh goaltender, said the players had hit Eagleson where it hurt during the summer meetings of June

1989. Herron felt the big shock from those meetings was the disclosure that Eagleson had loaned NHLPA money to "his own car dealer and his own law partner." A loan to his law partner? That was a new wrinkle to me, worth looking into.

Dick Lamby, a former player with St. Louis, said he could not recall voting on the NHL-WHA merger. "Not that I was any superstar, but I always thought every player should have had a vote on that. Isn't that how a union works?" Fred Ahern, whose NHL career ended in 1977–78, said of the merger, "The stupid thing about it was that it eliminated jobs. With the WHA alive, there were more teams and more players. When the WHA died, a lot of players were out of work. You'd think the people running the players' associations in both leagues would have been concerned with that."

But perhaps the most intriguing conversation I had that weekend was with Louis Robichaud, a former member of Parliament, former premier of New Brunswick, and now a Liberal senator in Ottawa. He was a talkative fellow, entertaining and animated, whose hands flew around when he spoke and who insisted on being called "Louie." We sat at the same table at a dinner hosted by Rosie Paiement. Paiement introduced us, telling Robichaud I was a reporter from Boston looking into hockey pensions and "one of your old pals, the Eagle."

Robichaud asked why I was interested in Eagleson. I said I thought his management of both the NHL Players' Association and Hockey Canada may have had something to do with the pitifully low pensions of retired players.

"He's one of the most powerful people in Canada," Robichaud said. "He's close friends with the prime minister, cabinet ministers, judges, many people in Parliament. Alan gets anything he wants. And he takes pretty good care of them, too."

"Does that mean you, too, Mr. Robichaud?"

"No," he laughed, though he said he had been treated to Eagleson's hospitality at a party back in the early 1970s. He said Eagleson was notorious among politicians for handing out gifts and free tickets to games, and for hosting social gatherings that centered on international hockey events: "I'd be able to do that, too, if I had an unlimited budget."

Robichaud said everybody in Canadian politics knew Eagleson ran Hockey Canada, with aid from the Canadian government. I asked why Canadian taxpayers would help foot the bill for free tickets, gifts, and parties that seemed mainly to benefit Alan Eagleson.

Robichaud said perhaps the gifts and tickets were paid for by advertisers, but it was well known that Eagleson ran Canada Cup events virtually unchecked. Canadians lived with it, Robichaud believed, because the good that came from Hockey Canada — the money raised for Olympic teams and youth hockey programs, the excitement of Canada Cup events and the Soviet–Team Canada series of 1972 — outweighed the bad. Besides, said Robichaud, Eagleson was viewed as a national treasure for getting Canada back into the forefront of international hockey.

Robichaud had been unaware that Canada Cup events were meant to generate pension money, and he seemed upset to learn that retired NHL players were receiving such low pensions. During the evening Rosie and Wilf Paiement, Don Marcotte, Dave Keon, and Rick Middleton, among others, told him about their low pensions and about the battle developing over millions of dollars in disputed surplus money. Robichaud seemed taken aback. He wondered aloud why Eagleson wasn't looking out for the retired players.

When the get-together ended, Robichaud suggested that, if I needed help researching my story or happened to be in Ottawa, I look him up. He added that, in his opinion, Eagleson would never be fully investigated.

"Why's that?"

"He has too many connections in high places."

HARRY SINDEN HAD SAID that Ice, which insured the NHLPA's group medical plan, was based in Bermuda. When I got home from the Florida get-together, I called the Bermuda Registrar of Insurance Companies. They had no "Ice Insurance Company" on record. I asked for any company starting with "Ice." Nothing. I asked for anything under "National Hockey League." Nothing. Perhaps the "I" in "Ice" stood for "International." I called again. There were many names beginning with "International" but none rang a bell. I also spoke to Rick Betterley, a captive insurance specialist in Massachusetts. He knew nothing of an Ice Insurance Company, but he did explain the advantages of a captive. Basically, it saved money and, if offshore, avoided U.S. taxes. It also avoided certain insurance regulations.

The break I needed finally came during a talk with a contact at the NHL. When I said I wanted to speak to somebody involved in running Ice Insurance, he said he'd have a word with Bill Wirtz, the Chicago owner, who also had an insurance business. My contact soon got back to me: "You're looking for International Advisory Services. Ask for a David Ezekiel. The real name of the company is Intra-Continental Ensurers Limited. Ezekiel manages it for the league."

I reached Ezekiel in Bermuda and said I was a hockey writer with two friends — retired players — who had ill children. I was curious about the NHL's company.

"We manage the captive insurance company of the National Hockey League," Ezekiel confirmed hesitantly. "I can't talk about the operation. I can't give out specifics about any of the companies we manage." He suggested I put my questions in a letter.

"What kind of insurance do you handle for the NHL?"

"The captive only handles very specific coverages for the league."

I asked if ICE insured current and former NHL hockey players.

"I can't tell you."

If the players' career-ending disability insurance or family health insurance was involved, I said, I needed to know and so did the players.

"They might be insured through ICE for certain of their coverages but, for instance, career-ending? I can't tell you whether they're insured through ICE or not."

"When was the business formed?"

Ezekiel said it was formed in 1985, and that was the last question he would answer. Other questions would have to be put in writing.

That same night I faxed him eleven questions. Some I already knew the answers to; I wanted to see if I got straight answers. Among other things, I asked:

"What are the specific insurance coverages you manage for the NHL?

"How many claims have been rejected through you concerning the NHL captive company you manage, and for what reason were these claims made?

"How many claims have been approved through you concerning the NHL captive company you manage, and for what reason were they approved?

"Who are the primary carriers you use to insure the NHL clubs and players and who are the secondary carriers?"

Despite repeated requests, Ezekiel never responded. From his silence I knew I'd struck a nerve. Then I got a call from an NHL contact, who said John Ziegler had issued an edict: administrative personnel were not to talk to me about league business matters.

I went back to the Registrar of Insurance Companies in Bermuda, explaining that the manager of ICE had refused to answer questions about the company. After transferring funds to cover the search fee in British sterling, I obtained a full membership list of ICE. Every NHL team was listed, as were team owners, general managers, team officials, and some league officials. How odd that not one of the many players I'd asked had any knowledge of the NHL-owned insurance company that covered them. Why was the league keeping it secret?

BRAD PARK'S AGENT, Larry Rauch, had attended the Florida gathering and promised to send me some old NHLPA-related correspondence when he returned to New York. One of the items he forwarded was a letter Alan Eagleson had written to all agents on May 27, 1987. It touched on a variety of subjects, including the NHLPA medical plan. "It was agreed that the NHL medical plan shall cover a player only when he is with the major league club. I have instructed Bill Sutton of these changes," Eagleson wrote, referring to the union's insurance agent. "It was agreed that the NHL clubs could add scouts to the NHLPA medical program" and that two trainers from each club "who are NHLPA members" would have disability coverage increased from $15,000 to $50,000.

I could understand Eagleson's involvement with NHLPA insurance matters, but why was he involved with NHL insurance? Wouldn't the league administer its own plan? And why was the NHLPA taking on scouts and trainers? Wouldn't they have been the responsibility of management? The letter heightened my interest in Eagleson's insurance dealings, particularly since the NHL seemed to be operating an offshore insurance company of its own.

Rauch also sent along some back issues of *Goals*, the newsletter sent by the NHLPA to the players. One issue noted that NHLPA meetings scheduled for July 24–25 of 1989 had been postponed to August at the urging of Detroit player rep Dave Barr. That meeting was to have been a follow-up to the players' coup of June 1989 in Florida, when they heard Ed Garvey's report. That date change, I recalled, had been the reason Steve Kasper couldn't attend the meeting at which Eagleson, to my surprise, had been given a vote of confidence by the players.

I knew Barr, who had broken into the league with the Bruins. He now played for the Red Wings, and I called him in Detroit to ask why he had suggested a date change for the meeting. He said he hadn't, calling the accusation "totally untrue," and adding, "I was pissed. Eagleson had taken the blame right off himself and thrown it on me." Barr had been so upset that he ultimately resigned as Detroit's player rep. He felt Eagleson had changed the date to throw the players off balance. It was summer; players schedule time with families and friends during the off-season. Eagleson had been buying time, Barr felt, mustering support among the reps he could count on.

Another story in *Goals* — under the heading "Blue Chip Mortgages" — boasted about three mortgages on the books of the NHLPA. "The borrowers, clients of Mr. Eagleson's law practice, are all financially solid. This fact and appropriate related details were disclosed to members of the Executive Committee when the mortgage funds were advanced."

Strange. Steve Kasper, and Ed Garvey in his report, had both said that nobody knew about the loans when they came up at the June 1989 meetings. Dave Barr, who was there, verified it. So did Pat Verbeek, Jim Korn, Ryan Walter, Mark Howe, Garth Butcher, and Mike Gartner, all of whom were in the room when Eagleson tap-danced around questions about union money being loaned to his pals. All told me that not one player at the meeting said he had any prior knowledge of the loans.

In a column called "Director's Notes," Eagleson talked about his contract, saying he spent "many more than 60% of my hours working for the union. Additionally, all office expenses, secretarial staff, executive assistant fees and rent come from my fees (with the exception of a $10,000 annual contribution to overhead which was negotiated as part of my contract)....The rent for my office and my secretaries' salaries are not paid by the NHLPA. Last season in accordance with my contract, I was paid $175,000 and that total was reduced to about $90,000 once these costs were factored in."

Eagleson also wrote about his involvement with international hockey. "Each event is audited and statements are, and always have been, available. All the work that I've done on the international front has been undertaken for the benefit of the NHLPA."

Eagleson, I knew, had rebuffed Dave Forbes, a former player who now worked as a financial adviser in California, when Forbes showed up in person at Maitland House seeking financial statements from international events. Eagleson had flatly refused to give him any information. Andy Moog had also told me Eagleson had refused to make international hockey or Canada Cup financials available to players. Yet here he was claiming the information *was* freely available!

There was also a reference to a car leased by the Players' Association for Eagleson, plus two other vehicles owned by the union, one a 1985 Buick for Aggie Kukulowicz, which was "part of our agreement with respect to international negotiations and operations." Kukulowicz was a Russian-to-English translator during international hockey tours whom I later learned was employed by Air Canada. Why was he getting a car, paid for by the NHLPA?

The newsletter noted that lawyer Bill Dermody had given a full report on NHLPA mortgages made under Eagleson's stewardship between 1987 and 1989. "The bottom line on the mortgages is that they are excellent investments," said the newsletter. Eagleson said he had agreed "to personally guarantee both of them."

And there was this tidbit in a newsletter under the headline: "U.S. Department of Labor Confirms NHLPA Actions." "Back in May of 1989, Mr. Ed Garvey told Bryan Trottier that he (Bryan) and Alan Eagleson could both be fined a million dollars and go to jail for 2 years. He alleged that the

NHLPA (and consequently Brian and Alan) was in absolute violation of U.S. Labor laws and that he was certain that they were breaking the law. Eagleson answered those allegations in June 1989 by stating 'As a Canadian Union, the NHLPA was not required to file with the U.S. Labor Department and that there was a U.S. Labor Department ruling to support this position.'

"On July 27, 1989, we received correspondence from Mr. J.F. Depenbrock, Associate Solicitor of the United States Department of Labor. His letter states the following. 'Based on your factual representations, it appears to us that under all the circumstances the Association (NHLPA) is not required to file reports with the Secretary (of Labor) under section 201....The activities of a foreign labour organization carried on under local law are not subject to regulations under the LMRDA [Labor Management Reporting and Disclosure Act].'

"In other words," Eagleson wrote, "in accordance with the legal advice received by the NHLPA, we are a Canadian Union and we file in Canada. The material that we file with the Canadian Government is very similar to the material which U.S.-based Associations file in that country. Thanks to Mr. Depenbrock and the U.S. Labor Department for clarifying this issue."

It defied logic. How could a union involving many U.S. citizens who derive their incomes in the United States working for U.S. corporations not be protected by U.S. labor law? Something didn't add up. The Labor Department opinion was "based on your factual representations." I wondered exactly what factual representations Eagleson had made.

Another document that pricked my curiosity was a scathing newsletter called *Players Voice*, which carried Ed Garvey's name and a Madison, Wisconsin, address on the front page. Garvey evidently published it as an antidote to Eagleson's propaganda in *Goals*. One story went into plans for an NHL expansion that would bring in an estimated $350 million. It suggested that retired players, current players, league owners, and even NHL president John Ziegler all share in expansion money. But "there is one person who thinks the players should not get one penny and the retired players should receive nothing. All $350 million would go to the owners!...Alan Eagleson, the players' friend. Here is what he said in Toronto: 'The rumor that the players want part of the expansion money is not true. We will be happy with the new jobs.'...Really, Alan? Who is 'we'?"

Under the headline "Eagleson Continues to Stonewall" was a story that pointed out: "Six months have passed since the June [1989] Rep meeting where Eagleson made promises to keep his job. Here are the ones he has not kept.

"1. Stop representing all individual players.

"2. Sever his ties with Eagleson Ungerman [Eagleson's Toronto law firm].

"3. Produce the lease for the NHLPA office with the Eagleson Family Trust.

"4. Produce the details of $483,000 spent on meetings over two years.

"5. Produce a list of people who received over $10,000 in gifts from NHLPA fund.

"6. Explain in writing the details of money loaned to friends and clients from NHLPA pension fund.

"7. Provide a copy of his pension plan that players are funding at the rate of $50,000 (U.S.) per year. (If players were receiving a similar benefit, the annual cost would be $26,250,000.)

"8. Open a new office for NHLPA away from Eagleson Ungerman.

"9. Work 100 percent of the time for NHLPA.

"10. Detail all funds received by Eagleson and his family from International Hockey.

"11. Turn over his tax returns for the past three years."

Yet another story in Garvey's newsletter was about Eagleson's position on free agency: "Once again Alan Eagleson has shown the players' cards to the owners, this time even before they have sat down at the bargaining table. In order to frighten players from demanding a change in the current disgraceful free-agency system, Eagleson was quoted in the USA Today (12/12/89): 'The only way we will attain free agency is by striking, and we might not get it then. The owners have made it clear there ain't no free agency without a strike.' The players themselves should decide their priorities for the upcoming negotiations. Likewise, the strategy to achieve those goals should not be shared with the owners.

"By publicly stating that the dismal free agency that exists in the NHL can only be achieved through a strike, Eagleson in essence compromises the players' bargaining power and gives comfort to the owners.

"Please, Alan — keep our cards close to your vest. At least wait until you get your management position before sitting on their side of the table."

Meanwhile, talking to Carl Brewer, I learned that current players had refused to meet with retired players about the pension dispute during the All-Star break in Chicago. The current all-stars had shut the door on them, Brewer said — per order of Alan Eagleson.

AFTER EAGLESON MANAGED to thwart the move to unseat him at the June 1989 meetings, the NHLPA members had hired William C. Dovey of Price Water-house, an accounting firm, to review union finances for fiscal 1987, 1988, and 1989. In August of 1989, Dovey had met with the players at the Toron-to Hilton to discuss his findings.

Eagleson recalled that August meeting in his memoirs, *Power Play*. The night before Dovey spoke, said Eagleson, audit committee members (and NHL players) Bryan Trottier and Kelly Miller met to go over the Dovey report. "Bryan phoned me once during the evening with a couple of questions," Eagleson wrote. "I referred him to [director of operations] Sam Simpson and our accountant, Marvin Goldblatt, so I knew on the Tuesday morning before the audit report was presented to the full membership that there were no problems....By eleven that morning it was pretty well over, the point having been made that any irregularities the auditor had uncovered were minor."

Eagleson also claimed vindication in a *Goals* newsletter before the 1989–90 season. "The Audit Committee report was presented by Mr. Bill Dovey, a partner of the firm Price Waterhouse," Eagleson wrote. "Dovey reported to the meeting that:

"1. There had been no misappropriation of NHLPA funds.

"2. The records of the NHLPA were properly kept and there were no unusual expenses.

"3. The reporting of the accounts of the NHLPA was within the rules and guidelines of accounting practices.

"Price Waterhouse spent more than a month going over our NHLPA records. They inspected each document from the past 3 years in accordance with the Audit Committee's instructions."

Pat Verbeek, a player rep, had been at that meeting. He told me that no audit had been issued to the players; he only remembered somebody getting up and giving a speech, the gist of which was that things appeared to be fine with Players' Association expenses.

I interviewed Dovey and got a copy of his report. A close comparison of the report with Eagleson's description of it revealed some major discrepancies. In reality, the auditor saw only what the Players' Association — meaning Eagleson — gave him: one-line financial statements, the working papers of the association's own auditors, and Eagleson's monthly expense statements. The auditor never saw Eagleson's tax returns; Eagleson refused to provide them.

Eagleson claimed that Dovey told the players "there had been no misappropriation" of union funds. In fact, Dovey's report said that the limited scope of the review did not allow him to determine if some spending was "necessary to or appropriate for the NHLPA." Dovey actually red-flagged spending for "promotion, gifts and awards," for which the NHLPA had been billed $216,965 over three years. Included in that figure was $24,000 for a London apartment in 1987 and 1988. An Eagleson family firm leased another flat in London at the end of 1988 and billed the Players' Association $4,000 for it in 1990. The promotion account was also charged $19,274 for golf and tennis club dues and expenses, and $2,130 for YMCA memberships for Eagleson and Sam Simpson.

"We have been able to identify the nature of expenditures," Dovey remarked, "but we were unable to determine how the NHLPA benefitted from them. It is an area we are concerned about from a control point of view" — a rather different spin than Eagleson put on it. Dovey found "some promotional expense related to Mr. Eagleson's annual golf tournament, Calgary Olympic tickets and hotel, and an annual party for the Premier of Ontario," which Eagleson defended as good public relations for the NHLPA.

It was also good public relations for Alan Eagleson, of course, a longtime Conservative who had once been president of the Ontario party and who was elected to the provincial legislature in 1963. As Louis Robichaud had said, Eagleson was a close friend of Brian Mulroney, the Canadian prime minister, a friendship cemented when Eagleson actively supported

Mulroney's first (unsuccessful) attempt to win the federal Conservative Party leadership in 1976.

Bill Dovey also questioned the lack of documentation for Eagleson's expense claims. "In most cases, a letter from Mr. Eagleson's law practice would detail the expenses but no supporting receipts or invoices would be provided." The Dovey report did not list a total figure, but individual expense statements ran into thousands of dollars. In December 1988, for example, Eagleson stayed in London twice on NHLPA business and requested $6,000 in expenses through Simpson.

According to Eagleson's statement, the first visit was to meet with the NHLPA's British insurance brokers. Expenses included $2,000 for accommodations at $500 per day and $1,150 for gifts to the insurance men. A note indicated the gifts were Wimbledon tennis tickets. The second visit, over Christmas, cost players $2,835. The reason for the trip was listed only as "S.M.," for special meetings. After a 1988 trip to Moscow and Helsinki, Eagleson billed the union $1,400 for "gifts (7 people)" with no indication of who got the gifts or why. In March 1988, Eagleson billed the union's special meeting account for expenses for two meetings in New York on March 31, but the expense request does not say with whom he met.

Dovey recommended that an audit committee be formed to oversee the union's financial operations and review Eagleson's expenses, and that Eagleson provide more documentation. Because players cannot pay much attention to union business during the season, Dovey also recommended that non-players experienced in business, labor, and legal matters keep an eye on spending. He further recommended the disclosure of any payments made to companies tied to Eagleson, who, Dovey said, was in the position of "directing and controlling" the Players' Association.

All in all, he painted a very different picture than Eagleson had claimed. In the end, Eagleson's attempt to use the Dovey audit to exonerate himself only made me more curious.

3

INADVERTENT DAMAGE

"I've had three back operations and I'm faking?
What did I do, dream up those operations?
Put those scars in my back myself?"
JIM HARRISON

WHEN I FIRST met him, in 1969, Jim Harrison was a skillful, hard-nosed center who played for the Bruins before being traded to Toronto for Wayne Carleton. During his eleven seasons as a professional he played for Boston, Toronto, Chicago, and Edmonton in the NHL, and Edmonton and Cleveland in the WHA. I knew his career had ended with a bad back, and Carl Brewer suggested I look him up. Harrison, said Brewer, had had problems with disability insurance and with Eagleson. I tracked him down in Kelowna, British Columbia, and during several long interviews he told me his story.

Harrison had already had two back operations — in May 1967 and February 1974 — when his back again began bothering him in early 1978, while he was with Chicago. He was sent to the Blackhawks' club physician, Dr. Louis W. Kolb. "Dr. Kolb told me I was going to have an epidural block — an injection into my back, dissolving parts of the bad disk." In fact, the epidural block was "a placebo shot, a sugar shot to see if I was faking." Harrison didn't learn about it until six years later, when a lawyer investigating his disability obtained his medical records. The doctor's notes on that January 1978 procedure state: "Epidural block not performed because

43

patient had complete relief with placebo...." Yet the following year, Kolb never made reference to the placebo in Harrison's case history, stating that "an epidural steroid injection" had been administered and that it "achieved only transient relief" for Harrison at the time.

When I spoke to Dr. Kolb, he recalled the Harrison case and described the placebo treatment as a form of trickery used to determine whether a medical problem is biological or psychological. "If you tell the patient before a placebo what it is, it defeats the purpose of the test."

The placebo test came only five days after Kolb had written a letter to Chicago coach and general manager Bob Pulford about his preliminary exam of Harrison. Kolb explained that Harrison had a sore back and had been treated with an "injection of medication into [his] lower spine, in an attempt to relieve discomfort....Surgery seems out of the question unless his condition worsens...."

Two days after the placebo, however, Kolb wrote Pulford again: "Neurosurgeon feels Jim may need surgery on his back as I mentioned to you....I do believe we should give Jim every opportunity to play (providing he does himself no harm and I will check him periodically to be sure he doesn't) before deciding any surgery is in order...."

Two weeks later Kolb wrote to Chicago trainer Skip Thayer: "This player is anxious to play but finds he is not able to perform without severe pain." Kolb described Harrison's problem this way: "Pain in his lower back, right buttock, and extended to his right calf." Kolb also made reference to an examination of Harrison after a game on February 15, 1978, saying Harrison could only bend forward "about 20 degrees.... Pain was more severe. He had more numbness in his calf and his heel."

Having informed Pulford less than a month earlier that back surgery was out of the question, Kolb wrote to Pulford on February 17: "Because of his increasing pain and inability to play effectively (in his mind), I suggest he be admitted to the hospital on Sunday, Feb. 19, 1978, to undergo an X-ray study of his back after dye treatment has been injected around the spinal cord." Kolb said that surgery, including possible spinal fusion, would be advised if Harrison's "myelogram proved to be positive."

So Harrison's inability to play effectively was "in his mind"? Five days after that letter to Pulford, Kolb assisted Dr. Jose Salazar's back surgery on Harrison. The operation took nearly three hours. A disk was removed, but no spinal fusion was done. Three months after the operation, Kolb wrote to Pulford: "[Harrison] should be able to perform for you with no restrictions during your coming season.... Jim's activities can be unlimited at this point in time."

Alakazam! Harrison was cured! Except that, in early November, he went to Kolb complaining about a knife-like pain in his back, shooting down through his buttock and into his right leg. The leg would get numb, and he'd be unable to move.

Kolb and Harrison went to dinner. Harrison told him he hadn't felt right since the operation and was thinking of retirement. Worse, he told Kolb, he and Pulford weren't getting along. He was upset that Pulford wouldn't give him time off to rest his back. He'd done his best, he said, but it wasn't good enough. Pulford was a slave driver.

Kolb reported back to Pulford with Harrison's medical update, and with their dinner conversation as well — including Harrison's feelings about Pulford.

Three days later, after being cross-checked by Dean Talafous in a Rangers-Blackhawks game, Harrison could hardly walk. Still, Pulford asked him to play. "I was their tough guy and he needed me," Harrison recalled. He did play, and his back worsened.

"One day I phoned the trainer at noon and said, 'I've just taken a couple of Valium and I don't think I can play tonight. Tell Pulford I'll come down for the game and have a whirlpool and dress for appearance.'" That night, while Harrison was having his whirlpool, "Pulford came in and said he needed me to play because me just sitting on the bench meant a lot to the hockey team.

"I said I'd do it, reluctantly, because I was in such pain I couldn't even bend over to tie my skates. I dressed and maybe stepped onto the ice once. After the game I had a treatment again, took more medication, and went home. The next day Pulford called me in, saying I'd been put on waivers the week before. I had to go to the minors. I said, 'You've got to be kidding me. You know I can't even walk.' He says, 'There's nothing wrong with you.' He said I'd played with a bad back all my life so what difference did it make now? He said I could go rot in hell."

Harrison refused to report to Moncton and was suspended without pay. He called his agent, Alan Eagleson; since 1974, Harrison had paid him 10 percent of his hockey salary. Eagleson urged him to come to Toronto for a medical consultation with Dr. Charles Bull.

CHUCK BULL, AN ORTHOPEDIC SURGEON, long-time friend of Eagleson, and Team Canada doctor, was no stranger to Harrison. As far back as July 10, 1974, after Harrison's second back surgery, Bull had examined him. His report from a December 15, 1978, examination at Humber Memorial Hospital in Weston, Ontario, noted that during Harrison's most recent operation, in Chicago, "inadvertently a nerve root was damaged" in Harrison's back. "His muscles are like a rock. There is intense spasm right from about the L2 down to the sacrum. He says with any type of forward flexion or pressure he gets discomfort right down the back of his calf into the great toe....

"I feel he has sustained more root irritation following that cross check two weeks ago and always the nerve has been fragile due to the disc pressure and trauma from inflammation postop....I have given him a prescription for Motrin." Bull advised Harrison to refrain from skating and "do nothing until January 11" of the following year.

Harrison's back trouble persisted and he again refused to report to Moncton. Still suspended without pay, he filed a grievance through his agent — Eagleson. Trouble was, Eagleson was also Pulford's agent, and Pulford was employed by Wirtz, with whom Eagleson had long been cozy. Judging the grievance, by the terms of the NHLPA collective agreement negotiated by Eagleson, was Eagleson's pal John Ziegler, the NHL president, whose salary was paid by Wirtz and the other owners. Harrison might be forgiven for thinking the deck was stacked against him from the start.

FOR THE GRIEVANCE MEETING on December 28, a room was rented at Chicago's O'Hare Airport. Attending were Harrison; his wife, Liz; Ziegler; Eagleson; Chicago physician Dr. Louis Kolb; Chicago general manager Bob Pulford; Chicago trainer Skip Thayer; and Bobby Orr, who by this time had retired as a player to be Pulford's assistant.

"As we were walking into the room," Harrison recalled, "Al said, 'Don't say a word. I'll handle the whole thing. Dr. Kolb and the trainers are against you.' He never asked one question. Pulford just said, 'You know we're sending him to the minors.' I said, 'I can't believe you guys are even saying this.' Eagleson said to me, 'I told you to shut up!' Right in the meeting he says this to me."

After the testimony, Ziegler sent everybody out except Pulford, Eagleson, and Orr. "They said they were going to make a ruling," Harrison recalled. "In about a half hour, Eagleson came out and said Ziegler had ruled I had to go to the minors." Harrison, crying, yelled, "I can't believe this! I can't even walk! You guys think I'm faking and I'm not!" "My wife was in a state of shock. Alan just said, 'That's the ruling.' I had to be on the airplane the next day at one o'clock." Eagleson insisted that Harrison shake hands with Pulford and Ziegler.

In fact, Ziegler, Pulford, and Eagleson had found themselves in a bind. Chicago hadn't followed league procedures in notifying Harrison of his demotion. "Ziegler didn't make a decision that day," Bobby Orr confirmed. "All he did was slap us [the Blackhawks] on the wrist because he said we hadn't properly notified Harrison that he was going to the minors. I left figuring he was still with the team. I remember that meeting well, because that's the day my car got stolen at the airport."

Ziegler verified that he never ruled Harrison had to go to the minors. He concluded that the meeting could not be considered a grievance hearing at all, but rather a discussion. "Ziegler said he never did rule," Harrison said. "It was just an agreement between Pulford and Eagleson." In other words, Eagleson — Harrison's agent and union leader — had cut a private deal with Pulford to the benefit of the Blackhawks and the detriment of his client.

Harrison reported to New Brunswick. One of his Moncton teammates was Trevor Johansen, who remembered him well from the 1978–79 season. "I lived with him in Moncton and there were days he couldn't get out of bed. The guy was on painkillers. He's hunched over. He had to lay down every hour almost. Here's a guy that was truly disabled."

In Moncton, Harrison was treated for his back problems before returning to Toronto in early 1979 for further examination by Dr. Bull on January 24 and January 30. After examining Harrison, Bull wrote two letters to Eagleson. The letters were marked "confidential — not for insurance or legal purposes." On neither occasion did Bull send a copy to Harrison, the patient. "He's been working on an upper body weight routine and found that pushing with his feet was straining his back," Bull informed Eagleson. "Following this maneuver he was tilted, couldn't walk and feels that this plus the leg raises caused pain to come back into his hip and go down his leg....

"Once the back spasms went down his leg he had pain as severe as he ever had and had to go to bed for two days....Presently he does definitely have spasm again in the lower L4-5 region, particularly on the right....He feels there is a radiation type of pain going into his buttock....told him to rest for three or four days and he is going to return to Chicago and rest, come back and see me on Tuesday, Jan. 30, when I can see about bracing him and sending him back to Monkton [sic] for skating and further therapy."

In a second letter to Eagleson, a week later, Bull wrote that Harrison "has had injections in his back on Jan. 24 and he feels they have definitely improved things. In essence, he has no back pain now." In the same letter, Bull wrote: "He still has numbness and discomfort down his calf. He can't stand for a prolonged period on his leg. He finds it hard to lie down due to discomfort in his leg. He says it's like a burning throughout his leg really. This is due to nerve root irritation. It could take three years to come back. It is sequalae of the previous disc herniation and the surgery." In the next paragraph, Bull wrote: "However, the back is good now."

So Harrison's real problem was inadvertent nerve-root damage suffered during the most recent surgery, damage from which it could take three years to recover. But "the back is good now." There was obviously something amiss, especially when Bull reported to Eagleson that "I have sent a letter to Eddie Johnston and a Xerox to you suggesting that [Harrison] return to practice and compete as soon as he feels his back is strong enough and that he can loosen it up enough to skate satisfactorily...."

Why were these letters sent to Eagleson and Johnston but not to Harrison? After all, they placed Eagleson in a serious conflict. Eagleson was Harrison's agent and the executive director of Harrison's union; Eddie Johnston was a part of Chicago management. Eagleson was allowing a doctor to send confidential information to management about a player he himself represented, a player from whom the information was being withheld. Whose interests were being served?

Harrison returned to Moncton, but not for long. When his wife, Liz, visited him there and saw his condition, she flew into a rage, calling Eagleson to tell him that Jim was drinking and popping pills to ease the pain. Eagleson told her he'd look after it. On March 24, 1979, Liz Harrison called Dr. Kolb, the Chicago physician, pleading with him to do something. Harrison's pain was excruciating. Kolb noted in a medical report that Liz Harrison was "somewhat distraught" and that he would see Harrison if he returned to Chicago. Harrison's coach in Moncton, Eddie Johnston, wanted to send him back. "He was dying," said Johnston. "I could see it in his face, see it the way he walked. He was hurting in a big way. I knew he needed help."

On Harrison's return to Chicago, Liz met him at O'Hare. She drove home with her husband laid flat in the back of their station wagon.

Kolb met with Harrison for another checkup, and by April 5, 1979, he was compiling a full case history. In it he referred to his November dinner with Harrison. "He made a comment to me that 'maybe the whole basis of this is that Mr. Pulford and I just don't get along,'" Kolb said in his report, adding that Harrison had told a nurse "he was interested in going on vacation and wanted a week or two off to go hunting."

"That was a complete lie!" Harrison said. "That's the kind of thing Pulford wanted from Dr. Kolb, so I'd look like I was faking. I'm faking? I've had three back operations and I'm faking? What did I do, dream up those operations? Put those scars in my back myself? Dr. Kolb knew my back was screwed up. Pulford knew, too, but he didn't want me to get my disability."

On April 16, Graeme Clark — an employee of Eagleson's player agent business — wrote to NHL vice president Brian O'Neill informing him of Harrison's disability. From Bull's report on Harrison and Harrison's own conversation with him, Clark noted the injury was created by the Dean Talafous cross-check the previous November. Harrison would be seeking career-ending disability insurance.

Urged to get other medical opinions — as required by the insurance carrier in such disability cases — Harrison went to the Mayo Clinic in

Minnesota for further evaluation and possible treatment. "All my medical records were supposed to be sent there," he recalled. But when Harrison arrived, nothing had been forwarded from Dr. Kolb, Dr. Bull, or the Black-hawks. Harrison spent three days at a hotel, waiting. "The doctor in Minnesota said, 'You've been through hell.' He phoned Chicago and said, 'Look, you send those records.' They said they'd send them right down. To this day they've never sent the records."

Three doctors at the Mayo Clinic examined Harrison. They agreed his back pain was created by a history of operations. One doctor suggested a spinal fusion would be needed. "I was hoping with proper medical care I would get better. Eagleson had told me if I got out of Chicago, I would be able to get proper medical attention. But my back just kept deteriorating."

Records of the Mayo Clinic examinations of Harrison were forwarded to Dr. Kolb in Chicago. One Mayo Clinic doctor said that if Harrison had a spinal fusion, there was "doubt that [he] could even then return to an active hockey career."

Adding insult to injury, Harrison kept receiving the bills for his Mayo Clinic exam. He finally paid them out of his own pocket, claiming the Black-hawks refused to refund the money. "They owed me around $10,000, expenses. They eventually covered part of the expenses, but I got stuck for the rest."

Harrison mulled over his future in the early summer of 1979. In the warm weather his back began to feel better. Then came a call from Glen Sather, coach of the Edmonton Oilers. Harrison had played one season for the Oilers in the WHA; along with Hartford, Quebec, and Winnipeg, Edmonton had just been added to the NHL as part of the 1979 NHL-WHA merger. Sather, who had briefly been Harrison's teammate and roommate in Boston, asked if he'd like to try a comeback and play on a team with "The Kid. Gretzky."

Still under contract to the Blackhawks, Harrison got permission from Chicago to try out. If he made the Oilers, Edmonton would owe Chicago compensation. "I went to their training camp and played three regular-season games with them. I played in Atlanta, and on the plane to Toronto afterward I couldn't get up from my seat."

During that game Harrison had been hit hard "because my whole right leg — every time I tried to skate — would shuck on me." He had earlier broken two ribs. Sather told him, "No way you can play. There's no hope."

On that Atlanta-Toronto flight, Harrison knew his career was over. It was time to call Eagleson to tell him this was the end. "Eagleson said he just talked to Pulford, who wanted me to go to Moncton. He said, 'The only option you have is to retire.' I said, 'Well, I retire. I'm quitting.'" Eagleson, seemingly surprised, said, "Okay, I'll draw up the papers." Harrison felt relieved; at least he had disability insurance to fall back on. In Toronto, he waited in Eagleson's office while the paperwork was completed. When he read the retirement papers, he was taken aback.

"Eagleson had agreed I would waive all medical disability, everything, any claims against anybody. I said, 'Al, I'm not signing that.' He got mad at me, swearing, saying, 'I made this deal for you! You bloody hockey players, who do you think you are?' He cursed me up and down.

"I said, 'Al, you know I've got three kids and I'm supposed to have another back operation. You know my chances of it taking are very slim. I'm going to be a cripple in ten years is what everybody is telling me.' Al said in his threatening way, 'If you don't like it, go get another lawyer!'

"So I got another lawyer, Don Affleck in Toronto. When Al found out, he phoned me and blew up. Told me if I didn't pick up my files, they'd be sitting on the doorstep on Bay Street. When I picked them up, three-quarters of the stuff wasn't there. Stuff we had done over the years, letters, like this one letter for my disability was not there.

"The way Al had explained it to me, when I retired I would get disability insurance through two policies — one through the Players' Association and one through the National Hockey League contract. But I got no place with these people because they all denied I was ever disabled. Everybody kept saying there was nothing wrong with me because that's what Pulford said."

Harrison got nowhere with Eagleson and the NHLPA. He obtained his medical files from Dr. Bull's secretary, but soon got bogged down by travel expenses and legal bills. He was told by the NHLPA he didn't qualify for career-ending disability insurance since he had a pre-existing back condition. "Eagleson always told me I was covered," said Harrison. "It was mind-blowing."

He later tried to file for worker's compensation. "I went to Buffalo on a wild goose chase for hearings. When I got there I found out Wirtz had canceled the hearing. I sat there all day to find out Wirtz's lawyer phoned and said he can't make it."

Harrison returned to the NHLPA, pleading for help. This time he was told to file for career-ending disability insurance coverage through North American Claims Facilities in Boston. He ultimately received $100,000 of the remaining $200,000 on his playing contract and settled for only $10,000 of $125,000 in NHL and NHLPA disability insurance coverage. "I was running out of money," he recalled. "It was down to taking ten thousand or nothing." His 1986 claim for worker's compensation for injuries as a Blackhawk in 1978 and 1979 was rejected for being late.

THE WIRTZ INSURANCE COMPANY, the Blackhawks, and Wirtz Corporation were all part of a multi-million-dollar empire partly owned by William W. Wirtz, owner of the team and chairman of the NHL's board of governors. "Workman's comp was written through us back then in the seventies and placed through us to an insurance carrier," said Edward Budzban, a long-time manager of the Wirtz Insurance Agency Inc. "Our records only go back to 1984. Those Harrison records have been destroyed....

"He couldn't prove he was hurt as a Blackhawk. We left it up to the insurance company and it kept getting bounced around. We had nothing to do with the decision. He filed too late, way beyond the filing deadline."

Budzban insisted Harrison had received a fair shake by the Blackhawks. "It's my understanding it was all settled and he was taken care of. We're being made whipping boys because we cut him from the team. To this day we honestly don't feel he was injured in one of our games. It's my understanding there was nothing really drastically wrong with him. I don't know why this is being resurrected.

"Bill Wirtz didn't own the insurance company. He owned the insurance agency. As agents, we don't deny claims. Bill Wirtz is one of the finest human beings you could ever find. It bugs me when people try to take advantage of him. We were more than fair and did everything we could do for this guy."

At the time Harrison retired, changes were in the works affecting disability insurance coverage. In October 1977, the NHL had switched carriers, from St. Paul Fire and Marine Insurance Company to Crawley Warren Group, a brokerage firm in London. Since the switch, both NHL and NHLPA disability insurance business was being handled by Eagleson. The league had put him in the unique position of overseeing all player disability coverages — the league's as well as the union's. You'll look long and hard to find another business in which a union leader is put in charge of handling the insurance for management.

Reinsurance of NHL and NHLPA career-ending disability policies had taken an unusual twist the season Harrison retired. Reinsurance — the common practice of double-insuring in case the first insurance carrier becomes insolvent — had been placed through two businesses. But the reinsurance policy, in force when Harrison made his brief comeback with Edmonton, was good for only two months, October 1 through December 3, 1979. The reinsurance policy was switched from Squadron Insurance to Continental Insurance Company of London for the period December 3, 1979, to October 1, 1980.

Reinsurance liability policies issued by Squadron covered both NHL and NHLPA career-ending disability insurance during that time. One of the exclusions for coverage on both policies caught my eye: "Does not cover losses directly or indirectly caused or contributed by...medical or surgical treatment...." In Dr. Bull's medical report, he referred to the third operation on Harrison, ordered and assisted by the Chicago team physician, Dr. Kolb. Bull had specifically noted that during the removal of the disk from Harrison's back, the two doctors "had to really work away to get it out and thus inadvertently the nerve root was damaged." The result of that surgery was that Harrison's whole right leg had become numb. And, referring to the Dean Talafous hit on Harrison, Bull had told Eagleson: "I feel he has sustained more [nerve] root irritation following that cross check two weeks ago and always the nerve has been fragile due to the disc pressure and trauma from inflammation postop."

Was there really any doubt that Harrison was hurt as a Blackhawk? More alarming yet, Bull's report indicated that Harrison had suffered inadvertent damage during surgery. This was a potential landmine. Such liability was specifically excluded in the NHL and NHLPA career-ending disability coverages. The Blackhawks would have been on the hook for damages.

Harrison didn't have access to his own medical records at the time; Bull's report was known only to Eagleson, the head of the union. If Eagleson went to bat for his disabled client, he might put the Blackhawks in financial jeopardy. Eagleson never did forward the report to Harrison, who therefore was unable to offer it as evidence for his disability claim. Indeed, by the time he finally got his hands on it, the report didn't even have value in his worker's compensation request, since the deadline for filing had passed.

Eagleson — Jim Harrison's lawyer, agent, and union boss — surely should have represented Harrison's best interests, knowing that the Chicago team doctor may have fouled up. But if Harrison had alleged malpractice, Wirtz might have been on the line for uninsured damages, and Eagleson would have had to lock horns with Pulford.

By the time I located Harrison, in 1991, he was in rough shape. "I still go to the hospital three times a week for treatments," he said. "I spent over $6,000 one year on acupuncture." He was heavily in debt. "I lost my John Deere tractor business, couldn't run it because I was laid up two years in bed. I lost my fishing launch. I lost close to $600,000, which I had when I retired. I have no feeling in my right leg. Mornings I can't get out of bed. I'm a cripple."

Harrison said that, swallowing his pride, he had approached Eagleson one last time, in 1990, "asking if I could get some help from the Players' Association." Eagleson told him to phone Sam Simpson, the director of operations. "I said, 'Sam, would you talk to Al? Tell him I can't walk. I can't lift anything. My back is getting bad. I don't want to go through a big lawsuit and court cases. I can't afford that. I'm nearly broke. Can the Players' Association help me somehow?' Simpson said he'd be talking to Al in the next couple of days. To this day, I've never got a call back."

The problem, as Harrison saw it, was that he had left Eagleson as a client. "When I wouldn't sign that agreement, waiving everything, Al all of a sudden would not even talk to me about disability insurance." Harrison's NHLPA membership was of no benefit. "Graeme Clark said, 'All Al Eagleson's players always get the disability insurance when they want.' Look at the guys who got it — Dale Tallon, Bill White. There's a list of six or seven.

"Tallon's a golf pro right now and he got $200,000," Harrison said. "Eagleson and him are the best of buddies. Nothing against Dale. He's a good friend of mine but Dale is in Al's back pocket. That's why he's working for the Blackhawks right now as a sportscaster."

As Harrison claimed, Chicago defenseman Bill White had also collected $200,000 in career-ending disability insurance after a concussion and neck injury. His agent — and, of course, his union director — was Eagleson. "The money, the checks, went right to Eagleson and Sports Management, his company," said White, now a business agent for a plumbing manufacturer in Toronto. "He put the claim through a company in Boston."

As he did for Jack Lynch, a former Washington Capitals defenseman and Eagleson client. Lynch's career came to an end in the 1978–79 season with a knee operation. I tracked him down at his home in Midhurst, Ontario. "I don't mind telling you I worship the land that man walks on," Lynch said of Eagleson, who helped get $150,000 in career-ending disability insurance money, which Lynch said he used to buy a house. "I had no problems at all. He's done nothing but help me. There will not be one foul word out of my mouth toward Alan Eagleson."

Jim Harrison was particularly critical of the Wirtz-Eagleson connection. "It's been that way ever since Eagleson got Bobby Orr to sign with Chicago," he said. "Tony Esposito [former Chicago goaltender] ends up president of the Players' Association. Dale Tallon ends up a sportscaster with the Blackhawks. Mike Keenan ends up coach and general manager of the Blackhawks, and coach of Team Canada. Bob Pulford ends up vice president of the Black-hawks. What did Pulford ever win in Chicago? Now they want him in the Hall of Fame?"

Harrison also mentioned former Hawks defenseman Keith Magnuson, who landed an executive position with Coca-Cola in Chicago. "Keith was supposed to come to the hearing," Harrison said of the O'Hare Airport meeting over his 1978 suspension and demotion. "He wouldn't show up for me because he was afraid for his job. My wife can verify this. Keith used to drive me to the games and practice. I had to literally lift my legs out of the car to walk to the house." Harrison says Magnuson told him, "'I can't come. I'm worried about my job.' He ended up being the Chicago coach the next year." (Magnuson told me he didn't make the hearing because he had something else to do that day.)

As Harrison said, members of the Hockey Hall of Fame selection committee — media members and management officials — received a letter from NHL president John Ziegler in 1991 urging that Pulford be considered for election. Pulford had played sixteen NHL seasons, scoring 281 goals and 643 points for Toronto and Los Angeles between 1956 and 1972, becoming coach of the Kings before moving to Chicago as coach and general manager.

Pulford grew up with Eagleson in New Toronto. Pulford was the one who introduced the young lawyer to other Maple Leaf players in the early 1960s — "Someone we can trust" is how Carl Brewer remembers Pulford introducing Eagleson. Pulford also served on the NHL Pension Society board of directors before the players lost their representation on the board in 1969.

"Ziegler was trying to influence the committee," one voter explained. "I thought it was insulting as hell, particularly when there were other candidates worthy of consideration. Here was the league president telling us who he thinks should go in."

Backed by Ziegler, Wirtz, and Eagleson, Pulford was elected to the Hall of Fame; arguably more worthy candidates await their turn. Dean Prentice, for example, played twenty-two NHL seasons, scoring 391 goals and 860 points. Doug Mohns also played twenty-two NHL seasons, scoring 248 goals and 710 points — mostly as a defenseman. Rick Middleton had 493 goals and 1,098 points over fourteen seasons. Eddie Johnston played eighteen NHL seasons, had 32 career shutouts, and was the last goaltender to play every minute of every game in an NHL season. None is in the Hall of Fame. Eagleson's pal is.

So is Eagleson himself, the only union chief in professional sport to be so honored. He was even appointed to the Hall of Fame Selection Committee, before being removed in 1993. By the time Jim Harrison told me his story, I was beginning to think Eagleson's picture ought to be hanging not in the Hall of Fame, but on the wall of the post office. And Harrison's was just one of dozens of horror stories I would hear from NHL players whose careers had been cut short by injury.

4

THE WALKING WOUNDED

"When I played in Montreal, Eagleson would come around
to the dressing room early in the season. Whenever
anybody asked a question about insurance, he said,
'Don't worry about a thing. That's why you have a Players'
Association.' Those were his words, and we believed him."
MURRAY WILSON

ED KEA WAS PLAYING for the Salt Lake Eagles, a
St. Louis farm team, the night he was bodychecked head first into the
boards. The 200-pound defenseman was knocked unconscious, carried off
the ice on a stretcher, and rushed to hospital.

Earlier that day — March 7, 1983 — St. Louis general manager Emile
Francis had phoned Kea's Salt Lake coach, Jack Evans, to recall Kea to the
Blues. At the time, Kea was on a one-way NHL contract with St. Louis,
meaning he was guaranteed NHL privileges — including his salary — even
if he were playing in the minors. Evans had asked Francis if he could keep
Kea for one more game. Francis had agreed. The St. Louis recall was in
effect, but Kea would play that night for Salt Lake before returning to
the Blues. Francis had already ordered a pre-paid ticket for Kea's return to
Missouri.

Francis got a midnight call at home. Evans told him, "I've got good news
and bad news. The good news is we won. The bad news is that Eddie Kea
got injured. He won't be able to report tomorrow."

Kea was in grave condition. "His brain was swelling so badly they needed
to operate and relieve the pressure," his wife, Jennifer, recalled. "They needed

to remove the blood clots that were forming." Kea underwent six hours of surgery. When Emile Francis got to Salt Lake, Kea's condition stunned him. "It was a matter of life and death. He just about passed away there. If he hadn't been such a big strong guy, he would have never survived.

"When it was time to bring him back to St. Louis, Ralston-Purina [owners of the Blues] loaned me a plane equipped with a nurse, a doctor, the whole works. I've gone through a lot of tough things in this business. Terry Sawchuk, when he was with the Rangers, got killed [rupturing his spleen in an off-ice fight] when I was there. Bob Gassoff died when I was in St. Louis [in a highway accident returning from a team party]. This one, though, it was really tough. Kea was a ten-year veteran. He had a family. You have to help the people who help you."

Larry Patey, the St. Louis player representative for the NHL Players' Association, called Jennifer Kea in Salt Lake shortly after the accident and assured her she needn't worry: "He told me there would be $100,000 from the league and $75,000 from the Players' Association." She had discussed insurance with her husband and they had decided he would not need added insurance because he already had coverage from both the NHL and the NHLPA.

Kea was in a coma for ten days. He spent eight weeks in hospital. Mrs. Kea never heard from Alan Eagleson or NHL president John Ziegler. She kept asking the Blues, and the team's player rep, about her husband's disability insurance coverage. Getting little response, she went to a lawyer. A year after the accident, she finally got a letter from Eagleson.

"He said he had done his utmost to get us $75,000," she recalled. "Parts of the letter were indelibly left in my mind. The letter suggested that I was causing trouble because I had insinuated to our player rep that I was not really represented." Jennifer Kea got the impression "I should be thankful that the money was sent to us so quickly because it was promptly done a year after [Kea's accident]. Ed was always known as a Christian athlete and that probably got some people's back up. There was antagonism toward people who would bring their faith with them to the arena. I think that was a little jab," she said of Eagleson's letter, "that we should have anything negative to say about anyone."

What about the $100,000 in NHL disability coverage? Emile Francis said he thought Kea was covered for two reasons: he had a one-way contract guaranteed by the Blues, and he'd actually been recalled at the time of his accident. Francis learned from the league, however, that Kea didn't qualify for disability. "The insurance had changed so that if a player had gone through waivers, he was no longer on a major-league roster. Even though he was on a one-way contract, the disability was null and void."

"Did the NHL or the Blues make any attempt to inform Kea he had no NHL disability insurance when he went to Salt Lake?" I asked Francis.

"Disability insurance was being carried through Lloyd's of London," he said. "There were so many claims, evidently it cost a lot of money. Some were illegitimate. Lloyd's of London canceled out the disability insurance for the league."

"Was it canceled at the time Kea was injured?"

"I can't specifically say yes or no," Francis answered. "I've got a gut feeling it came after Kea."

In fact, both the NHL and the NHLPA had mirror policies offering the same coverage in effect on March 7, 1983, the date of Kea's accident. There had been an earlier time when premiums paid by the NHL for health insurance coverage weren't forwarded. Did the same thing happen, I asked NHL president John Ziegler, with the league's career-ending disability coverage?

"If it did," said Ziegler, "it was very brief."

As to whether Kea knew his NHL disability insurance wasn't in effect in Salt Lake, Emile Francis said he didn't tell Kea because he felt that was the responsibility of the Players' Association. "This was just at the end of the season, before the [trading] deadline. By that time, representatives of the Players' Association would have had meetings with the players. They made a tour through the league. The thing that was unfortunate was that here was a really legitimate claim put in by Eddie Kea, but the insurance had changed."

I tracked down Blair Chapman, a teammate of Kea's both in St. Louis and Salt Lake. Chapman said he was never informed by either the NHLPA or the St. Louis player reps that insurance rules had changed. In fact, Chapman didn't recall Eagleson or Sam Simpson telling the St. Louis players of any insurance change before or during the 1982–83 season.

Jennifer Kea was a high school teacher when she married Ed. She graduated from Waterloo Lutheran University in Ontario, majoring in English and history. When I first spoke to her, she was working part-time in an antique shop. "Basically, we live on disability money and savings. We receive three different types of income related to Ed's injury. One is Social Security, which is the greatest portion of our disability income. The second is worker's compensation, about $189 a week. That is what the State of Missouri gave to anyone who was injured in 1983 no matter what their income was.

"The last portion is from the NHL Players' Association, $750 a month, which is $9,000 a year. Ed's life insurance is being diminished by $9,000 a year until it reaches zero. I believe that's in about two years, or about age forty-five.

"William Sutton is the provider of our family health insurance," she said of the NHLPA insurance agent at the time. "After Ed's accident we were able to continue on the plan and price until two years ago. It was $2,400 a year, about $250 a month. The price today is in the area of $561 a month, about $7,000 a year."

Of their $9,000 annual insurance income, in other words, the Keas were spending $7,000 for life and health care insurance. "We have in the past tried to find ways of reducing the cost of the health care and seeking other carriers to cover us. But because of Ed's medical history, no one will take him on."

And what of the $100,000 the Keas believed they had coming from their NHL disability insurance? "Nothing was paid initially," Jennifer Kea remembered. "Five thousand dollars was offered to our lawyers from the NHL. It was explained to me that a new policy [that would exclude minor-league players] had come into effect in October of 1982. The only trouble was that nobody had told either Emile Francis or the players themselves."

The $5,000 offer was eventually increased to $20,000; the money finally came to her about three years after her husband's accident. "To get the check for $20,000, we had to sign papers that said we gave up all rights to any legal recourse."

Ralston-Purina made up the $80,000 shortfall, or at least about $72,000 of it. "When Ralston-Purina sold the team to Harry Ornest, he refused to buy Ed Kea along with the team," she said. "We were blessed in that Ralston-Purina wanted to do right by Ed. Because he did not receive the [NHL] insurance money, they tried to make up for what the NHL had not done."

The Keas and their four children live in a St. Louis suburb, "just getting by the best we can." Jennifer Kea said that John Ziegler, the NHL president, wrote her once. "Mr. Francis appealed to him on our behalf. Mr. Francis asked me to write a letter to Mr. Ziegler, which I did. To which he replied that if we were ever destitute, he would then make an attempt to assist us." She was disappointed, she says, "but I basically did not dwell on those things because I had far more important things to deal with. I thought having negative attitudes would not enhance my situation."

Kea still has seizures from the injury. Constantly on medication, he's in and out of hospital. He can speak only in short sentences. "He's partially blind and only has short-term memory. He becomes so depressed. Ed's totally disabled and probably, short of a miracle, will be for the remainder of his life."

BLAIR CHAPMAN, KEA'S TEAMMATE in St. Louis and Salt Lake, played seven seasons with the Blues and the Penguins before he too suffered an injury that ruined his career. "I took a shot in Colorado and fell on my right side, on a goal post," he recalled. "They kept telling me it was a bruise. After a month I had numbness in my leg. I had a CAT-scan done and found out it was a ruptured disk." St. Louis team doctor Jerome Gilden reported four times in sixteen days that the injury would not keep Chapman out for long, but just before Christmas 1981 — a month to the day after he first examined the injured right winger — Chapman was undergoing major back surgery.

Less than two months after the operation, the team doctor noted in an examination that Chapman had suffered a "strained back while skating." On February 13, 1982, the doctor noted that Chapman was "not ready to play at this time." Just three days later, he revised his report. "Player has 80 percent range of motion — should start hitting in practice next week." Nine days after that, Chapman was sent down to Salt Lake, where he reinjured his back in his first game. He eventually returned to St. Louis and skated in three April playoff games.

The following September, at the Blues training camp, Chapman suffered more back problems. He played twenty-two of the team's first twenty-seven games, but sprained an ankle and was again demoted to Salt Lake. Recalled to St. Louis, he was hurt yet again. On December 10, a St. Louis injury report noted that he "complained of neck and low back pain." On December 18, he stretched his left knee ligaments in a game against Hartford. Dr. Gilden noted that Chapman "should be OK with [knee] brace and treatment."

Chapman returned to action, but not for long. His medical reports from December 1982 and January 1983 record a litany of injuries: "strained right knee," "sprained right anterior collaterial ligament, right knee," "contusion to back — strained dorsal," "strained right shoulder." A day after noting the shoulder injury, Dr. Gilden downgraded it to "a slight strain...should be OK with treatments." Sent back to Salt Lake, Chapman appeared in twenty-two games, never to return to the NHL.

Why was he injury-prone after four and a half consecutive seasons in which he missed only 30 of 388 games? "The major surgery was basically the end of my career," he said. "Eight weeks later, I was released to play and hurt it again [in Salt Lake]. I tried to come back for a couple of seasons but basically I couldn't do it any more. I couldn't keep up. I kept getting hurt with all those other injuries because I couldn't react right with my back the way it was. I was always trying to protect it. As soon as I'd get hit, my back would get sore with muscle spasms and I couldn't play."

Damaged goods, Chapman was placed on waivers as the 1983–84 NHL season began. When no team claimed him, he was released. His career was over.

Chapman tried to collect his career-ending disability insurance, citing his 1981 disk surgery and the injuries he received during the 1982-83 season. He was turned down. "He missed three games with the flu, sat out the next five games and played four of the next six games before being sent on loan again to Salt Lake City on Feb. 14, 1983," wrote Helen A. LaPorte, claims manager at North American Claims Facilities in Boston, in a letter dated April 18, 1985. "That wasn't true," said Chapman, who now lives near Pittsburgh. "I don't know where that information came from." Sure enough, as I discovered, the Blues' medical reports revealed a different story. Why were those reports never forwarded to North American Claims? Why did Chapman's union not help him?

When Chapman was released, St. Louis wanted to buy out his contract at one-third its $135,000 value. He objected and filed for arbitration. This was a dispute between a player and a team, yet by the terms of the collective bargaining agreement the arbitrator would be NHL president Ziegler, whose salary was paid by the team owners. "When we got to New York for the hearing," Chapman recalled, "my lawyer said he thought Ziegler wasn't a good arbitrator, we'd like to have one who was impartial. Ziegler wouldn't let anyone arbitrate other than himself."

Eagleson had arranged for an NHLPA representative, Greg Britz, to attend. Britz had been a general manager at American Airlines in Canada; his association with Eagleson had been reported in the July 1984 *Sports Illustrated* story. Back in 1980, Eagleson had arranged for NHL players to take part in a golf tournament sponsored by American. For doing business with the company, Eagleson received free travel passes. So many passes ultimately went to his use that American conducted an internal investigation, which led to Britz's resignation. Eagleson hired him to represent NHLPA members in arbitration cases. Britz hadn't practiced law in nearly ten years. "It was a joke," Chapman recalled. "He might as well have not been there. He hardly said anything.

"They made my wife, myself, and my lawyer fly to New York — which I had to pay for — for that hearing. Ziegler had been in St. Louis twice before that, but couldn't give us a half hour of his time. No, we had to fly to New York."

Nearly a year after St. Louis sent Chapman packing, Ziegler ruled that he would receive $56,929 from the Blues, plus interest, reasoning that Chapman was due 68 days' pay out of a 181-day NHL regular season, his contract having been terminated on December 10, 1983. That date was significant. It was the day after Chapman's lawyer, Michael Flynn, gave the Blues an ultimatum to pay Chapman or face "equitable disposition" — a request for arbitration. From then on, Chapman said, "my contract was null and void. In other words, if I had waited the whole season and *then* applied for arbitration, I would have got my full contract."

By now Chapman's life was in turmoil. He had no income. He was being denied what he thought would be $175,000 in NHL and NHLPA career-ending disability insurance. He had to hire a lawyer to process his arbitration. He'd been paid only $11,000 by St. Louis, pending Ziegler's decision. "And a month after St. Louis let me go, my wife lost a baby," he recalled. "I was so bitter. Nobody cared. I tried to get away from hockey. I'd wasted my life believing that you do everything you can to play for the team, revolve your life around the game since you were old enough to skate, sacrifice whatever you can. For what — to get treated like this? Having to fight to get insurance coverage you were supposed to have?"

Chapman said he was never told he'd have trouble collecting if he was forced to retire because of injuries. "Eagleson and whoever was with him would come around visiting the dressing room at the beginning of each season," he recalled, echoing dozens of disillusioned players who'd suffered serious injuries, "assuring us we had good coverage as both NHLPA members and NHL players.

"When you retire hurt you're not getting paid any more. You have to hire a high-priced lawyer. The Players' Association knows that and the NHL knows it. Most guys can't afford it. Lawyers aren't going to take it on a contingency basis and it's going to take two or three years. Even Ed Kea had a hard time getting it, and he's definitely disabled."

In 1991, Chapman still walked with a pronounced limp and considered himself down and out, trying to get "any job." He again had tried to collect career-ending disability insurance, but again had been denied. This time the claims manager ruled that he had exceeded a policy limit by playing in more than twenty games after his back surgery — the so-called "cured rule."

At the time of Chapman's injury, the NHLPA's 1981–82 coverage was in force. Players were informed of the policy change during a June 1983 meeting in the Bahamas. The twenty-game cured rule was not officially added to the policy until a Lloyd's of London notice was passed on to Alan Eagleson. That notice was dated May 17, 1984 — two and a half years after Blair Chapman's original ruptured disk and back surgery.

IAN TURNBULL PLAYED TEN NHL seasons, mostly for the Maple Leafs, before suffering a back injury in 1982 while playing for the Baltimore Skipjacks, a Pittsburgh farm team. He, too, required surgery for a ruptured disk.

"I had $200,000 insurance I had bought through Robert Bradshaw and Associates as an optional disability. That basically came through Al Eagleson's office. Bradshaw was recommended as the underwriter by Eagleson — that's the choice you had." But when Turnbull filed for his disability, he was informed in a March 7, 1983, letter from William J. Sutton & Company, a Toronto insurance agency, that his coverage had been denied because he'd been playing in the minors at the time he was injured. (A former Bradshaw employee, and a close friend of Eagleson's, Sutton had taken over the disability insurance business in 1982.)

Turnbull turned to Eagleson for help. "He said he wasn't an insurance company," recalled Turnbull, now an investment and real estate business-man in California. "He said it wasn't his responsibility to pay claims. I could appreciate he wasn't an underwriter, but he was running the show. Everything was generated from his office, everybody knew he was in charge. He was pulling the strings. That was common knowledge. Other players who were Eagleson's clients had collected. They didn't seem to have problems."

Three doctors supported Turnbull's claim. One wrote: "I have strongly recommended to Mr. Turnbull that he abandon professional sports in any player capacity." Another assured North American Claims Facilities in Boston, which had denied the claim: "He is totally and permanently disabled for contact sports, especially hockey and football." Yet eleven months later North American Claims wrote to Turnbull's lawyer: "We have received nothing in the way of documentation which would indicate that Mr. Turnbull is permanently totally disabled from continuing his occupation as a professional hockey player...."

Turnbull was getting the fast shuffle. He hired Ron Roberts, a Dallas lawyer who had been the WHA Players' Association executive director. Roberts, a college friend of John Ziegler, had played a key role in the NHL-WHA merger of 1979. A five-page letter Roberts wrote to Helen A. LaPorte, claims manager of North American Claims Facilities in Boston, turned things around. In it, Roberts outlined Turnbull's disability case as a member of the Players' Association under NHL contract and raised the possibility of a "bad faith" multi-million-dollar punitive damage award that could be sought "against all concerned parties....As a matter of fact, I can't help but wonder how many other claims have been improperly denied without any review...."

Turnbull got his insurance settlement less than three months later. He received $75,000 on his NHL Players' Association policy, as well as $200,000 in additional coverage he had taken out on Eagleson's advice. He paid Roberts $50,000 in fees. He never did collect his $100,000 NHL disability policy because he was playing in the minor leagues at the time he was injured. Like Ed Kea, he was still under NHL contract. He did not fight that decision, however, because Roberts wanted another $25,000. "I wanted to get on with my life. This was just wearing me down."

IN HIS FOURTEEN NHL SEASONS, Pierre Larouche was a prolific scorer. During the 1975–76 season he scored 53 goals with Pittsburgh, a club high until Mario Lemieux came along. In the 1979–80 season, with Montreal, he scored 50 goals in seventy-three games. Over his career he averaged better than a point a game; fewer than 40 of the NHL's all-time top 100 scorers had done that. He was playing for the Rangers when his career ended in 1988.

"The left part of my back and my left hip caused me to retire," said Larouche. "I couldn't pivot properly. Lost a lot of my strength in my left leg and hip. We tried all kinds of treatments. I swam for six months. It's just that the damage was done. The muscles were damaged. I was thirty-two and every time I tried to come back it didn't work."

Through his New York agent, Rob Ingraham, Larouche notified the NHLPA of his intent to file for $30,000 in disability benefits. (NHL and NHLPA insurance coverage had changed from earlier years. NHL players thirty and over were insured only to a maximum of $30,000; coverage amounts increased for younger players. Older players ran higher risks of injury, went the thinking, but had already enjoyed good earning power in their careers; younger players were at less risk of injury and had not met their NHL salary potential.) Larouche knew he had that much coming to him from a booklet issued by the Players' Association, containing the 1986 NHL-NHLPA collective bargaining agreement, and from the meetings Alan Eagleson held with every team: "He bragged to us about our great insurance, how we should not worry, knowing we have the best coverage in sports. He'd come at least once a season. I was with three teams and he'd have these meetings every year. He'd say, 'One thing you don't have to worry about is disability insurance.' Nothing about 'This isn't covered or that isn't covered.'"

Larouche's disability claims for NHL and NHLPA insurance were denied by North American Claims Facilities in Boston, representing Crawley Warren, the Lloyd's of London company in charge of both the NHL and the NHLPA disability insurance. Larouche was told his claim was denied because his back injury was recurring. He had injured the back in 1981 but had never been informed that the original injury might one day jeopardize his insurance. "I didn't know that if you got hurt and then came back — in my case for six or seven years — that I was not covered because I was hurt before. It's not fair. I didn't know that I'd hurt it again. And that this time my hip would be affected, too." In fact, said Larouche, "my hip is probably more the cause of my retirement than the back. It never came around again. I also always thought that if you got hurt playing hockey, you were protected for whatever the amount of money was at the time of being hurt. That's what Eagleson always said. That's what he led us to believe."

Larouche was shocked that his claim was denied. And he was dumfounded that his own union wouldn't help him. "All of a sudden they were saying tough luck. I was always under the impression if I couldn't belong to the NHLPA anymore because I couldn't play, disability would get paid to me. It's not like I had three years left on my contract. When my injury occurred it was in my option year. It's not like I retired just to take three years' money...."

Now living in Scarsdale, New York, Larouche has limited hip movement. The hip sometimes locks. His left leg is shorter than his right because of muscle damage in his back that extends to his hip. "The left side of the hip is still numb today and it comes all the way up the front. It's still painful."

Larouche eventually gave up his fight for disability insurance. "I'm not going to hire a lawyer, wind up paying $15,000 to $20,000 in fees, go through all that time, just to break even."

LOUIS SLEIGHER'S NHL CAREER was cut short in 1987 when muscle tore away from the bone in his upper right leg. Orthopedic specialist Dr. Bert Zarins performed two operations, said Sleigher, "trying to reattach the muscle." Both times Sleigher attempted to skate after rehabilitation and therapy; both times his groin was reinjured. His playing days finished, he tried to collect $150,000 in NHL and NHLPA disability insurance as specified in the 1986 collective bargaining agreement.

"My agent, Steve Freyer, notified the NHLPA and NHL. It took a long time to go through the process," Sleigher said. "Alan Eagleson gave me no help at all. Steve used to call him every second week. Finally, I called Sam Simpson and asked what was going on. He just said, 'We're working on it.' They were working on it, all right. I was out of work and getting no satisfaction."

According to Freyer, the Players' Association directed him to insurance agent William Sutton in Toronto. Sutton forwarded Sleigher's claim to Crawley Warren, the London brokerage company. From there the claim went to a Lloyd's underwriter and back to Boston for paperwork. Freyer recalled: "I was extremely frustrated by the speed, or lack thereof, that the whole process moved at."

Getting bounced around from the Players' Association to Sutton's insurance company, waiting for word about the claim from London, Freyer was contacted by North American Claims in Boston, which handled the processing. Sleigher and Freyer were kept jumping though hoops, setting up doctors' exams, getting medical records in order.

"To me, that was the really aggravating, annoying part of it," said Freyer. "They're not efficient. They did not process the claims quickly. They were not speedy in contacting medical people. It was just an egregiously slow effort by the local people. I was very frustrated by that. Ultimately, that blame falls on the Players' Association.

"I found it to be an adversarial relationship. It seems to be a system of barriers set up, rather than 'How can we help you? How can we expedite this thing?' I can't tell how many phone calls I had to make to assertive people to get the thing moving. In a clear-cut case like Louis Sleigher, who today walks in pain, it was nonsense."

Freyer finally did an end-run. "I had enough of the B.S. We went around

Sutton and directly to the underwriters at Lloyd's. I had a friend, with a good working relationship with London, call Lloyd's directly, saying, 'Cut the baloney, cut the checks!' More than anything else, that's what got Louis his money."

Freyer still sizzles about it. "If Louis had been living paycheck to paycheck, which is not unusual for many NHL players, he would have been in real deep trouble because of the stupid bureaucracy they had developed and the way they were impeding a legitimate claim. Sutton didn't get in there and battle for us. Eagleson didn't get in there. This was Louis Sleigher and his agent, left hung out there on our own. If it wasn't for that friend, I'm not sure what would have happened."

THOUGH HE PLAYED ONLY five years in the NHL, Trevor Johansen paid a high price in scar tissue. He's had four operations on his right knee, surgery on his left knee, and two shoulder operations. A defenseman with Toronto, Colorado, and Los Angeles in the late 1970s and early 1980s, he had his career ended by a knee injury.

Johansen's agent for much of his career was Eagleson. Eagleson's friend, Dr. Charles Bull, who had played a role in the Jim Harrison case, performed Johansen's first knee surgery. "He didn't take the whole cartilage out, which was the procedure another doctor I consulted would have used. Bull was the doctor with Team Canada. So I went to Eagleson after the [1981] tournament and said, 'Al, my knee still hurts and that doctor friend of yours, who's a very nice man, he might have screwed it up.' Al says, 'Well, I don't know if that's true and it's tough to prove. You can't get anybody to testify in court.'" Johansen was thinking of a malpractice suit, but Eagleson, he says, talked him out of it.

The knee got worse. "I was playing on a lot of medication, anti-inflammatories." Facing another surgery, he retired during the 1981-82 season. He stopped in to see Eagleson and Marvin Goldblatt, an Eagleson employee whom Johansen had known long before turning pro; he remained friendly with Goldblatt even after he left Eagleson and went with Bill Watters as his agent. (Watters, a former CFL football player, became a player agent for

Eagleson's agency business before going on his own in 1979; he is now assistant general manager of the Toronto Maple Leafs.) He told Eagleson and Goldblatt he was retiring and needed their help in filing for disability. "I was in Marvin's office and told him it was clear, I'm disabled. I met all the requirements to collect my insurance....They both offered their condolences."

But nothing happened, so Johansen started calling them again. "I talked mostly to Marvin. He did not believe I could collect on a disability claim. I had played two or three years after my first injury." Johansen finally got the insurance papers and filed a claim himself. It was denied because of pre-existing conditions. Eagleson was no help. "Nobody from the Players' Association said, 'Let me handle that for you. This is how you go about it. This is what you need to do. These are your rights.'"

With the aid of Bill Watters, Johansen ironed out the remainder of his pro contract. And he hired Ron Roberts, the Dallas lawyer and ex-WHA Players' Association executive director, to help with his insurance. He eventually got his money — all $325,000 in NHL, NHLPA, and added disability coverage — but only after Roberts threatened to sue. He paid Roberts $75,000 in fees to collect what he'd been led to believe by Eagleson came automatically with his NHL contract and his membership in the NHLPA.

Despite the grief and the cost, Johansen felt lucky to collect at all, because he knew of many other deserving players who failed to. "The problem with hockey players is that they just want to play. The average NHL player is very young and extremely focused. In my case I always felt it was a responsibility to rush back after an injury. The insurance companies know that players will make heroic efforts to return. And the pre-existing clause is built around that. The classic examples are the Jim Harrisons and Ed Keas, who are ignored after dedicating themselves to their teams and quickly forgotten."

WILLIE HUBER'S FIRST KNEE SURGERY came in 1976. "Between '76 and '89, I had a lot of injuries with that left knee," recalled the ten-year NHL defenseman. By the mid-1980s, his medical history included another major knee surgery and two arthroscopic operations. But it was a knee injury suffered in Vancouver during the 1987-88 season, while he was playing for Philadelphia, that knocked him out of the league. "I was out eight weeks," Huber said. "Then I came back and played twenty-five or twenty-six games. Just before the playoffs we played the Rangers and I got hit. I was trying to keep the puck inside the blue line. My body was twisted, and Kelly Kisio's knee hit the outside of my knee and pushed it in, tearing some more ligaments."

Surgery was not recommended by Philadelphia team doctors. "They said sometimes it's not as good to have surgery on your knee because I'd already had surgery twice before." Instead, Huber knew he faced more therapy. "That's all I ever did. Stationary bikes every day, lifting weights with my knee, stuff like that."

A West German by birth who moved to Canada and later became a U.S. resident-alien, Huber decided to have another doctor examine him. He knew a team physician with the Detroit Pistons of the National Basketball Association. The news wasn't good. "The doctor said I might not be able to ever play again because my knee wasn't strong enough."

Huber decided to take a year off to rest his knee. "I was still young enough to come back," he reasoned, informing Philadelphia general manager Bobby Clarke of his decision. "He said, 'Fine. If you can't play, you can't play. No sense killing yourself.'"

By the fall of 1989, when training camp opened, the knee still hadn't healed. Huber's Detroit doctor left him no choice. "I tried to skate and there was no way. My knee's so bad, it's like spaghetti in there. If I didn't retire, the doctor said I'd be walking with a cane by the time I'm fifty." Huber quit hockey for good, and in April 1990 he filed for $30,000 in career-ending NHLPA disability insurance.

Huber had no doubt he was insured. Like every other injured player, he recalled that Eagleson toured the league at the beginning of each season, conducting meetings with each team about union business. Disability insurance was one of the subjects. "'When you get hurt, if you have a career-ending injury, that's what you get compensated for.' Eagleson always said that." But when Huber went to file his claim, he learned from NHLPA director of operations Sam Simpson that he had missed the filing deadline by four months.

"I said to him, 'I didn't know anything about filing within a certain period.' He said guys in years past were filing four, five, six years later.

They had changed the amount of time you had after you retired from hockey, which I didn't know."

Huber talked with Eagleson. "Mr. Eagleson said, 'Well, geez Willie!' He was in a bind to help because he said I filed too late, so I was entitled to nothing. He said he'd go back and talk to the insurance company and maybe try to settle for fifteen or sixteen thousand. Ten minutes later I get a phone call back. Eagleson says, 'Well, we got you sixteen thousand — it's better than nothing.'"

That's when Huber decided to hire a lawyer. He felt entitled to the full $30,000. Why was Eagleson deciding which players would get disability claims paid, and how much they would get? How would he know within minutes, without even filing the claim, that Huber would get $16,000 if he wasn't directly involved in the decision?

Eventually, it cost Huber $4,000 in legal fees to get two career-ending disability checks, one for his NHL coverage and the other for his NHLPA coverage, totaling $16,000. His net was $12,000. "I thought I was entitled to a minimum $30,000. I was putting my body in jeopardy for all these years and to get only $12,000? That doesn't make sense to me."

Huber was most aggravated by the explanation Eagleson and Simpson offered. "They said I filed too late, and I didn't know when I had to file — that's what I got out of this."

DISK SURGERY ENDED MURRAY WILSON'S seven-year NHL career with Montreal and Los Angeles. The speedy winger was advised by Dr. Ted Percy at the University of Arizona and Dr. James Garrick of San Francisco not to play because of the removal of a herniated disk in 1977. Wilson's back "prevented me from playing without pain. I had trouble turning on the ice, turning to my right."

Sent to the minors by Kings general manager George McGuire, Wilson refused to report because of his back trouble. When the Kings suspended him, he turned to Eagleson, his players' union executive director, phoning him at home. He needed Eagleson's help to settle a $210,000 injury grievance with Los Angeles and to get his disability insurance claim processed. Ironically, Eagleson told Wilson he had a bad back of his own.

"He was on his way to London, England, to have his back looked at. He wanted to know why I was calling him at home. He said, 'You're not a client of mine. You're a client of Art Kaminsky's. Tell him to take care of your problems.' He told me he had no goddamn use for Kaminsky.

"I said I was a paid-up member of the Players' Association for seven years — since '72 — and I was calling him because he was the director of that association. I told him, 'Even when George McGuire suspended me, I paid the dues. I thought you could help me answer some questions or advise me how I can handle this disability issue. Isn't this what we're covered by insurance for?'

"He said he didn't care what my problem was, that Kaminsky was my agent and I should go have him solve my problems. He said being paid up with the Players' Association made no difference. It was a five-minute conversation, tops. I never heard from him again."

Wilson took both his suspension and disability insurance problems to the NHL for arbitration. "It dragged on — oh, God! — for a couple of years. I went without an income from November '79 to '81. I got notified my $210,000 disability had been settled in '81, when my brother Doug got married. By then my house had gone into foreclosure. I didn't have any money."

Actually that money, I discovered, was a settlement of his contract. Wilson hired his own lawyers, eventually paying $70,000 to process the insurance claims and help with his arbitration case. "The NHLPA was useless for me. It was a farce. Eagleson couldn't care less and he made that clear. The league couldn't care less. It's a part of my life I'd like to forget. I went through hell." It took nearly four years for him to get $83,500 in disability insurance.

"When I played in Montreal," Wilson recalled, picking up the refrain, "Eagleson would come around to the dressing room early in the season to discuss Players' Association matters. He always said, 'Don't worry. If anything ever happens to you playing hockey, the NHL Players' Association can take care of it.' Whenever anybody asked a question about insurance, he said, 'Don't worry about a thing. That's why you have a Players' Association.' Those were his words and we believed him."

GARY CROTEAU FIRST INJURED his left knee in 1968, playing college hockey at St. Lawrence University in Canton, New York. The surgery was successful and Croteau went on to an NHL career with Los Angeles, Detroit, Oakland, Kansas City, and Colorado. In 1979, at the Rockies training camp, he slammed into a goal post. He injured the same knee.

"I came back but the knee did not respond. I was taking a lot of treatment, started on anti-inflammatories, packing it in ice, and it was still inflaming." Croteau's coach at the time was Don Cherry. Croteau recalls that Cherry "wouldn't allow me to practice. Just light skates the morning of a game, then go out and play that night. I started walking with a limp after that. I continued to play and then around the first of March I started taking painkillers. Soon as Cherry found that out, he called me into his office and said, 'You're not playing the rest of the season. Your knee isn't strong enough. We'll get you ready for next year.'"

Croteau tried to rehabilitate the knee, but knew he was finished when it "continued to inflame." He reported to Colorado's minor-league club in Fort Worth, Texas, and played a couple of games, "but it just didn't respond." After playing fifteen games of the 1979–80 season, he retired, notifying the Players' Association and Alan Eagleson.

Croteau was on a one-way NHL contract with Colorado, assuring him of all NHL benefits including disability insurance. Eagleson had told the Colorado players that they need not worry about disability insurance, that every player on an NHL contract was covered in case of career-ending injury. Yet Croteau was now told he didn't qualify for the career-ending insurance because of the old injury from college. He told Cherry what had happened. "Don and I had developed a nice relationship," Croteau recalled. "He was the one who suggested I talk to Eagleson. First he made a phone call to Eagleson on my behalf."

I'd known Cherry since his Boston days and knew he was a player's coach. He considered Eagleson a good friend. "Al had represented me," Cherry told me. "Actually Billy Watters did, through Eagleson's sports management company." Eagleson's company had negotiated Cherry's coaching deal in Colorado after Harry Sinden fired Cherry as the Bruins' coach after the 1979 playoffs.

"When Gary said he was being stiffed on his insurance," Cherry recalled, "I said I'd call Al and I did, just to crack the ice for him. Al said he'd help."

"When I talked with Eagleson," Croteau said, "he felt there may be a claim. I could submit a claim to the Players' Association. They would review it and take appropriate action."

I asked who the "they" were.

"I asked the same thing. Eagleson said he would, with Sam Simpson and an insurance man."

Hearing nothing, he phoned Eagleson again. In the meantime Croteau had realized he not only had NHL and NHLPA disability coverage, he had also purchased added disability coverage through insurance agent Robert Bradshaw at the urging of the NHLPA. Reminding Eagleson of this in their second phone call, Croteau said, Eagleson backed off. Now he told Croteau it was "a fifty-fifty proposition" as to whether he could get the claim paid. "He said maybe he could help, but it would cost money. He didn't have time to chase insurance cases." Croteau was livid. "Back when I was playing in Oakland [1970–74], we asked him about disability. We were assured, if hurt by a hockey injury, we would be insured." Now that Croteau's career was over, however, his claim was denied.

"Because I'd had surgery twelve years earlier, they kept saying it was a degenerative disease, then a recurring injury. So the twelve years I played on it without a problem didn't count. Why didn't anybody ever tell me my knee wasn't covered? That didn't stop them from taking my added insurance premiums. After going through all the effort, popping all those pain pills, now they were saying I'm not covered? Bull! That wasn't right."

Croteau also hired Dallas lawyer Ron Roberts. "We had the doctors write letters," said Croteau. "They supported our position that up until that [1979] injury, the knee was performing at 100 percent. That it had passed the test of time. That the reason I was no longer able to play was because of the last injury and the last surgery." Of the $175,000 Croteau believed he had coming to him, he eventually settled for about $90,000. His legal bill ate up about 10 percent of that.

AT SIX-FOOT-THREE AND 215 POUNDS, Pat Quinn was a hulking defenseman in his playing days with Toronto, Vancouver, and Atlanta, perhaps best remembered for the devastating check he put on Bobby Orr during a Toronto-Boston playoff game at Boston Garden in 1969. Wayne Cashman, Orr's roommate, recalled the next day, "Bobby got up three times during the night and answered the phone, but it never rang." Quinn went on to a successful coaching career in Philadelphia, Los Angeles, and Vancouver, where he became the Canucks' president and general manager.

Quinn's career ended with an injury suffered not on the ice but in his driveway. While captain of the Atlanta Flames in 1976, he fell off a skateboard and broke his left ankle. He tried a comeback but was never the same. He filed for disability insurance (which covers players off the ice as well), expecting to collect a combined $200,000 in coverage from the NHL, the NHLPA, and the added disability insurance he had purchased from NHLPA insurance agent Robert Bradshaw.

Quinn's claim was denied because he had appeared in fifty-nine games after his injury. As I would find, the exact number of games a player could play after an injury and still be eligible for disability was not an issue until the early 1980s. Even in 1980, two years after Quinn filed his claim, Eagleson was assuring NHLPA player reps by letter that they could play and still get their disability insurance. "To be a valid claim the disability must be continuous from the date of accident for a full twelve months. That's not to suggest the player is not allowed a reasonable time to try to return to play," Eagleson wrote, specifically addressing Lloyd's of London disability coverage. "But this cannot be a situation whereby he returns and plays for a season or more, and then decides to submit a claim."

Every team had an eighty-game regular season in 1980. So how many games could an injured player compete in after being hurt? Eagleson didn't say. Presumably, any number less than eighty. After Quinn's broken ankle had mended and he'd tried a comeback, he found he wasn't rehabilitated. On what grounds could he be denied his insurance?

Quinn hired former U.S. Justice Department prosecutor Robert J. Vedatsky of Philadelphia, who drafted a $3-million lawsuit against the NHL Players' Association, insurance agent Bob Bradshaw, and Lloyd's of London. "We couldn't get to first base with the Players' Association or anybody else," Vedatsky recalled. "They wouldn't even answer my phone calls until we wrote that suit and it was sent to the Boston insurance claim manager. We mailed copies of it before it was to be filed. I was a federal prosecutor. It was written like an indictment."

He never had to file the suit. "Eagleson came to Philly to talk with the speed of lightning," said Vedatsky, chuckling as he recalled a snowstorm that had Eagleson worried because his flight to Philadelphia was delayed. He said Eagleson appeared relieved when they met, evidently concerned that Vedatsky may have filed the suit anyway, thinking Eagleson had stood him up. "We settled Pat's insurance case in a short time."

An upshot of Quinn's case was an investigation by the Insurance Commissioner's Office of the Commonwealth of Pennsylvania into added insurance coverage endorsed by Eagleson and sold by Bradshaw through the NHLPA. The Pennsylvania state insurance commissioner determined that Bradshaw had violated state regulations, including selling insurance without a license to members of the Pittsburgh Penguins and Philadelphia Flyers. Bradshaw did not admit wrongdoing but paid a $10,000 fine.

Charles Dettrey, a former supervisor of investigations for the state insurance regulatory board, headed the investigation. He said the case didn't go further only because of time constraints. The issue could have been pursued as a criminal matter but Dettrey was discouraged by his superiors. "I had put two months into the case and they thought that was enough."

Why didn't he think the case went far enough?

"Eagleson," Dettrey replied. "I wanted to add him next. As the evidence shows, he was the one pushing players to buy insurance through Bradshaw. They weren't even licensed to carry on that business in Pennsylvania. And when it came time to collect on a legitimate claim, as was the case with Pat Quinn, many players were having a helluva time getting the coverage they were entitled to."

AFTER QUEBEC CENTRE ANDRÉ SAVARD was checked into the boards in a game against Buffalo just before Christmas in 1984, his knee swelled up. He tried to play against Montreal a few days later but the pain was intense. It turned out that the knee was badly damaged, and the team doctor told him, "You won't be able to play again." After more than 900 games in twelve years with Boston, Buffalo, and Quebec, Savard was through.

The following summer, he brought up the subject of insurance with Eagleson. "Al told me he'd get my disability insurance for me, but it would cost money for lawyers," said Savard, who was thirty-one at the time and had been the Nordiques' player representative. "He said $100,000 was the best he could get for me. And maybe he'd get me some money from the team toward what would have been my contract for playing. I said, 'That sounds good. Sure.'"

Savard said his disability insurance claims were processed "with no problem" within six months. He was notified that the NHL insurance payment was to be in U.S. funds, but later received a letter from NHL vice president Gil Stein stating there was a mistake and the payment would be in Canadian funds. Savard received $60,000 from the NHL and $40,000 from the Players' Association, both in Canadian funds. The NHLPA check came with an invoice from Eagleson asking Savard to send an $8,500 check "to my attention...with respect to legal fees as agreed."

Savard sent Eagleson the money, and in February 1986, he got a letter from Marvin Goldblatt, treasurer of Rae-Con Consultants Limited. "Mr. Eagleson has sent the $8,500.00 check to us as a payment in full for fees. Thank you." Enclosed was invoice Number 548 from Rae-Con: $7,860 for "retaining counsel and obtaining settlement of claim under Lloyd's policy." There also was a notation about work done with the Nordiques "to resolve all contract matters in conjunction with insurance policy." The remaining $640 was billed as telephone, air travel, and hotel expenses.

I asked Savard, whom I'd known since he was a rookie with the Bruins, about Rae-Con.

"That was the law firm that helped me out," he explained. "It had nothing to do with Al Eagleson."

"Do you know what Rae-Con is?"

"Well, the law firm that worked on my insurance."

When I told him that Rae-Con Consultants was one of Eagleson's companies — that RAE stood for R. Alan Eagleson — and that Goldblatt was an employee of Eagleson's, Savard's jaw dropped. "I never knew this," he said, shaking his head in disbelief. "He billed me for a company that's his? Great deal. He sets up our insurance as Players' Association director, then he charges us to get it? He gets paid both ways."

Eagleson was well aware that Savard's coverage should have totaled $175,000, not $100,000, and that the funds were to be paid in U.S. dollars. I asked why Savard agreed to pay a fee when he felt he was entitled to the insurance.

"I was afraid," he said. "My career was over. I told Al and he said, 'Don't worry about a thing. It'll be tough, we'll need lawyers, but I'll get your insurance, André." Eagleson also promised Savard he'd talk with Quebec owner Marcel Aubut about a job. Savard ended up coaching a minor-league team the next season.

In 1984, NHL disability insurance called for $100,000 in coverage and NHLPA insurance another $75,000. The coverage had been arranged by Eagleson, who clearly knew Savard was entitled to $175,000 U.S. I wondered why Savard — even after paying a fee to the Eagleson company — did not receive the benefits he was due. At the time, Savard's $100,000 Canadian was the equivalent of only about $70,000 U.S. And that was before his $8,500 payment to Rae-Con.

I consulted three disability insurance experts familiar with Lloyd's coverage. All agreed Savard should have received $175,000 U.S. All agreed he should not have been charged a fee by the head of his union to collect it.

"I wouldn't want to be involved with anything like that, charging somebody to get their insurance payments," said Jim Edgeworth Jr., a fifteen-year sports disability insurance specialist based in Houston. "Players' associations have always been there to help the players. They exist to best represent the interests of their players."

"The $8,500 is nonsense," said Ted Dipple, president of American Specialty Underwriters Inc. in Woburn, Massachusetts, whose clients include players in major-league baseball, the NBA, the NFL, and the NHL. "The insured should get 100 percent of a valid claim, even if London appoints an adjuster."

"It's astounding," said Allan Checkoway, a disability insurance expert based in Boston who is often consulted by law firms on insurance issues, of the $8,500 fee. "I would say that's a conflict."

All three also said Savard should have received payment in U.S. funds. "I would deliver U.S. funds if that's what the certificate said," Edgeworth noted. "I would go to the wall for my client to make sure he got every penny for his premium." Dipple added: "If you're not going to honor the currency spelled out in the agreement, why not pay him in yen or lira?"

A FIRST-ROUND NHL DRAFT PICK, chosen by Colorado in 1978 before being traded to Boston in 1981, Mike Gillis — "Dobie" to his teammates — was a Bruin when he suffered a badly broken leg at training camp in September 1984. Alan Eagleson was Gillis's agent; Eagleson's company, Rae-Con, also handled Gillis's financial affairs. And Eagleson, of course, was the head of the union to which Gillis belonged.

Rae-Con reported the injury on September 28, 1984, as a broken ankle to William J. Sutton & Company, the insurance agency that handled NHL and Players' Association business. It soon became clear to Gillis his recovery was not going well and, at twenty-five, his career was over. On March 29, 1985, Eagleson wrote to Sutton on Players' Association stationery with a completed career-ending disability form, claiming Gillis was finished and wanted his insurance benefits.

Gillis was covered for $75,000 on his NHLPA policy, $100,000 on his NHL policy, and $100,000 in optional insurance offered to NHLPA members, which Eagleson had suggested he take. The three policies were issued through Crawley Warren Group of London, England, headed by Bernard J. Warren.

In late October 1985, North American Claims Facilities of Boston — the adjuster for Crawley Warren — refused payment on the basis that Gillis could still play pro hockey. By this time he had enrolled as an undergraduate at Queen's University in Kingston, Ontario. Eagleson, while at Queen's for a speaking appearance, met with Gillis and asked him to get additional medical reports. Gillis did so. On December 13, 1985, Eagleson forwarded the medical information to North American Claims, again requesting that Gillis be paid his insurance. The claim was denied a second time.

In February 1986, Dr. Charles Bull — Eagleson's buddy and the Team Canada doctor — issued a report confirming that Gillis was unable to play pro hockey. Eagleson sent Bull's findings to North American Claims on March 26, 1986, as further evidence that Gillis deserved his disability insurance.

Marvin Goldblatt told Gillis that lawyers may be the only answer if the insurance matter was not settled. At Eagleson's request, Gillis and his wife drove from Kingston to Eagleson's Toronto office to discuss the claims. Eagleson told Gillis that lawyers in the United States and England would be needed to put the heat on Lloyd's. Gillis agreed and a letter was dictated, authorizing Eagleson and Rae-Con to act for Gillis.

Eagleson and Goldblatt also asked Gillis to authorize Goldblatt and Kingsmar Holdings Limited, another Eagleson business, to act for him in processing his claims. For lawyers, accountants, and "special advisers," Gillis agreed to pay 15 percent of whatever he received.

A few months later, Eagleson told him the claims had been settled in full. Of the $275,000 U.S. coverage for his three claims, Gillis received $233,750. The remaining $41,250 went to Kingsmar.

Clean deal, no problems — or so Gillis thought. In fact, a telex, dated April 4, 1986, from Eagleson to Bernard J. Warren showed the true nature of the deal. On April 3, Eagleson had sent a letter to North American Claims requesting that the Gillis claim be paid. On April 4, in his telex, Eagleson reminded Warren that in the André Savard disability claim, processed four months earlier, he had helped the insurers (save $105,000) and that he had saved them money on another claim by former Philadelphia Flyer Bill Barber. Savard had been paid out in Canadian dollars instead of U.S., hadn't got the full coverage he was entitled to, and — adding insult to injury — had paid Eagleson's company for the privilege.

Now Eagleson was calling in the chit. In the telex, he stated: "I feel strongly on Gillis. He is absolutely honest and has refused to go to an outside lawyer in Boston or Toronto because he trusts me." The same day, Warren responded by telex, promising to "do whatever possible" to get the Gillis claim resolved. A week later, Lloyd's insurance man Dennis Johnson sent Eagleson another telex from Warren's office in London, suggesting Eagleson attend a meeting in London the following week to discuss the Gillis claim.

On May 19, 1986, North American Claims of Boston wrote to Eagleson.

Lloyd's of London had agreed to pay the $75,000 Players' Association disability insurance in full. The same day, another letter from North American Claims went to NHL vice president Gil Stein, informing him the $100,000 in NHL insurance coverage for Gillis had been approved in full. A copy of the letter was sent to Eagleson.

It was ten days *after* the two claims, totaling $175,000, had been approved — and three days *after* Eagleson had been informed by the NHL that documents were being sent for Gillis to execute — that Eagleson met with Gillis and his wife. Eagleson led Gillis to believe he'd have to hire outside professionals to fight for the money. Unaware the claims had already been approved, Gillis agreed to pay Eagleson 15 percent of whatever came from the claims. Since $175,000 had already been settled, Eagleson's company made $26,250 before the ink was dry on the agreement Gillis signed. And since both claims had been approved, it was a formality for Gillis to collect on his third policy, the optional coverage, a mirror policy placed through the same agent and the same broker. "That is the reason for taking optional insurance to back up the NHL and Players' Association coverage," said insurance expert Ted Dipple, whose experience with Lloyd's dates back more than twenty-five years. "If the two disability policies were satisfactory for full settlement, the third was a *fait accompli*."

On September 10, 1986, Kingsmar — Eagleson's company — billed Rae-Con Consultants — Eagleson's company — for $41,250 U.S., 15 percent of the $275,000 total for all three Gillis claims. The bill was stamped "paid" on September 9, the day before the date on the Kingsmar invoice. Marvin Goldblatt, Eagleson's Rae-Con employee, signed the check payable to Kingsmar. Kingsmar had been paid before issuing a bill, but who'd know the difference? Gillis had been led to believe he'd won a hotly challenged insurance case. Eagleson's company cashed in by withholding information from Gillis and by taking 15 percent of the insurance benefits, negotiated and placed by Eagleson, contractually guaranteed to NHL players and members of the NHLPA.

Gillis himself went on to become a lawyer and a sports agent, representing such players as Geoff and Russ Courtnall. On May 17, 1994, through a Toronto lawyer, Charles Scott, he filed suit against Eagleson and two of his companies, Rae-Con and Jialson Holdings (Jialson had taken over Kingsmar in 1993). The suit sought more than $500,000 in damages, plus the $41,250 U.S. slice Eagleson had taken off the disability payout.

Eagleson, who bragged that he'd never backed away from a fight, filed a countersuit. As executive director of the Players' Association, he argued, he "owed no duty to Gillis to act in his best interests, nor any other duty." Why? Because Gillis, having suffered a career-ending injury, had "ceased to be a member of the NHLPA" at the time he filed for his disability insurance.

DALE TALLON SOUGHT $215,000 in career-ending insurance after he suffered a compound fracture below the right knee while playing for Pittsburgh in a game against Vancouver in 1980. Eagleson was his union executive director and his agent. Tallon said he had no problem collecting the insurance — "None whatsoever. Eagleson handled it for me. He never charged me a fee." As Jim Harrison had said, Tallon went on to become a Blackhawks TV commentator (an appointment approved by Blackhawks owner and Eagleson buddy Bill Wirtz) and a golf pro at Tamarack Golf Club in Naperville, Illinois.

Straightforward deal, no wrinkles? So it would seem if not for the letter, dated May 10, 1982, that Crawley Warren chairman Bernie Warren sent Eagleson.

Dear Alan:

In accordance with our agreement in London last week, I enclose herewith a receipted invoice in the amount of $4,950.00 U.S. funds concerning the Tallon claims.

Although we had originally anticipated that a 5% collection fee was to be attached to the payment, in the circumstances we have accepted your figure of 3% for a total in the amount of $4,950.00 U.S. funds for which payment we thank you.

If you require any further documentation please advise me further.

Yours sincerely,

Bernard J. Warren

The attached invoice, also on Crawley Warren stationery, was addressed to Eagleson and signed by Warren himself.

The NHL and the NHLPA were paying premiums to cover their players for career-ending disability insurance placed by Eagleson. The Lloyd's broker was collecting a premium commission. Now the broker was also collecting a "collection fee" to process the claim of an injured player? It didn't add up. Why was Eagleson steering almost $5,000 U.S. of Dale Tallon's money to Bernie Warren for something Warren had already been paid to do?

"I've never heard of that in my life," said Ted Dipple, "a broker collecting a fee to process a claim. And I've been in this business all my adult life."

"Would you pay your car insurance agent an extra fee to get your coverage if your car was damaged in an accident?" said another expert, Jim Edgeworth. "Those costs are included in the premium. That's part of what you pay for, to process the insurance if there's a claim."

GLEN SHARPLEY PLAYED FOUR SEASONS with Minnesota between 1976 and 1980 before being traded to Chicago. During a game against Washington in 1981, he was highsticked in the face by Darren Veitch, suffering an eye injury that ended his NHL career. Sharpley had a handshake agreement with Eagleson to be his agent in return for 7 percent of his hockey salary. "That's how we worked until I got hurt," Sharpley recalled. "When I got hurt, he wanted a contract with me."

Sharpley filed for career-ending disability insurance coverage totaling $340,000 — including optional insurance he'd taken out through the NHLPA. Eagleson told him the insurance company "didn't want to pay." Sharpley was twenty-five at the time. Through his old friends Pulford and Wirtz, Eagleson got him a two-year contract with Chicago, a scouting job that paid $25,000 a season.

The disability claim hung in limbo, according to Sharpley, until he threatened to leave Eagleson. He said Eagleson told him he would "have a hard time collecting the insurance" if Eagleson wasn't his agent. "My back was against the wall," said Sharpley. "There was no question in my mind with him at the helm, I'd get my money. There was no question I'd have trouble if I had anybody else. He said his expenses would be high and therefore he had to charge a fee to get the insurance."

Sharpley finally collected his insurance, but had to pay Eagleson a $15,000 fee. Part of the money, said Eagleson, was to pay for a plane trip made by Bernard Warren and his wife to the United States.

"I had breakfast with the insurance man, Mr. Warren, his wife, and Al," Sharpley said. "I told him, 'If I could play, I would play. I'm young enough, but my vision isn't right from the injury.' The doctors had all examined me. The insurance company knew that. Al knew that. I think the man and his wife had a nice vacation. That's about all we said about my injury....I don't think it lasted long enough for me to finish a cup of coffee."

In a letter to the players, Eagleson mentioned the Sharpley claim: "Glen had a difficult case with the insurance company. We retained counsel to assist Glen. In normal circumstances, Sharpley would have paid 35 percent on a contingent fee basis to a U.S. lawyer....Glen was paid $325,000 and his fees were approximately $15,000. Glen had agreed in writing to the fee schedule before any action was commenced...."

"Imagine having to pay that son-of-a-bitch to get insurance I was already owed," said Sharpley, who now operates a sporting goods store in Haliburton, Ontario. "Here he is my agent, whom I'm paying to represent me, charging me a fee to get my insurance, which I had already paid for. Not only is he my agent, but he's the Players' Association executive director in charge of matters involving the players — including insurance! He's collecting a fee from me as a lawyer, collecting a fee as the Players' Association director through membership dues, and now he sticks it to me with another fee to collect my disability insurance. He was making it on three ends."

BOB DAILEY WAS A RUGGED NHL defenseman between 1973 and 1982. He spent his final five seasons in Philadelphia, where his career ended with a badly broken ankle. When Dailey sought his career-ending disability insurance, Eagleson — who had represented him throughout his career — told him he would have to pay for Bernie Warren to fly to the United States to accelerate the claim.

The Warren trip cost Dailey $5,000. A small price to pay to collect $375,000? Yes, except that, as in the Sharpley case, Eagleson wasn't just Dailey's agent, he was also his union boss. Again, here was the executive director of the union charging a member to collect insurance coverage guaranteed by the collective bargaining agreement.

Warren came to the United States in January 1983, during an NHL-Soviet mid-season tour of exhibition games. Sharpley had met with him at The Marriott in Bloomington, Minnesota, the day after a North Stars–Soviet exhibition game. Dailey met with Warren and Eagleson in Philadelphia for dinner before a Flyers-Soviet exhibition game on the same tour.

"Not a lot was brought up about the insurance," recalled Dailey, who lives in suburban Philadelphia and works as a cellular phone salesman. "I didn't know what position Warren was in to expedite the disability claim, or what his whole purpose was."

Four days after their meeting, Dailey got a letter from Eagleson saying that Sports Management, Eagleson's agent business, had paid for the Warrens' trip. "I arranged to bring Mr. and Mrs. Warren to North America at Sports Management's expense in order to expedite [Dailey's payment]," wrote Eagleson, who also said he made a special trip to London to work on the claim. "The expenses Sports Management has incurred in the September trip and for Mr. and Mrs. Warren will exceed $10,000. The Warrens flew to New York by Concorde and then on to Minnesota and Philadelphia in order to accommodate my request to have Mr. Warren meet you and Glen Sharpley." Eagleson asked Dailey for $5,000 "as a fee for Sports Management to offset the expenses incurred. This will be matched by Glen Sharpley so that the total expenses will be met...."

How many chairmen of insurance companies fly from Europe to the United States to meet with a claimant? How many bring their wives to such meetings? I thought I'd ask Bernie Warren that question. I got the Crawley Warren number in London and his secretary took a message. A few days later, Warren called my home. I managed to get a few answers before he realized what was up.

Warren denied that Eagleson had paid for that 1983 trip. "I can confirm Mr. Eagleson has never, ever paid for my flights, particularly Concorde flights," Warren said. "The hockey people don't pay for my flights. I make my own expenses." He remembered discussing insurance claims with only one player: "I recall meeting Mr. Sharpley. I don't remember Mr. Dailey. I think we discussed a claim with Mr. Sharpley during that trip." I told him about Eagleson's bills to Sharpley and Dailey. Warren was surprised to learn Eagleson had billed them for his expenses.

In the same interview, I asked Warren if he had any other business or property interests with Alan Eagleson. Several people had told me that Eagleson had a place in London, and I wondered if Warren might know anything about it. Warren got huffy, saying no, he had no other interests with Eagleson, and accused me of being a typical American journalist looking to turn up dirt. He hung up.

His irritation was out of all proportion, his bristling denial more emphatic than necessary. All of which — together with the correspondence from the Mike Gillis and Dale Tallon claims — suggested that their relationship deserved further scrutiny.

5

SIMPLE ACTS OF FRIENDSHIP

"If a claim is filed, the claim has been paid, but
the recipient has not received the full proceeds —
I'm not a lawyer, but it sounds like fraud."
ROBERT TIERNEY

A SOURCE IN CANADA had told me that, in
London, Eagleson stayed at a place he referred to as "Pimlico." I phoned
London information to see if perhaps Eagleson or his wife was listed, but
the London directory was organized by area, and I didn't know the right
one. I called Scotland Yard and was told, "There's a Pimlico Road not far
from Buckingham Palace." I called the *Daily Telegraph* and found a reporter
kind enough to go through the entire directory, one area at a time. After
a long search, he said, "There's a listing for an R.A. Eagleson at 17 Pimlico
Road."

I asked if anyone in London was up on hockey.

"Field hockey or ice hockey?"

He gave me the name and number of someone considered knowl-
edgable, Vic Batchelder, who published a hockey newspaper or magazine. I
called Eagleson's number, but got no answer, so I called Batchelder. He
turned out to be familiar with Eagleson and the Players' Association,
remembering that an NHLPA meeting had been held in London in the mid-
1980s. He also recalled, on another occasion, seeing Eagleson and John
Ziegler together there.

I told Batchelder I'd covered NHL hockey and the Bruins for years and was checking into Eagleson's questionable practices involving player pensions and other matters. I needed information on 17 Pimlico Road. Could he help by looking up the deed to the place, finding legal papers, talking to neighbors, providing any information he could about Eagleson's connection to 17 Pimlico Road? He wondered if I was willing to pay for his time. I said I was and was also willing to pay for photos of the Pimlico place. We struck a deal, and Batchelder was off and running.

MEANWHILE, I HAD DISCOVERED IN 1983, at a players' union meeting in the Bahamas, insurance discussions had been conducted by a group led by none other than Bernard Warren, representing Crawley Warren Ltd., the disability insurance brokers for the NHLPA. Other speakers included Robert Tierney, vice president of Boston Mutual Insurance Company, the carrier of NHLPA life, accidental death, and major medical insurance; and Bill Sutton of William J. Sutton & Co. Ltd. of Toronto, administrators of the NHLPA insurance programs.

Looking through a report of those meetings, one item jumped out at me. "A discussion ensued around the recent provision in the policy that allows a player twenty games to rehabilitate from a serious injury, following which no [career-ending disability] claim can be submitted for that injury." Well, how about that — "the recent provision." It hadn't been in place when the 1982-83 season began.

The summary noted that Buffalo Sabre Ric Seiling had had a problem with that "recent provision." Seiling had suffered an eye injury and was concerned with the rehabilitation rule, believing twenty games were insufficient and "might encourage more players to claim rather than continue to rehabilitate." Hockey players, as Trevor Johansen had explained and as I knew from covering the Bruins, invariably try to come back from injuries as soon as they can. I'd watched Terry O'Reilly play nearly a full season with a torn rotator cuff. Why would anyone play if he knew he was putting not only his body but also his insurance coverage on the line?

Eagleson had answered Seiling's question, pointing out that the twenty-game condition had been negotiated with Lloyd's underwriters who had sought a ten-game limit. The twenty-game condition, or "cured rule," was a means of disallowing career-ending disability claims for an injury. Yet the reason St. Louis player Blair Chapman had been given for having his disability claim denied was that he had come back and played within a year of having major surgery. In fact, the old NHLPA disability policy was still in effect when the union discussion on insurance was held in Nassau.

At the same meeting, underwriter Dennis Johnson told the players the total premium from all NHL and NHLPA hockey disability coverage for the most recent year "was in the region of $800,000, whereas claims were approximately $1.2 million." Johnson was concerned that the disability plan was in jeopardy. "Too often," he said, "claims had been submitted by players who were retiring anyway and who intended to try and link the end of their career to the most recent injury they suffered. In truth, the retirement was caused by normal degeneration of the body, perhaps contributed to by a series of relatively minor injuries...."

This meeting took place nearly three months *after* Ed Kea's near-fatal accident left him in a coma. It was his misfortune that the accident happened at a time when claims were already high. Sure, Kea eventually got his NHLPA insurance, but the league offered only $5,000 on what should have been $100,000 in coverage.

Robert Tierney, who had also spoken at that 1983 meeting and done insurance business with the NHLPA, was from my part of the world, so I called Boston Mutual. I learned he had retired and lived on the South Shore of Massachusetts. I reached him and set up a meeting.

Tierney turned out to be a garrulous, florid, silver-haired fellow. Though his firm had been involved on the group health side of NHL and NHLPA insurance, he was able to explain the disability insurance business to me. NHLPA disability insurance went from Eagleson through Robert Bradshaw (and, in later years, Bill Sutton, who left Bradshaw to form his own business), to Bernard Warren and Dennis Johnson, the London brokers, and to Bert Stratton, the underwriter who took it to the floor of Lloyd's for Crawley Warren. At Lloyd's, insurance coverage is split among a syndicate of buyers. Insurance risk is sold in percentages to Lloyd's "names." The syndicate of names shares in any loss, as it does in profits. The final premium is charged when the policy is issued through the broker back to the agent and then to the policy holder. That final premium includes an excess billing over and above the actual cost of the insurance.

Thinking of Ed Kea and Blair Chapman, I asked about the responsibility of supplying updated information to those covered by disability insurance. Was there any obligation to inform the insured of any changes in policies?

"I believe there is," said Tierney. "Each individual is entitled to have a certificate which outlines benefits, eligibility requirements, the limitations of the policy, and how to file for claims." An insured player had "a right to know from his employer who is providing benefits, what the level of benefits are, and how he collects in the event of death, disability, or retirement."

Thinking of Terry O'Reilly and Brad Park, I asked if NHL players knew about reinsurance of their whole life and group family policies. "In my day, the players were young," Tierney said. "They really weren't interested in details of insurance. They were more interested in contracts, big bucks, and playing hockey. And winning the Stanley Cup."

"The purpose of self-insurance in a captive in Bermuda by the NHL would include profits for the owners, is that correct?"

"The potential for profits, always the potential for profits."

No wonder the players didn't know about ICE. The NHL didn't want them to know. The league itself had an offshore insurance business, and insurance companies don't necessarily make money by paying out claims.

Tierney was surprised to learn of the problems facing the O'Reilly and Park families, saying that "if the youngsters had pre-existing conditions" they should have been covered, unless the NHL and NHLPA insurance programs had changed.

Thinking of Bob Dailey and Glen Sharpley, I asked Tierney whether, when a disability claim is paid in full through a conduit (the Players' Association, meaning Eagleson) and the full amount is not paid to the player, would that be proper?

"If a claim is filed," Tierney answered, "the claim has been paid, but the recipient has not received the full proceeds—I'm not a lawyer, but it sounds like fraud."

When I asked about Bernard Warren, Tierney made clear he preferred to move on to other topics. I asked his impressions of Alan Eagleson.

Tierney had had "numerous meetings" with Eagleson over the years, he said, and found him to be "bright, articulate, and sometimes crass." He remembered that former Bruin Mike Milbury had been an early antagonist of Eagleson's. At the 1983 Nassau meeting, Milbury had suggested another insurance agent to handle NHLPA business as a possible replacement for William Sutton. If that had happened, there would be no guarantee that Bernard Warren's company would retain the brokerage business, or that Eagleson could control what transpired. Eagleson strongly opposed the idea.

"I know that there was one comment [by Eagleson, about Milbury]," Tierney said, "something about Mike being a smartass, since he went to Colgate or one of those schools.

"He's the only man I know," Tierney said of Eagleson, "who in a social gathering, in a restaurant, would blatantly use the word 'fuck,' and no one would say anything to him. Everything was 'fuck this' and 'fuck that.' It was awful. I was always taught that if you couldn't find the proper word, then rearrange your sentence, but you certainly don't stoop to vulgarity."

"Was it your impression," I asked, "that Eagleson had a firm understanding and a control on who would operate insurance for the NHL and NHLPA?"

"I'd certainly say if Alan said yea, it was yea, and if Alan said no, it was no. I'd say he was in control. More so than the owners, that was my impression. He would purchase the insurance not only for the NHLPA, but the NHL coverage as well. The owners in those days said fine, negotiate these benefits, whatever they are. It's going to cost x, you take care of it. So yes, he was controlling it."

Can you imagine the board of directors of General Motors asking the executive director of the Teamsters to go out and take care of GM's insurance as well as the union's?

I had discovered an NHLPA memo sent to all player representatives about the terms of disability insurance that would take effect October 1, 1983. In that correspondence, base disability coverage was described as being $100,000 U.S. provided by the NHL and $75,000 U.S. provided by the NHLPA. "The Lump Sum Benefits totaling $175,000 U.S. are payable in the event a player becomes permanently and totally disabled, defined as being unable to play Professional Hockey ever again, due to accident. Coverage is 24 hours per day, 365 days per year, on and off the ice.

"For the benefits to be payable, the injury must result in a player being prevented from playing hockey for 12 continuous months from the date of accident, and at the end of that time, in the opinion of a qualified medical practitioner, to be beyond the hope of improvement. The disability must be the result of a single accident, and not the result of a previous condition or injury....

"As you are aware, all playing contracts in the NHL are guaranteed in the event of disability resulting from your duties for the team, including while playing, practising and while travelling on behalf of the team."

The letter made no mention of a twenty-game "cured" rule. Blair Chapman had not played a full month of hockey after his back injury and disk surgery, yet his claim was disallowed. And if games played in the minors could be used *against* Chapman, why didn't Ed Kea's minor-league status support his claim?

Most important, why was Eagleson not protecting the interests of his union members? Here he was informing players that "all playing contracts in the NHL are guaranteed in the event of disability." Where was he when Chapman went to settle his "guaranteed" contract after being disabled? Where was he when John Ziegler shredded Chapman in the arbitration process and Chapman settled for forty-two cents on the dollar? And where was he when Kea crashed into the boards in Salt Lake? This 1983 Players' Association notice—which members depended on for their understanding of disability insurance—didn't even mention that players on NHL contracts were not covered when playing for a minor-league affiliate. And that notice was mailed seven months *after* Ed Kea had been left brain-damaged.

ROBERT BRADSHAW WAS THE insurance agent who handled NHL and NHLPA disability coverage before 1981, when Bill Sutton took over. I tracked him down in England, interviewed him by phone, then met him when he was next on this side of the Atlantic. A strapping, white-haired, six-foot,

240-pounder, Bradshaw had done insurance business with Eagleson since 1969. Over the years, he said, Eagleson became more and more demanding. He started asking to use Bradshaw's chauffeured limo and New York apartment. Then he started phoning Bradshaw and telling him when he was going to use them. Then he by-passed Bradshaw altogether.

"He didn't ask," said Bradshaw, "he demanded. He'd get hold of my driver directly. He used the car fifteen, twenty times a year." Eagleson's use of his apartment also became bothersome. He would phone, said Bradshaw, and say, "I'm coming to town. I need the flat." On one occasion, said Bradshaw, Eagleson got jealous that one of his employees—Bill Watters—also used the Manhattan apartment. Watters confirmed the story.

Bradshaw explained that all NHL disability insurance business used to go through a Canadian-American insurance agency in Detroit, operated by the Norris family, former owners of the Red Wings. That business was apparently sold, and the business went to another company, St. Paul Fire and Marine Insurance, between October 1, 1974, and October 1, 1977. Bradshaw was chosen by Eagleson to be the agent in charge of placing it with underwriters at Lloyd's in 1977, when Crawley Warren became the exclusive broker.

I asked about Ed Kea. "If he was on an NHL contract," said Bradshaw, "then he'd be eligible for NHL benefits. As a matter of fact, the underwriters went out of their way to try and not develop wording that opened the area of degree of competition. If somebody had an NHL contract and was injured while that contract was in effect and his insurance was in effect, and if the premiums were paid, it would strike me he'd have to get the benefits."

Bradshaw said that Eagleson took a hands-on role in processing disability claims. "He took a very active role whenever there was a claim or a potential claim. My concern always with Eagleson was that he was the pilot, the co-pilot, the engineer, the cabin crew, and everything else. He not only owned the airline and flew it, but decided who sat in the seats. He would get deeply involved in the various intricate ramifications of how the insurance operated. He felt some sort of ownership or governorship over any policy he was involved in. He wanted to dictate whether the benefits should be paid in full or in part."

John Ziegler claimed, in a September 1991 interview I had with him in New York, that the disability insurance business had dried up in the early

1980s—there were so many claims, Ziegler said, that insurers simply didn't want the business—which was why Bradshaw had been released in favor of William Sutton.

"Dried up? I had competition," Bradshaw insisted. "There were competing sources within different Lloyd's brokers. Crawley Warren no longer had the direct handle. He [Warren] had competition amongst brokers." Bradshaw suggested that the real reason he was dumped was that Eagleson wanted more favors from him—more perks—which Bradshaw was unwilling to provide.

When it came to Eagleson's own coverage, "His family got free insurance," said Bradshaw, adding that he absorbed the cost himself. "And travel accident insurance for him and his family because they traveled a lot." Did Bradshaw offer this free insurance voluntarily? "With Mr. Eagleson," said Bradshaw, "you never did anything voluntarily."

Bradshaw also insured other companies with which Eagleson was involved. "Arthur Harnett ran Eagleson's companies that did the rink-board advertising along with the promotional work for the Canada-Russia series," Bradshaw said, explaining that Canada Cup insurance had also come to him.

"When you did the Canada Cup insurance, who gave you that business?"

"Eagleson," said Bradshaw. "All negotiated with him."

I asked Bradshaw about Bernie Warren's relationship with Eagleson. Bradshaw confirmed that Eagleson had a place in London but didn't know if there was any connection to Warren.

It seemed odd that many people seeking to do business with the NHLPA did not have to wine and dine Eagleson, as Bradshaw had been expected to do. The executive director of the union, it seemed, wined and dined them. Expense records I examined showed Eagleson charged players thousands of dollars to entertain and provide gifts to people doing business with the NHLPA, some of whom were his personal friends.

NHLPA records showed the union spent more than $200,000 on "promotion, gifts and awards" in the fiscal years 1987–89. Gifts alone cost $36,917 during that period. The union also bought almost $60,000 worth of game tickets, which Eagleson distributed. Agents and brokers who were paid to arrange disability insurance for NHL players were among the beneficiaries.

Bill Sutton, the insurance agent with whom Eagleson did union business after Bradshaw got bumped in 1981, got perks from the NHLPA: free golf, free tickets to games at Maple Leaf Gardens, paid for by the players. Besides disability insurance, Sutton was also the agent for $90,880 in NHLPA dental coverage. His company also drew consulting fees from the Players' Association. On November 17, 1988, the NHLPA issued a $20,000 check to "Wm. J. Sutton & Co. Ltd." The bill from Sutton noted the money was for "consulting fees and advice in respect of insurance policies for both medical and dental coverage for NHLPA members including travel to and attendance at various related meetings."

In July 1987, Eagleson traveled to London to talk with representatives of Crawley Warren. On his return, he billed the union $360 U.S. for meals with the insurance men, and $200 U.S. for theater tickets for Bert Stratton and Dennis Johnson. In January 1988, Eagleson bought a liquor "gift" for Bernard Warren, charging it to the union, and dinged the union another $286 U.S. for a meeting with Warren in London.

Peanuts, perhaps, but why was the NHLPA paying for gifts for an insurance company chairman when the union was the customer? Ordinarily it's the client who gets stroked, since the client has the option of taking the business elsewhere. Why was Eagleson buttering these guys up? On another trip to London, in February 1988, he treated Warren and his associate, Dennis Johnson, to the theater and billed the "special meetings" union account $200 U.S. Other expenses he charged to the NHLPA included $1,150 U.S. for gifts to Warren and Johnson, with a notation "Wimbledon tickets." I couldn't help but wonder who was benefiting from the union's largesse—the union, or Eagleson?

VIC BATCHELDER, THE BRITISH hockey writer, came through. One day, in my letterbox in the newsroom of the *Eagle-Tribune*, I found Title Number NGL623724 for Flat B, 17 Pimlico Road, registered on October 4, 1988. It was an eighty-six-year lease, beginning March 3, 1988, for £350 a month (at the time, about $775) "plus additional rent."

The place turned out to be a quaint brick building behind a black iron fence, near Buckingham Palace. The front door is blue, with a gold handle and door knocker. Inside are five flats, or apartments. According to the Greater London land registry, flat B at 17 Pimlico Road had four names on the lease. Grosvenor Estate Restorations Limited was the first. Things came into focus when I read the other three names: Jialson Holdings Limited, an investment firm whose president was R. Alan Eagleson; Dennis Johnson; and Bernard James Warren.

I contacted Grosvenor Estate Restorations in London and was told that Grosvenor restored buildings and managed property. It looked after land owned by the Duke of Westminster, an estate administered by trustees. The Duke of Westminster owned the land through the Royal Family. Grosvenor owned the building at 17 Pimlico; the lease was owned by whomever appeared on the property register at the land registry.

The members of the NHLPA were paying Eagleson to be their executive director; some were also paying him to be their agent. His duties included placing the union's disability insurance business. They were paying rent to an Eagleson company that owned the building on Maitland Street in Toronto where their association was headquartered. And, though they didn't know it, they were also paying Eagleson to stay at his own flat in London—a flat he owned jointly with the head of the firm to whom he had directed the disability insurance business.

A couple of weeks after I wrote in the *Eagle-Tribune* about Eagleson's involvement with Warren, I received faxed copies of two letters. The first was stamped: "Received NHL Oct. 15, 1991." The letterhead read: "Crawley Warren Group PLC — Bernard Warren, Chairman and Chief Executive Officer." It was dated October 10, 1991, and addressed to Mr. J. A. Ziegler, National Hockey League, 33rd Floor, 650 Fifth Avenue, New York, N.Y. 10019.

Dear John,

I have recently seen the article in the Lawrence Eagle-Tribune which again "rakes the coals" on hockey matters.

I note that the article was a new slant on Alan Eagleson regarding his Pimlico Road apartment.

The article stated that you were unaware of the Eagleson/Warren connection with the Pimlico flat, which might represent a conflict of interest, and I would just confirm that I have no ownership interest in the apartment whatsoever.

I believe my name appears on the lease as I was prepared to act as one of two guarantors in connection with the rental payments.

The purpose of this letter is just so that you are aware of the actual facts. With kindest regards.

Yours sincerely,

Bernard

Warren's story didn't match with what I'd found. Grosvenor Estate Restorations Limited required two British residents to be on the lease with the Eagleson family company. By signing on with Eagleson, Warren agreed (in the words of a London lawyer) "to take a Lease of the premises in the event of the existing Lease being disclaimed by the Liquidator on liquidation of Jialson." Warren, of course, had specifically denied being associated with Eagleson in anything other than the insurance business.

I had asked a senior employee of Grosvenor Estate Restorations why Grosvenor would be on the lease. In case of non-payment of rent, I was told, Grosvenor was positioned first on the register to hold clear title to the lease. Did Jialson own part of the lease? Yes. Jialson, second on the register, was actually the proprietor of the lease, responsible for fulfilling its terms. And did Dennis Johnson and Bernard Warren own part of the lease? Yes. If Jialson failed to meet its commitments, Johnson and Warren would be held responsible. So all four parties owned the flat together? There was no hesitation: "Absolutely."

The second letter faxed to me showed how John Ziegler administered NHL matters involving Eagleson. This one, on NHL stationery from the New York office, was Ziegler's reply to Warren, dated October 16, 1991.

Mr. Bernard Warren
Chairman and Chief Executive Officer
Crawley Warren Group plc
8 Lloyds Avenue
London EC3N 3HD
Dear Bernie,

Thank you for yours. I was not concerned.

It is rather sad that a sleaze can wrap himself in the cloak of "Media"
and thereby take on the protected privilege of being able to label simple acts of
friendship as evil.

Cest La Vie.

All the best.

Sincerely,

John

Ziegler's letter indicated that a copy was being sent to Eagleson.

IN 1991, EAGLESON was widely rumored to be seeking the presidency of the
International Ice Hockey Federation. That position would solidify his power
over international hockey, making him overseer of everything from Olympic
hockey to the World Championship Tournament. When Vic Batchelder got
wind of the rumor, after helping me locate the London Land Registry documents linking Eagleson and Bernard Warren, he wanted out.

"I can't afford to buck Mr. Eagleson," he explained. "I don't know if I
want involvement with your story anymore. If Mr. Eagleson becomes head
of the IIHF and decides to get his claws into us, he could make life very
difficult for me."

TED DIPPLE, THE DISABILITY INSURANCE businessman in Massachusetts who'd
once had dealings with Eagleson, lived in Andover, not far from my *Eagle-
Tribune* office. I called him one day and we arranged to meet.

A native Englishman with a polished wit and an air of educated refine-
ment, Dipple specializes in high-risk sports coverage and is a leading insurer of
athletes. He had started in the insurance business in 1957 with Lloyd's and
come to the United States in 1973. He had an interesting tale to tell.

In 1982, Dipple said, he became interested in landing the NHLPA disability
insurance account. At the time he was doing some business with Boston
player Mike Milbury, and he asked Milbury how he might go about bidding

on the NHL disability business. Milbury steered him in Eagleson's direction, and a meeting was set up in Toronto.

Dipple was planning to make a pitch, but Eagleson, he said, made a pitch of his own. Eagleson was then organizing a series between NHL teams and players from the Soviet Union. "He asked me whether I was interested in purchasing rink advertising," Dipple recalled. "When I asked how much that would cost, the figure $100,000 was thrown out. I think that's when I said, 'I'm not interested.' I was there to talk about insurance. He brought up the subject of advertising. I didn't tie the two together."

Eagleson himself tied the two together in a subsequent letter to Milbury. He said he thought he could use Dipple's bid to land the business "as an inducement to have Crawley Warren participate again in the rink-board advertising scheme related to international hockey. I have advised Crawley Warren of the upcoming series," Eagleson wrote, "and will be twisting their arm to participate in the rink board or television program."

Sure enough, I discovered, for the 1981 Canada Cup, Crawley Warren had indeed purchased $100,000 in advertising. So Bernie Warren was involved in Eagleson's Canada Cup undertakings as well.

CRAWLEY WARREN, IT TURNED OUT, handled many types of insurance. Perhaps the most intriguing part of the operation was a Canadian travel insurance company called Voyageur, which offered coverage for lost baggage and hospitalization away from home.

By 1985 Voyageur Travel Insurance had six offices in Canada. In Crawley Warren's 1985 annual report, Bernard Warren noted a pre-tax profit in excess of £2 million. The next year, 1986, pre-tax profits were just under £2 million and Crawley Warren added a new company in Canada, Assured Assistance Associates Inc.

Warren noted in the chairman's statement of the 1986 report that "professional sports insurance is an important segment of our business, in which Crawley Warren continues to be predominant....Overall the market has continued to provide the flexibility to respond to the business which we have been able to develop," because, he said, "co-operation has been established between underwriters and the client."

Cooperation indeed. I thought of Eagleson's favors to Crawley Warren — reducing André Savard's claim by nearly $100,000 U.S., then pointing it out to Warren when he wanted Mike Gillis's claim expedited; paying Warren's company a "special fee" to process the disability claim of Dale Tallon; the gifts provided by Eagleson and billed to the NHLPA; the cozy set-up at 17 Pimlico Road.

In the 1987 annual report, Warren noted that Voyageur Travel Insurance had opened another office in Halifax and the group had increased pre-tax profits to nearly £2.4 million. In the report, Warren touted Crawley Warren's "close relationship with the National Hockey League and National Hockey League Players' Association." On page 14 of the annual report was a color photo of Brian Mulroney flanked by John Ziegler and Alan Eagleson. The chairman's statement from Bernard Warren said he was pleased to advise shareholders of a major development: "Following an eighteen month study, a decision has been made to transform Voyageur's travel insurance business in Canada from that of a broker to that of a Federal insurance company. Voyageur currently underwrites holiday travel insurance by way of binding authority from certain underwriters at Lloyd's, but in future will underwrite the business for its own account. It is anticipated that the insurance company will be incorporated, licensed and underwriting by January 1st, 1988...."

In July 1987, the Canadian government's office of the Superintendent of Insurance and office of the Inspector General of Banks were amalgamated into the office of the Superintendent of Financial Institutions, under Michael Mackenzie. At the time, Eagleson's friend Roy McMurtry was Canada's High Commissioner to Britain (McMurtry ended up a director of Voyageur before being named a provincial justice and chief justice of the Ontario Court's trial division). In 1988, an election year in Canada, Mulroney and his Conservatives were returned to office. Among his supporters was Alan Eagleson. Voyageur Insurance Company commenced underwriting in Canada on April 1, 1988. It was given privileged access to customers of Air Canada, then a government-owned airline.

"We made a bid," recalled Robin Ingle of John Ingle Travel Insurance in Toronto, a competitor of Voyageur. "It sort of disappeared. We got dead-ended.

All of a sudden, Voyageur had the business. We asked why and never got an answer. We had an extensive proposal. Our price was better, our product was better, and Air Canada would have made more money. I couldn't believe it. They wouldn't even reply."

In Crawley Warren's 1988 annual report, Warren informed shareholders that Voyageur was taking off. "With the potential of Voyageur Insurance Company, I cannot see any boundaries to the continued expansion and well-being of the Group." According to the annual report, "The initial year recorded the most important change in the history of Voyageur when its activity as a Lloyd's coverholder was transformed into that of a Canadian insurer with the incorporation and licensing of Voyageur Insurance Company....Worldwide travel and tourism reached new heights and as host country to the Calgary Winter Olympic Games, business volumes both domestic and international showed significant gains and growth, allowing Voyageur to make a meaningful contribution to the up profitability....The Voyageur subsidiary, Assured Assist-ance Associates Inc., in its capacity as provider of worldwide assistance, main-tained its valuable role of offering affiliated services to Voyageur policyholders."

In the 1989 annual report, Warren noted that Voyageur "is now a sig-nificant Canadian federal insurance company and clearly the market leader in its field of specialty, providing a variety of products for both the vacation and business traveler." Crawley Warren's financial statement showed an eighteen-month pre-tax profit of £5.1 million, versus £2.2 million for the previous twelve-month period. Management service costs for directors increased by more than £500,000. Warren, as chairman, received £255,000, excluding pension.

The 1989 Crawley Warren Group report also included some bragging. The company had been granted armorial bearings, its coat of arms and motto proudly displayed on the cover of its financial report. "It is my belief that the motto, 'Trustworthy and Honourable' is synonymous with the character of the Group," Warren wrote in his chairman's report. "As we enter 1990, the Crawley Warren Group is finely poised to take advantage of situations that present themselves during the next decade."

The next year, 1990, was even more lucrative, with the group declaring a pre-tax, twelve-month profit of nearly £5 million. Warren said in the annual report: "Voyageur Insurance Company performed superbly and continued to be a market leader in Canada....We believe Voyageur holds a unique position as the only insurer in Canada with a total commitment to providing travel insurance to the vacation and business travel markets."

What had happened to boost Crawley Warren's fortunes? Basically, the company had taken a federally approved grip on the travel insurance industry. The vast majority of Voyageur customers boarded Air Canada flights. Air Canada was a federally owned corporation at the time Warren's company got the approval. (In mid-October 1988, 43 percent of shares in Air Canada were sold publicly, with the remainder sold in 1989.)

Warren's company had a good thing going, as James I. McCartney, publisher of the *Buyer's Guide to Travel Health Insurance*, explained to me. There was simply no meaningful regulation of the travel insurance industry in Canada. "On the regulatory side, you won't get any bureaucrat able to answer: What are the standards in registration? What are the criteria for licencing? What's the approval process for insurance programs? What's the checklist done on these companies? And who sits on the review board?

"Here we are facing a major issue worth billions of dollars in Canadian expenditures in the payments of medical bills over the years, and it could be millions in premium income, but there's no control. Travel insurance companies are simply not required to file the same information as other companies."

In fact, much of the medical coverage for travelers was already provided to Canadian citizens by the country's universal health plan. "The losses or risk was minuscule because the provinces covered just about everything," McCartney explained. "The claims have been so small it's not important."

He used the example of an Ontario resident taking a travel insurance policy before flying from Toronto to Miami. "With the typical claim being a stubbed toe while on vacation, most of the time what was paid out was recouped from OHIP [Ontario Health Insurance Plan], so there was little liability and they kept all that premium money."

It was a no-brainer. Voyageur collected premiums from Canadian citizens, particularly snowbirds who vacationed in Florida. If there was a claim for hospitalization, Voyageur would pay it, submit it to the government, and get reimbursed. Air Canada was a major transporter. A travel insurance application in a ticket sleeve — what could be simpler? No need even for a travel agent. The customer could put the premium on a credit card. "It's a major advantage for an insurer to land that account," said McCartney. "They got access to a market they'd never have access to."

And what about the other Crawley Warren company, Assured Assistance? Its business was to help sick Canadians get home as quickly as possible. If a Canadian in Florida became ill and needed, say, heart surgery, the assistance company would get the customer back to Canada. Why?

"They move quickly and pay the flight home rather than risking a long hospital stay and paying the medical bills," McCartney said. "The problem is in cases when a patient flies home and ends up on a waiting list, whereas they would have been treated in Florida. And of course people have bought the insurance to cover just that — treatment in Florida."

While Voyageur was pumping profits into Crawley Warren, Lloyd's of London was suffering the worst crisis in its 305-year history, incurring losses of about $9 billion from 1988 to 1991. (In July 1993, the High Court in London ordered five Canadian banks to pay Lloyd's $4 million covering credits to various Canadian clients.) Some of the tremendous hit at Lloyd's came from losses on claims that had been reinsured through underwriters. When Voyageur insurance coverage exceeded maximum limits of provincial health plan coverage, the excess was reinsured through Lloyd's, so Voyageur was spreading what little excess risk there was.

Voyageur's profitability was jeopardized when OHIP began changing its rules in 1990. "Travel insurance was costing OHIP $200 million a year," recalled Dr. Robert MacMillan, the executive director of OHIP between 1989 and 1993. "The risk was very low for the companies. I trimmed [the loss] by recommending the rates be changed, and they were." The Ontario government, which had been paying 100 percent of emergency hospitalization costs outside Canada, trimmed the benefit to $400 a day, then $200 a day. (Recently the benefit was raised to $400 a day again.)

"OHIP changed coverage and it became significant. The whole system had been reversed," said James McCartney, the travel insurance expert. "In effect, you had to cover yourself (with insurance) out of the country."

"Voyageur has reached a point in its history where the company should now rest in Canadian hands," Warren announced in the 1992 annual report, and in January 1993, the company was indeed sold to a subsidiary of the Royal Bank, resulting in an after-tax profit of almost £6 million, or $11.7 million. As a major shareholder, Warren made a fortune.

"With the change, Voyageur bailed out," said McCartney. "The Canadian taxpayers were footing the bill for most Voyageur claims. It was an extremely lucrative business. When you've got Air Canada, you only need one account. A lot of people got away rich off that deal."

6

BEST-LAID PLANS

"I have a $10,000 pension in Canadian funds for sixteen seasons in the NHL, and he gets a $50,000 pension in U.S. funds. You figure it. How many goals did Alan Eagleson score?"
BOBBY HULL

TALKING TO NHL PLAYERS past and present, I heard again and again about their lousy pensions. Some believed their pension fund had been mishandled. Delving into the matter, I learned that a group of retired players was becoming increasingly militant, demanding information about the administration of the fund and threatening legal action. As I soon discovered — and as Bruce Dowbiggin makes clear in *The Defense Never Rests*, his comprehensive account of the NHL pension dispute — Carl Brewer, the former Maple Leaf defenseman, and his partner, Sue Foster, were driving forces behind the initiative from the start.

When I spoke to Brewer about it, he insisted that the NHL, with Eagleson's approval, had converted "millions of dollars from the pensions of retired players" for its own use and to pay the pensions of current players. He said he was forming a group to sue the league and hoped that current players would meet with retirees to discuss the issue. "Eagleson is in cahoots with Wirtz and Ziegler," Brewer said. "It's been going on for years. The NHL is run by a very small inner circle — Eagleson, Wirtz, and Ziegler. We're going to get to the bottom of this." Brewer said he'd been trying to get answers for more than a year, ever since he'd learned that his pension had been increased.

"Why would you complain when you were getting an increase?"

"I got this Merry Christmas letter in the mail signed by Eagleson and Ziegler. It said my pension had been increased because of an agreement in 1986. But the letter came two years later. I wanted to know where the money came from. I called the Pension Society and couldn't get a straight answer. I still haven't been able to get a straight answer."

I told Brewer I planned to call the NHL Pension Society myself. He said he doubted I could get information since I wasn't a member of the plan. "If I can't get answers as a retired player, you sure won't." He also said that frankly he was leery of reporters because so many had promised to check into Eagleson. I assured him my interest was genuine, and we agreed to stay in touch.

Not long afterward, I got talking with Bill Shaheen, an old friend, who'd been the lead U.S. Attorney in New Hampshire before forming his own law firm and then going on to become a judge. Shaheen said that in the United States pensions were a sensitive area; laws outlined in the Employee Retirement Income Security Act (ERISA) must be followed to the letter. If members of a plan couldn't get information about their pensions, he said, that would throw up a red flag with the government.

I told him the NHLPA was based in Canada. Shaheen thought that wouldn't make a difference. Players on U.S. teams such as the Bruins were employed by U.S. corporations, which fall under U.S. law. Some of the players were also U.S. citizens. Besides, he said, Canada must have similar laws.

As Brewer had predicted, the NHL would not provide me with pension figures, so I began asking retired players to supply them. It quickly became clear that NHL pensions were the worst in major professional sport. Brad Park's seventeen seasons were worth a $13,000 annual pension. Dallas Smith had played sixteen seasons but his pension at age forty-five would be only $7,514. Don Marcotte's fifteen seasons meant $11,000 a year. Hall of Famer Jean Ratelle had a twenty-one–season NHL career and a pension worth $12,924. Another Hall of Famer, Johnny Bucyk, got $13,200 a year after playing twenty-three seasons. Brewer's pension was $13,000; Bobby Orr's was $8,400. Colleen Howe confirmed that her husband's pension, after twenty-six NHL seasons, was about $14,000. Yet another Hall of Famer, Milt Schmidt, had played sixteen seasons for a pension of $5,800. "Fortunately I'm getting an executive's pension as well," Schmidt said. "Believe me, the NHL executive pension plan is a whole bunch better than what the players get. The owners made money off the players for years." Wayne Cashman, after seventeen seasons, had a $13,200 pension — "Canadian," he pointed out. "That's more like $11,000 U.S. Of course I don't know much about the pension plan. The NHLPA and Eagleson never sent me much information. I did get a pen-and-pencil set once."

Lou Angotti's pension was about $6,000 for ten seasons. Ralph Backstrom put in seventeen NHL seasons for an annual pension of about $10,800. When he died in 1989, Montreal Hall of Famer Doug Harvey was down and out, trying to make ends meet on a pension of $8,556. Maurice Richard collected $7,200 for eighteen seasons. Harry Watson, who spent fourteen seasons in the NHL, was sixty-eight when I asked about his NHL pension — $4,800 a year. Tod Sloan's pension paid him $4,176 a year for thirteen NHL seasons. As Ferny Flaman had told me in Florida, the pensions of many retired NHL stars, himself included, fell below the U.S. poverty level of $6,624 annually for a single person. (Fortunately, Flaman worked as a scout for New Jersey.)

Until 1967, the pension funds of NHL players and officials were commingled. One of the most pathetic stories I heard came from Judy Hayes, the widow of Hall of Fame linesman George Hayes, who worked 1,704 National Hockey League games between 1946 and 1965 and died in 1987. I found her working as recreational coordinator for the town of Ingersoll, Ontario. When her husband died, she said, she was offered a lump sum of $1,032 or a monthly pension of $16.98. "I think it's ludicrous, to be quite frank. It's the funniest thing I've ever heard."

She turned down the lump-sum offer, made in a letter from Manulife, the Canadian insurance firm that handles pension benefits for the NHL Pension Society. "I wouldn't take it for a couple of reasons. It's a great conversation piece. And I wanted them to deposit it in my bank account because I figured it would probably cost them more than $16.98 a month to do that. I thought if they can be that ridiculous, I could be just as ridiculous."

CARL BREWER'S "MERRY CHRISTMAS" letter, which he sent me, made for interesting reading. Dated November 21, 1988, it was signed by Eagleson and Ziegler and was written on letterhead with both the NHLPA and NHL logos. "As a result of the negotiations between NHLPA player representatives and NHL owners," it read, "we are pleased to be able to advise of an increase in your pension. Although the agreement was reached in August of 1986, it has only been in the last 90 days that the final approvals from all Government authorities (Canada, Ontario, U.S.A.) have been obtained. We hope this helps in making your Christmas even merrier."

The letter prompted many questions. If there was a surplus in 1986, how long had it been accumulating? Did the players get all the surplus? If Eagleson had been negotiating the increase for the retired players as well, why weren't those players even consulted?

Perhaps the collective bargaining agreements and NHL pension documents would shed light on the matter. I obtained the 1981 and 1986 NHL CBA booklets and pension information. The legalese made for tough sledding, but it was clear the pension plan had been amended on December 9, 1983, and that funds were invested "in a manner determined by the Plan trustees." Who were the trustees? I also found the NHLPA contribution to the pension perplexing. Evidently, players were obliged to pay 25 percent of the pension costs each year from revenue generated by international hockey. If they didn't play an international series, the league was responsible for the full pension cost. Why, then, would players risk injury in a Canada Cup tournament, earning peanuts, when they'd get the same pension benefits anyway? When they did play, they were simply reducing the league's pension expense by 25 cents on the dollar. What kind of deal was that?

As mentioned, Brewer, who locked horns with the hockey establishment throughout his playing career, had engaged Mark Zigler, an intense, bearded lawyer with Koskie & Minsky in Toronto. Zigler had helped Dominion Stores employees in a similar, much-publicized battle with Conrad Black and the other owners of the grocery chain, earning his reputation as an astute pension specialist. Zigler's preliminary report on the NHL pension issue — which Brewer and Sue Foster paid for out of their own money — claimed that records of the NHL Pension Society filed with the

Pension Commission of Ontario "[did] not indicate any kind of contribution ever made by the Players' Association to the Pension Fund or the Pension Society" from international hockey. Further, it appeared that in 1987 "the Pension Society received a refund from the Manufacturers Life of some $23,488,280."

No contribution from international hockey? Eagleson had long persuaded NHL stars to play in Canada Cup tournaments by assuring them they were topping up their pension fund. And what was this huge refund from Manulife?

"Documents filed with the Pension Commission indicate that the League has used the surplus to reduce its contribution," Zigler's report claimed, "in the amount of some $2.9 million in 1987, $2.5 million in 1988 and $2.3 million in 1989." Of the roughly $24-million refund, only $4.4 million had been used to improve pensions of retired players.

An NHL contact provided me with his pension certificate. It made clear that players had shared in surplus pension funds back in the 1960s. Evidently, somewhere along the way, the rules had been changed. The owners had taken the surplus and given Brewer and the other retired players a small increase. The rest was being used to offset current player pensions.

And the head of the NHLPA had gone along with it?

CARL BREWER SPENT COUNTLESS HOURS and dollars trying to rally other retired players to the cause. He got help and financial support from Andy Bathgate, Allan Stanley, Eddie Shack, and Bobby Orr among others. For a meeting with Mark Zigler at the Ramada Inn in Toronto a couple of weeks before Christmas 1990, he and Sue Foster got out more than a hundred former stars — including Bathgate, Shack, Orr, Gordie Howe, Frank Mahovlich, Johnny Bower, Red Kelly, and Bobby Hull — journeyman players, referees, and linesmen. Gradually, thanks to his and Foster's tireless organizing efforts, support was building for his position that the NHL Pension Society had wrongly diverted money that should have gone to the retirees.

While in Toronto, several players also met privately with Tom Lockwood, a lawyer retained by the Law Society of Upper Canada. Rich Winter, the Edmonton-based agent whose questions about Eagleson had helped spark the June 1989 uprising, had filed a complaint with the law society accusing Eagleson of unethical conduct.

A couple of days later, Dave Forbes, the former Bruin now in financial management in California, who'd come to Toronto for the Zigler meeting, dropped in unannounced at Eagleson's Maitland Street office. He reminded Eagleson's secretary that he had spoken with her the day before, requesting past NHLPA financial documents.

"She asked me to wait and she said she had a letter from Alan to me," Forbes wrote in a report about the meeting. "She returned shortly with the letter and was followed quickly by Eagleson who said: 'Dave, Forbsie, hey what's this going on with you, running around telling this guy and that that I won't give you this or that. Every time you've asked me for anything I've always gotten right back to you. When I heard your name attached to Salcer and Winter I was really disappointed and now that you're involved with them you're turning into a jerk.'

"I had anticipated this kind of reaction and began by mentioning I was here on my own, not connected with Salcer, Winter or anyone else, and that I was continuing in my quest for information that would answer my growing list of questions....He agreed this was reasonable.

"Then he said, 'Well good, how can I help?' I began with the surplus in the pension plan, to which he interrupted me and raised his voice about Garvey and Winter and about them putting all these ideas in everyone's mind and causing all sorts of confusion. I asked him what the surplus was...because I heard $23M and he said he was sure it was $30M. He then said, 'I understand Mark Zigler was saying at your meeting the other night that this surplus belongs to the players. Well it doesn't. It's the owners'. I've retained counsel to look into this and they have assured me that this money is the owners'. However, if someone wants to file a lawsuit maybe they could get it.' (Is that an interesting statement?) I then asked him if he would file a lawsuit on behalf of players and he said no. It appeared clear that he had resigned himself to this surplus being the owners'."

Forbes referred to the 1967 NHL pension plan document, which made clear surplus money was to be used solely for the benefit of players. "He said he hadn't heard of that. This in itself I found surprising. I mean, here I was informing the executive director of the NHLPA about language in the document itself that said surpluses were the players' and he didn't even so much as say, 'Could you get me a copy of that document? I'd like to look into it.' He couldn't care less."

Forbes also asked about Hockey Canada. "I mentioned I had noticed in the CBA that the players' share was a function of 'net proceeds' and that he knew as well as I that 'net' can be just about whatever you want it to be. In light of this I thought it would be helpful to see the financials to see what was above the line, and know where the gross proceeds were going.

"He said that information was none of my business and that these records would not be available to me. I then began to discuss 'fiduciary duty' and mentioned my own position as a fiduciary and how I was not only required to disclose any and all pertinent financial issues but that I was willing and desirous to do so. I asked if he shared the same perspective.

"His response was most interesting. He said that he preferred not to be called a fiduciary because he didn't see himself to be one. But that rather as a lawyer he was accountable to a higher ethical standard and he felt that was sufficient."

CARL BREWER SAW AN OPPORTUNITY to take the retired players' case to the active players and enlist their support during the 1991 NHL All-Star break in Chicago, where they were refused admission to a Players' Association meeting. When I learned that the current players had shut out the retired players, turning their backs on their predecessors, I spoke with Andy Moog in the Boston dressing room after a Whalers-Bruins game. Moog, the Bruins goalie at the time, was a Players' Association vice president. What had happened? Why did the retired players get the cold shoulder?

Moog explained that the players had been informed by Eagleson and NHLPA president Bryan Trottier that some retired players were looking to take away some of the current players' pension money. His account was later verified by Bobby Hull. When the current players refused to meet the retirees in Chicago, Hull said, it prompted a heart-to-heart talk between two of the great goal-scorers in NHL history, Hull and his son Brett.

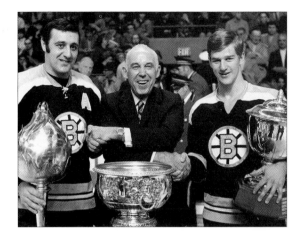

Led by Phil Esposito and Bobby Orr (with former NHL president Clarence Campbell), the Boston Bruins won two NHL championships in three years in the early 1970s. Orr was Eagleson's prize client and steered many other players Eagleson's way.

In the early days, Eagleson and Orr were like brothers, sharing everything from Bobby Orr Enterprises Ltd. to a Stanley Cup embrace in the Bruins dressing room. Their relationship soured after Eagleson engineered Orr's move to Chicago in 1976.

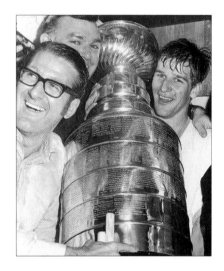

Orr's Stanley Cup-winning goal against St. Louis in 1970. It was at a reunion of that championship team in 1990 that author Russ Conway decided to look into the players' growing dissatisfaction with Eagleson's leadership of their union, the NHLPA.

Ed Garvey, a Madison, Wisconsin-based labor lawyer and former head of the NFL Players' Association, produced a scathing assessment of Eagleson's performance as head of the NHL Players' Association.

John Ziegler, the NHL president until 1992, was a close friend of Eagleson's, a friendship that drew Garvey's censure. Many players believed the NHL owners had the union leader in their back pocket.

Hall of Fame defenseman Brad Park, who has a son needing specialized care, learned that the NHL had its own captive insurance company in Bermuda after he lost his group health benefits.

Former Bruin Dave Forbes, now an investment adviser, repeatedly sought information about union finances and pensions — even showing up unannounced on Eagleson's doorstep — but was rebuffed.

When Bill Watters worked for Eagleson, Hockey Canada — a nonprofit organization supported by Canadian taxpayers — ended up, in effect, subsidizing Sports Management Ltd., Eagleson's agency business.

Edmonton agent Rich Winter was one of the first people to openly question Eagleson's apparent conflicts of interest. He filed complaints with the RCMP and the Law Society of Upper Canada.

Former Boston captain Terry O'Reilly resigned in disgust as the Bruins player representative after learning he had supposedly endorsed changes to the NHL-NHLPA collective bargaining agreement — changes he strongly opposed.

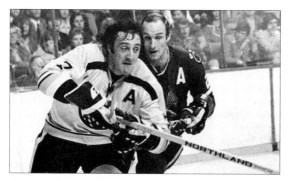

Phil Esposito — at Eagleson's behest — urged players to support the NHL-WHA merger without understanding why it was in their interest to do so. Bill White (right), an Eagleson client, collected disability insurance without difficulty.

Permanently brain-damaged, Ed Kea was shabbily treated by the National Hockey League and Eagleson.

Bob Dailey, who suffered a badly broken ankle, was charged dubious expenses to collect his disability claim.

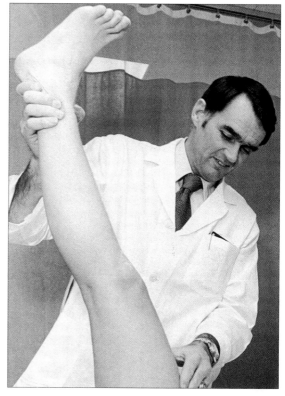

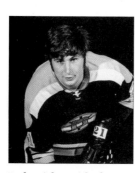

In the nightmarish aftermath of his back injuries, Jim Harrison remains in almost constant pain.

Dr. Charles Bull informed Alan Eagleson that Harrison's back problems may have been caused by botched surgery while Harrison was with the Chicago Blackhawks, yet withheld the information from Harrison himself.

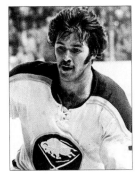

After a knee injury ended his career, Rick Martin won a $2.5-million medical malpractice judgment.

When a back injury ended his career, Murray Wilson (right) approached Eagleson, the head of the Players' Association, who told him, "You're not a client of mine. You're a client of Art Kaminsky's. Tell him to take care of your problems."

The consulting firm hired to help with André Savard's claim turned out to be Eagleson's own company.

When Ian Turnbull sought help, Eagleson "said it wasn't his responsibility to pay claims."

Eagleson companies pocketed $41,250 U.S. from Mike Gillis's disability insurance money.

Dale Tallon's disability payout came with a perplexing Crawley Warren "collection fee" of $4,950 U.S.

To collect his disability claim after an eye injury, Glen Sharpley had to pay Eagleson's firm $15,000.

Pierre Larouche was dumfounded that the players' union refused to help with his disability claim.

Bernard Warren's London-based company, Crawley Warren, handled NHLPA disability insurance; his travel insurance company, Voyageur, made out handsomely in Canada after the Mulroney government gave it preferred access to Air Canada passengers.

Roy McMurtry, an Eagleson pal and fellow Ontario Conservative, met Bernard Warren while serving as Canada's High Commissioner to Great Britain; he ended up a director of Voyageur Insurance before being appointed to the bench.

A Crawley Warren annual report shows Eagleson with John Ziegler and Brian Mulroney. Eagleson has been friends with Mulroney since working on the former prime minister's first bid for the leadership of the federal Conservatives in 1976. Voyageur Insurance commenced underwriting in Canada in 1988, the year the Mulroney Conservatives were re-elected.

Businesses connected to Norman Donaldson, an Eagleson friend and business partner, received favorable loans from NHLPA funds. When the loans fell into arrears, they were extended.

Arthur Harnett, who worked on Eagleson's successful campaign for the presidency of the Ontario Conservative Association in 1968, became involved in the sale of Canada Cup rink-board advertising.

Marvin Teperman got a $1.2-million loan from NHLPA funds. Eagleson claimed such loans were approved by the union's "investment committee," but an NHLPA employee admitted there was no such thing.

An accountant and close associate of Eagleson's, Marvin Goldblatt was contracted by Eagleson and Chris Lang to provide financial expertise for the international tournaments Eagleson organized.

Eagleson bought the lease for this London flat, near Buckingham Palace, with the assistance of Bernard Warren.

Eagleson's neighbors at La Coquille Club Villas in Florida, where he kept a winter home, included General Alexander Haig.

When Eagleson moved the NHLPA into 37 Maitland Street, most players didn't know their union boss was also their landlord.

Although 37 Maitland had only four legal parking spaces, as many as ten spaces were leased out at the same time.

Eagleson's Collingwood, Ontario, home (left) adjoins that of his friend and business partner Norman Donaldson.

Eagleson sold this home, in the Rosedale section of Toronto, to Donaldson, who planned to convert it into apartments.

"Brett, out of the blue, said, 'What are you trying to do, Dad? Take $250,000 out of my pocket?'" Hull recalled. "I said, 'Brett, this is your dad you're talking to. I wouldn't try to take money out of anyone's pocket, least of all yours. Whoever's been beating on your ear has been telling you a bunch of falsehoods. All we're looking for are answers about surplus benefits that are supposed to be in our pension fund. You're likely to find out the surplus monies that should have been in our pension funds were used for your $250,000 [the senior-player benefit negotiated in 1986].'

"The current players had no understanding what our questions were about," said Hull, who still has the bull-like physique of his playing days. "They thought we were a disgruntled group of old has-beens trying to take money out of the pension fund that didn't belong to us."

After the all-star debacle, Dave Forbes wrote John Ziegler. "No matter what we have gone to for information about our pension plan we have come away with little substance," he wrote, adding that NHL treasurer and vice-president of finance, Ken Sawyer, appeared to think "the NHL pension plan is his, not ours." Forbes questioned $415,993 in pension administrative charges. He complained that retired players had come away empty-handed after requesting information about their own pensions. He asked Ziegler several questions:

"Are you aware that a surplus exists in our pension plan that the owners now claim belongs to them?

"Are you aware that in 1983 the plan was apparently retroactively amended to change the beneficiaries of surplus monies from the players to the owners?

"Are you aware this was done without any apparent authorization and that the player/beneficiaries were never notified of this illegal change?"

Forbes noted that Ontario pension law required that at least half the trustees of multi-employer pension plans represent the employees. "In light of this we are somewhat surprised with the ease with which you have brushed us off. Our group consists of the very people who have built hockey into the great game it is today."

Forbes sent copies to Andy Bathgate, Carl Brewer, Gordie Howe, Bobby Hull, Bobby Orr, Dennis Owchar, Rene Robert, Allan Stanley, retired referee Bruce Hood, Ed Garvey, the owners or governors of every NHL team,

Eagleson, and incoming NHLPA deputy executive director Bob Goodenow.

His letter prompted a nasty response from Ziegler. "You have joined your colleague Mr. Brewer in publishing inaccuracies and misstatements, including some which you know are inaccurate," he wrote Forbes. "I am not knowledgeable as to whom you refer to as 'we.' The Pension Society has no information on file which suggests you are authorized to represent anyone as to his pension other than yourself. Any person who has questions as to his pension receives an answer to the best of our ability."

Ziegler noted "certain former players have announced they intend to launch litigation over this subject matter. Others have said you are a part of this group." He told Forbes that such actions "were not conducive to a non-adversarial atmosphere."

WHEN I FIRST SOUGHT INFORMATION about the NHL Pension Society, phoning the Ontario Pension Commission, I was refused because I was not a member of the plan. I asked Dave Forbes and Brad Park to officially designate me as their representative in obtaining documents related to their pensions. They did so, and at the Pension Commission of Ontario, on Bloor Street in Toronto, I photocopied reams of documents and took them home to Massachusetts.

The records showed that in 1947, when the NHL Pension Society began, players contributed $900 a season. For the first ten years, only players contributed. "It was quite a chunk out of your pay in those days," Gordie Howe remembered. "A player would make $5,000 to $7,500 a season before taxes, and $900 was being taken out for pension." In 1957, the six team owners began matching player contributions.

The year the owners began to contribute, the NHL Pension Society — which managed player pensions — realized it would have a surplus at the end of the year and asked for a legal opinion on what to do with the money. "The opinion received," according to the society's 1958 annual report, "was that this surplus belonged to all of the 'participants' and that the money could only be disbursed to provide additional pension benefits for the 'participants' on an equitable basis." Players shared a surplus of $310,243 that year, each player getting $315 per season played.

In 1964, the annual player contribution increased to $1,500 per player. Each season in the NHL was expected ultimately to be worth nearly $1,000 a year in pension, payable at age sixty-five. That year, the regulations were revised so that any surplus could be used to offset new contributions to the fund with the approval of the NHL Pension Society.

In 1967 the NHL expanded to twelve teams. The plan was again changed so that players could collect retirement at age forty-five or fifty-five, whichever they preferred. The revised pension agreement again specified that any surplus would be shared by the players every five years. That year, players shared about $460,000 and were notified that the surplus would be divvied up again in 1972.

Two NHL owners at the time confirmed that the players were entitled to any pension surplus. "It is certainly my understanding that the lion's share, that's where it was going," said Weston Adams Jr., president of the Boston Bruins from 1969 to 1975. Bill Putnam, a former part owner of both the Philadelphia Flyers and Atlanta Flames, said flatly, "The surpluses were for the benefit of the participants — the players."

Players had been represented on the board of the NHL Pension Society from day one. In 1969, however, the owners assumed the entire cost of funding the pension plan. "In view of the assumption of this obligation, the player representation on the Board of Directors of the Pension Society shall cease," stated the minutes of the 1969 meetings of the NHL Player-Owner Council.

"It was the owners' idea to put us out," recalled Hall of Famer Norm Ullman, a former Detroit and Toronto center — and former NHLPA president — who now lives in Unionville, Ontario. "It was just done. I don't think the players had any notification of changes."

Other players agreed that there had been no discussion of the issue. "One minute we had representation, the next minute we didn't," said former player Lou Angotti. "But I was always under the impression the pension was for the players. Whatever kind of monies it generated, in surplus or interest, I never thought it would go anywhere but to the benefit of players."

One owner who attended the meetings that removed players from the Pension Society board said the owners were well aware that this was an important step. "The league could do whatever they wanted with the pension fund," said Bill Putnam. "I doubt the players really understood the ramifications of it." Putnam said he was surprised that Eagleson agreed to the change. "At the time, as the owner of a financially struggling franchise, I was in favor of it. But it really was not a fair situation for the players.

"It was a joke, really. We [the owners] all saved money on the deal and Alan just went along with it. Now I look back at it and I'd have to say it wasn't right, not at all proper. The money in the pension plan was always intended to go to the players, not to benefit the owners by offsetting expenses."

There was considerable doubt whether Eagleson even had the right in 1969 to speak for the players. When he agreed on behalf of the new "informal" players' association to remove them from the Pension Society, there was no collective bargaining agreement between the NHL and the NHLPA. (The first CBA wasn't signed until 1976.) In the United States, where ten of the twelve NHL teams were based, Eagleson was not even a legal representative for all players and retirees.

International hockey featuring NHL stars began with the Team Canada–Soviet Summit Series of 1972. In the 1976 collective bargaining agreement, the pension plan changed again. Beginning in the 1975–76 fiscal year, 50 percent of profits from international hockey were earmarked for the pension fund. Yet even though the players had resumed contributing to the fund through their participation in international hockey, they did not regain representation on the Pension Society.

Players who risked their careers by injuring themselves in these international tournaments were paid a relative pittance. "By the time you get done paying taxes, there isn't much left," said Brad Park. "A lot of players played a lot of international games — Canada Cups, World Tournaments, NHL-Soviet games — during the late 1970s and early '80s. When you boil it all down, split by the number of games played, was it really worth risking your career for a few thousand dollars? I don't think so."

The players were told that some of the international hockey profits went into a bonus pension fund. Both Eagleson and NHL president John Ziegler were on record, I discovered, as referring to a "bonus pension" or "supplemental pension." But there was no such fund, at least not officially. According to the Pension Commission of Ontario, the escrow account that held the money in question was never registered as a pension fund. That meant the money was not subject to the strict rules that govern pension funds.

In 1983, fourteen years after the players lost their representation on the Pension Society, the society changed the rules governing surplus money. Many players active at the time — including Gord Roberts, Wayne Gretzky, Denis Potvin, Rick Middleton, Pat Verbeek, Ryan Walter, Mike Gartner — told me they were never notified of these changes, which were contained in a revised plan filed December 9, 1983, with the Pension Commission of Ontario and made retroactive to January 1, 1982. The change stated that the Pension Society could allocate any surplus money among the NHL teams and the players in proportion to their contributions to the fund. It also stated that any surplus amounts allocated to the clubs could be used by the owners "to reduce member club contributions to the Club Pension Plan."

And reduce their contributions they did. For the 1982–83 fiscal year, NHL owners used $900,435 in surplus money to offset nearly 50 percent of their pension contributions. The next year another $74,405 of surplus was used; the year after that, a further $265,809.

By now, the surplus was growing quickly. Investment profits soared during the economic boom of the 1980s. As of July 1, 1986, the pension fund held an unallocated surplus of just over $24 million, money earned by Manulife on annuities purchased with NHL pension contributions. Instead of battling for the surplus, Eagleson allowed owners to use the money without consulting the players. Besides giving themselves a contribution holiday, the owners used more than $9 million of the surplus to fund the $250,000 lump-sum pension negotiated in 1986.

Gordie Howe said he knew nothing about these rule changes, yet he was listed as a member of the Pension Society from 1982 to 1986. He did not even find that out, he told me (and repeated under oath), until 1991. In his affidavit, Howe said the only time he was ever consulted about membership in the Pension Society was in the mid-1980s.

"I received a notice from the National Hockey League that I had been elected to a position with the Pension Society. I recall subsequently telephoning the office of the National Hockey League and indicating I did not wish to accept any position with the NHL Pension Society." The Pension Society continued to "elect" him anyway. Howe said he was never told of his "election," nor did he ever receive notices of pension meetings he was supposedly attending.

NHL vice president Ken Sawyer, a pension society director between 1981 and 1992, said meeting notices were usually sent to the club with which a Pension Society member was affiliated (Howe was employed as an executive with the Hartford Whalers in the 1980s). "I'm very surprised he didn't get them, because all directors would be sent material," Sawyer said in a deposition. "Whether or not it didn't get from the club to him, I don't know."

Jimmy Fox, a former Los Angeles player rep now employed by the Kings in a front-office job, remembered the pension surplus coming up during collective bargaining in 1986. "The owners wanted to use the surplus to help fund the increase," Fox recalled, referring to the $250,000 lump-sum retirement benefit for players with at least 400 career NHL games. "I recall the number of $15 million being discussed. [Eagleson] did not come out and say who owned it. Everybody realized that the money was not new money. It was old money. My beef is not that the owners took it and did what they wanted with it. My beef is that the NHLPA did not fight harder for that money. The position of the executive director should have been that it's 100 percent players' money, as opposed to 'I don't know.' His job was to fight for every cent of that dollar."

Most players did not realize that the new $250,000 lump-sum benefit was being paid for with the pension surplus, meaning it cost many of the owners far less to fund. Some found out from Ed Garvey in 1989. When they learned the owners were using the surplus to meet their pension obligations and fund the lump-sum payments, said Garvey, "they were wild." Garth Butcher, then with the Vancouver Canucks, stood up and said, "You mean to tell me the money contributed for Bobby Hull, Bobby Orr, Gordie Howe, and those players is being used to pay current player benefits? Well, that sucks!"

"Players had no idea of a $20-plus million surplus in the pension plan" when they approved the 1986 contract, said Garvey. Ironically, their first clue may have come when the clubs used a small part of the surplus to increase pensions in 1988 — the "Merry Christmas" letter. That's when Carl Brewer sensed there was more where that came from — surplus money the owners, unchallenged by Eagleson, were effectively keeping for themselves.

IN 1987, THE PROVINCE OF ONTARIO — where the NHL plan is registered — adopted a new rule guaranteeing representation for pension fund participants. It had been almost twenty years since Eagleson had agreed to remove players from the Pension Society. Now the owners' exclusive control was jeopardized. Rather than bring the players back on board, as the new Ontario law intended, the NHL sought an exemption. And they needed Eagleson's help to get it.

"The National Hockey League Players' Association represents all hockey players who participate in the National Hockey League Club Pension Plan," Eagleson wrote to Murray Elston, then chairman of the Ontario Management Board of the Finance Ministry in the Liberal government of the day. Elston's role was to recommend to the Pension Commission of Ontario whether to grant the exemption. "This letter will confirm the NHLPA's support of the application to have the National Hockey League Pension Society exempted by regulation from the plan....We have discussed the matter with the Pension Society and understand that the exemption will permit it to continue to act in its present capacity in respect to the Plan. In our view, this is in the best interests of our membership." After his signature, Eagleson added: "Murray, Personal regards, Alan."

Elston sent Eagleson's letter to the Pension Commission as evidence in support of the proposed exemption; with all retired and active players apparently in agreement, the Pension Commission approved it. The NHL owners thus kept exclusive control of the Pension Society as it made decisions concerning the players' multi-million-dollar pension fund.

But there were three problems. First, contrary to Eagleson's assertion, the NHLPA did not represent all players covered by the plan, since retirees no longer belonged to the union. Second, according to several NHL officials I interviewed, Eagleson wrote the letter at the specific request of NHL vice president Ken Sawyer. Third, Eagleson's claim that the NHLPA supported the exemption was untrue, or so said the current and former players — including player reps — I interviewed.

Andy Moog was stunned when I showed him Eagleson's letter to Elston: "I never saw that. I wasn't aware of it until now, and I was a team rep for the Bruins when it was written." Cam Neely said he never knew about it. Ray Bourque, Lyndon Byers, Terry O'Reilly, Ken Linseman, Jean Ratelle, Gerry Cheevers, Reggie Lemelin, Marty McSorley, Glen Wesley, Don Marcotte, Milt Schmidt, Brad Park, and Johnny Bucyk were all participants in the plan, and all said the same thing. "It was business as usual, another example of The Eagle going along with whatever the league wanted," said Pat Verbeek, an NHLPA player rep at the time. "I never knew about any pension exemption supported by the Players' Association."

When Eagleson wrote Elston — August 1, 1989 — he was at a critical juncture as executive director of the union. Less than two months earlier, at the 1989 meetings in Palm Beach, Ed Garvey's questions about his chummy relationship with the NHL bosses had almost cost him his job of twenty-two years, and one of the most contentious issues had been the pension fund. Eagleson had survived the move to oust him, but he was put on notice that his handling of union affairs was under scrutiny. Another meeting was scheduled for late August in Toronto.

On August 1, in other words, Eagleson did not know if he would be dismissed by the players. Many suspected he might end up working for the NHL. The letter showed that Eagleson kept the players out of the NHL Pension Society even as Carl Brewer — and a fast-growing number of other plan participants — were futilely seeking information about their pensions.

IN APRIL 1991, BREWER and six other former players — Andy Bathgate, Gordie Howe, Bobby Hull, Allan Stanley, Eddie Shack, and Leo Reise — filed suit against each NHL club, NHL president Ziegler, and the NHL Pension Society. In essence, the suit claimed that the owners had misallocated surplus pension money.

While Mark Zigler was masterminding the legal attack against John Ziegler *et al.* in Canada, Ed Ferren, a Philadelphia lawyer who represented former players Bob Dailey and Reggie Leach, was also looking into the pension issue. He called it "a scam" and in June 1991 filed a class-action suit at

U.S. federal court in Camden, New Jersey, on behalf of Dailey, Leach, and other former players against Ziegler and the twenty-one NHL clubs. Ferren's complaint charged that the players had received only $4.4 million of a $24-million pension surplus and that nearly $2 million had been "removed altogether" from the plan without notice to former players. It accused Ziegler and the NHL of failing to allocate funds to the exclusive benefit of retired players as required; "diverting pension plan and trust assets"; breach of contract; and breach of fiduciary duty. The suit also claimed that Ziegler and the NHL had violated federal Employee Retirement Income Security Act (ERISA) laws in the United States.

At about this time, an unlikely ally rallied to the league's defense. Larry Regan, a former Bruin and Maple Leaf, was president of the International Professional Hockey Alumni Association (later called the National Alumni Association), based in Ottawa. Regan sent a letter to all alumni members, implicitly supporting the league's position in the pension surplus dispute. And in a *Toronto Star* story about the disputed $24-million surplus, he was quoted as saying, "The league has carried out its commitments." Noting that the NHL had given close to $5 million of the surplus back to retired players, Regan said, "I am not even claiming our organization was responsible for getting this piece of the surplus applied to benefits under the pension plan. I would like to think we had some influence...."

When I called Regan, he said he had a letter from Alan Eagleson verifying that the pension surplus belonged to the NHL — too bad, but those were the breaks. Besides, Regan said, it wasn't the business of a reporter to snoop into these affairs.

I asked him to send me the Eagleson letter. It had been written in December 1990, just days before the retired players met with Mark Zigler at the Ramada Inn in Toronto. "In the 1986 collective bargaining agreement negotiations," Eagleson wrote to Regan, "one of the principal bargaining items of concern to the NHLPA membership was the creation of a 'Security Package' to provide additional income to players after retirement. We knew, before the negotiations began, that Manulife had made a substantial refund to the Pension Society."

Eagleson noted that the total surplus was approximately $25 million. Of that, NHL Pension Society accountants and actuaries had determined that approximately $4.4 million belonged to former players. The league agreed, Eagleson said, "that $4.4 million had to be used, through some fair method of allocation, for the benefit of former players." He said the money had been held up for nearly two years because of tax concerns, involving Revenue Canada and the U.S. Internal Revenue Service; these concerns had finally been resolved in October 1988. Eagleson claimed, as did the NHL, that the surplus had been a refund from Manulife for overpayment in pension contributions made by the league.

Reading Eagleson's letter, I wondered why Regan didn't go to the Ontario Pension Commission himself. It didn't seem to have occurred to him that players in the plan, including himself, never had a say because nobody had notified them. Small wonder — why would the NHL want retired players to know they had received only a small portion of the $24-million surplus that many felt was rightfully theirs?

A FEW DAYS AFTER REGAN sent out his letter to all alumni members, Bobby Orr called my home. He'd just received some interesting correspondence himself. "Guess what?" he said. "The NHL wants to sue me."

"For what?"

"Libel, slander, defamation of character. They say their reputation and business have been harmed because of me, Dave Forbes, and the story that came out in *The National* [a now-defunct U.S. sports newspaper] on the pension."

The NHL was suing the man responsible for selling more NHL tickets from the late 1960s through the mid-1970s than any other player? I couldn't imagine it. I asked Orr to fax me the complaint.

Sure enough, Orr, Forbes, *The National*, its editor, Frank Deford, and a lawyer and sportswriter, Lester Munson, were named as defendants. The notice centered on Munson's feature stories, which zeroed in on the disputed NHL pension surplus and Eagleson's background with Hockey Canada. The complaint challenged the accuracy of the story and of quotes attributed to Orr and Forbes. Orr was quoted as saying: "Our money is now being used to pay pensions of current players." And Forbes: "We have been stonewalled by the people at our pension, our union, and our league."

On letterhead listing fifty-three different lawyers with the firm of Lerner & Associates, Toronto lawyer Earl Cherniak wrote Orr: "If Mr. Munson has misquoted you in these articles, copies of which are enclosed herein, kindly advise the writer of the manner in which you were misquoted and any communication you have had or propose to have with the National Sports Daily concerning a retraction and public apology."

Having gone through the documentation I'd collected at the Pension Commission of Ontario, I knew the league didn't stand a snowball's chance in hell. Forbes had indeed been given short shrift by Eagleson and by Ziegler. So, I knew, had Gordie Howe. And Orr was correct that current player pension costs had been paid from the NHL pension accounts held for former players. The surplus was being used to offset owners' contributions; some teams were contributing nothing to the fund, using the surplus to subsidize their contribution holiday.

"Were you misquoted?" I asked Orr.

"No."

"Well, as I see it, they're trying to set up Munson, hoping you or Forbes will say you were."

"I wasn't — I said it."

Forbes also said he was correctly quoted.

Ziegler sent a copy of the complaint, with a cover letter, to all current and former NHL players. Ziegler's letter, dated May 2, 1991, said in part: "The NHL has traditionally practiced restraint in dealing with public criticism, so as not to divert the fans' attention from the game — especially during a time such as now when the Stanley Cup playoffs are underway." (Many players chuckled at this, since Ziegler was perceived as a non-fan who sometimes didn't even bother attending playoff games.) He continued: "The untrue accusation that the NHL is failing to honor its obligations to former players cannot go unanswered. Because of the attack upon the integrity of the NHL, the NHL Pension Society, and the NHL Member Clubs, we have directed that action be taken by outside counsel against those spreading these untruths."

The message was clear: keep your mouth shut. If the NHL was willing to move against Orr, anybody was fair game. Ziegler's letter brought a swift response from former NHL stars Brewer, Vic Hadfield, Keith McCreary,

Allan Stanley, and Eddie Shack, who wrote him on May 12: "It is indeed sad that players, who contributed greatly to the development of the NHL, have, in their view, experienced difficulty getting what they believe to be fair and above board support and accounting from such entities as the Pension Society.

"It is sad that many players who played international hockey and were told that their pensions would be improved because of their involvement and participation have developed the sense that they have never had true and straightforward fully disclosed accounting for the revenues granted.

"Further, it is regrettable the NHL and the member clubs would resort to such treatment of one of our game's icons, Bobby Orr.

"Perhaps your recent tactics of filing this notice and distributing it widely to all hockey players is seen by you as a worthwhile intimidation and scare tactic. We believe that you will find this effort on your part to discredit the two players in question will succeed, instead, in rallying tremendous support for the players being maligned by you."

On May 15, the NHL filed another legal notice, this one against Gordie Howe, Billy Harris, the *Toronto Sun*, the Toronto Sun Publishing Company, and reporter Jack Saunders. Charging libel and slander, the complaint alleged that the NHL clubs would suffer damage to their business and reputation because of the *Sun* story on the dispute. Howe, in particular, was cited for having the audacity to comment publicly on the league's handling of Brad Park and Terry O'Reilly when they sought help for their ill sons. The complaint chastised Howe for suggesting that Ziegler and the NHL clubs, as well as the Pension Society and an insurance company, "have caused considerable hardship" to children. The story quoted Howe as saying: "Brad Park has a child in a wheelchair. Terry O'Reilly has a child with a liver condition. They went to the league and were told to go instead to organizations set up for those purposes. There's a sensitivity lacking."

That same day, the NHL and its member clubs filed yet another legal notice, this one against Brewer, Billy Harris, *The National*, editor Deford, and sportswriter Munson, alleging libel and slander in a story about the pension suit.

"It's the way they function," said Hall of Fame goaltender Ken Dryden, himself a lawyer. "Intimidation. Sue. It's the nature of the NHL. It's insanity."

"Imagine Ziegler and the NHL suing Bobby Orr and Gordie Howe?" said former Bruin and Islander Eddie Westfall. "No two players built the game more than they did. It's an absolute disgrace, even thinking of suing those two."

"The last I knew, everybody has a right to their opinion," said Gerry Cheevers, "but all bets are off when it comes to freedom of speech in the NHL."

The overall response was perhaps best summed up by Andy Moog: "Mr. Ziegler and the league have shot themselves in the foot."

ON OCTOBER 21, 1992, Ontario's Mr. Justice George Adams Jr., in a 150-page decision, ruled that NHL clubs must reimburse pension surplus money the league had improperly used since 1982. His order specified no figures until an updated accounting had been done, calculating the interest and annuity amounts that retired players would have received since 1982 had league executives and club owners not unilaterally changed the rules of the pension plan. The profits earned on annuity money belonged to the pensioners, not to the team owners.

Eagleson's role did not escape Judge Adams's censure. "When the NHLPA negotiated with the NHL in 1986, it was representing only active or present players, and the NHL and NHLPA had no power to extend the NHLPA's authority to former players without their consent....

"The apparent moral shortcoming in the NHLPA's conduct captured by its Executive Director's participation in the November 21, 1988 'Merry Christmas' letter to former players, should not be confused with the Association's then limited mandate."

The NHL Pension Society appealed the ruling, but the tide had turned in the players' favor. Once they understood what had really happened, they joined ranks and, in early 1993, sent a petition to Floyd Laughren, minister of finance in the Ontario NDP government of Bob Rae, requesting that the 1989 exemption be revoked. Laughren in turn wrote to Ken Sawyer at the NHL: "Representations have recently been made into the government concerning the appropriateness of this exemption. The exemption was agreed to by the previous government on the basis that it was endorsed by both the plan sponsors and the representatives of members. We are now being advised that a significant number of the plan's beneficiaries do not support this exemption." Laughren demanded that the Pension Society provide documented evidence that the exemption had the support of a majority of the members. "In the absence of this evidence, serious grounds will exist in my view for the revocation of the exemption." He set a deadline of April 30, 1993.

When I interviewed Murray Elston, the Ontario government official who had recommended the exemption, he admitted he'd been had. "From the letter, I understood anybody, retired or current, a person accessing or accruing benefits, was represented by [Eagleson] in the pension exemption endorsement. I don't think I ever gave it a second thought. It led me to believe all was fine. It's clear now that participants had no knowledge. In light of the controversy now, it would make sense to revoke the exemption.

"If I had knowledge the participants hadn't endorsed the exemption, we would have sent it back to the NHL Pension Society and said get your act together, no exemption. Absent of approval of players — knowing what is being represented now — I think it was a drastic misrepresentation of the facts."

Laughren's request for evidence that the exemption should remain in force prompted an eight-page letter from Toronto lawyer John M. Solurush, representing the NHL Pension Society. Solurush claimed there was no evidence that "a significant number" of players objected to the exemption. He also noted that the NHLPA was "the collective bargaining agent for hockey players" and had consented to the agreement.

"Sure — without their knowledge," said Mark Zigler, who also emphasized that the union was not the bargaining agent for retired players covered by the plan. "Eagleson wrote the letter on behalf of players he didn't even represent."

As for the Pension Society's position that there was no evidence "a significant number" opposed the exemption, the petition delivered to Laughren included the signatures of 118 retired players, sixteen of them members of the Hall of Fame. And through a notice filed by Bob Goodenow, Eagleson's successor as head of the NHLPA, all active players effectively notified Laughren they no longer supported the exemption. In May 1993, the exemption was revoked.

Soon afterward, Laughren told Bruce Dowbiggin, "I think the importance is that in any pension fund, there should be employee representation on the board. That is just justice." He pointed to the letter from Eagleson supporting the exemption. "I'm not blaming the former minister, Mr. Elston. I think he acted in good faith, [believing] that the letter he received certainly implied that [the exemption] would be fine with the players and the officials.

"Hopefully we can go forward now. I'm sure that the retired players, players and officials, will be vigorous in pursuing justice on their own behalf. And so they should."

In February 1994, during the Winter Olympics in Lillehammer, Norway, Mark Zigler called me to say that the Ontario Court of Appeal had upheld the lower court decision awarding the retired players their disputed pension money. The phone rang all day.

"It's my wife's birthday and she said this is the greatest birthday of her life," Gordie Howe told me. "Justice is served. I'm happy for all the players who have made the game what it is. The courage of your newspaper to take something on like this was so impressive. It was a catalyst to wake people up."

"This is about the best thing that has ever happened to us older players," said Ferny Flaman. "I'm beyond words, really."

Calls from Carl Brewer and Sue Foster, Milt Schmidt, Johnny McKenzie, Brad Park, Terry O'Reilly, Don Marcotte, Bobby Orr, Eddie Westfall, and many others made it a wonderful day. But I knew the battle wasn't over when a league official called me with a statement from NHL senior vice president Jeff Pash.

"We believed there was merit in pursuing the appeal," said the statement. "We understood the league's use of the surplus to be both permissible and in accordance with the results of collective bargaining negotiations with the NHL Players' Association." Pash said league officials would review the decision with NHL lawyers "to determine the appropriate action." I knew then that the issue was headed to the Supreme Court of Canada.

The following week, I spoke to Gary Bettman, who had succeeded John Ziegler in late 1992. He confirmed that the NHL Pension Society was going to appeal to the Supreme Court of Canada. I said I thought it was a disgrace that the retired players were being forced to fight to the very end for their money. Bettman explained that the NHL had to exhaust every legal avenue before taking action against Baker & McKenzie, the Chicago law firm that had advised it about the surplus in the early 1980s. "I'm just digging out from the past," he said. "Nobody told me there were so many termites in this house I moved into."

In July 1994, the Supreme Court refused to hear the appeal. The original decision stood, although it would be another six months before lawyers for both sides had agreed on adjusted pension increases. The four-year war was over. Thanks largely to the insight and grit of Carl Brewer, more than 900 retired players — and a few current players who had been in the league before 1983 — would be getting better pensions.

The increases vary from $1,000 a year for some players to more than $10,000 for others. A retiree's increase depends on the number of years he played, which years, and when he began collecting retirement money. For such Hall of Famers as Gump Worsley, Maurice Richard, Frank Mahovlich, and Johnny Bucyk, the increases are significant. In certain cases, pensions will nearly double. For some former players, the NHL pension is their major — in some cases, sole — source of income.

"Those articles really woke up hockey people around the country and Canada, particularly the players. We had no idea what was going on," Gordie Howe said in a personal call that meant a lot.

"I don't think any of us knew the owners were offsetting their pension contributions for current players with money already in the fund, until we read those newspaper articles out of Massachusetts," said Allan Stanley, the former Maple Leaf defenseman.

Eddie Shack was upset that the retired players hadn't received coverage or support from many Canadian journalists. "Up here they didn't want to listen to us. Didn't want to pay attention. They were playing up to Eagleson and Ziegler and the rest of them, taking the easy way out. It took an American newspaper to wake up Canada about what was happening to us older players.

"Those buggers got away with treating us like dirt. They thought we'd go away and we didn't. But we wouldn't have been successful if it hadn't been for Carl Brewer."

7

BETRAYAL

"Eagleson and Ross Johnson were close, and Eagleson
knew we weren't going to be doing business with Johnson's
company. Maybe that's why he took Orr to Chicago —
because he could do business with Wirtz, and get all that
Standard Brands sponsorship for international hockey."
PAUL MOONEY

B ACK IN JUNE 1990 — not long after the 1970
Bruins reunion — a column appeared in the *Globe and Mail*, chastising
Bobby Orr for not fulfilling a $90,000 pledge he had supposedly made years
earlier to a sports injury clinic at York University. The gist of the column, by
Marty York, was that Orr's name was mud because he had stiffed the clinic
for some of the money he had promised.

Something didn't add up here. Orr wasn't the kind of guy to stiff anyone. I'd known him since 1969 when, just two years out of high school and
enrolled at Northeastern University in Boston, I began covering the Bruins.
At the time, the young Orr and the veteran winger Johnny Bucyk had been
unusually kind to me, going out of their way to make me feel comfortable.
In those years I was close in age to many of the players; I knew the game,
having played since I could skate; and, like many of the younger players,
I was single and not averse to chugging a beer or smiling at a pretty face.
I became friends with some of them, Orr in particular.

On my first road trip with the Bruins, the day before a game in Montreal,
Orr realized I had never covered the team on the road. "Nervous?" he asked.
"This is the big city, you know. Where you going tonight?" I didn't have

a clue. Orr made a point, getting off the bus, of telling me where he'd be that evening — "Stop by if you like." It was one of those little gestures that stays with you.

One morning in 1971, when the Bruins were riding high and capturing every heart in New England, Orr showed me a side of him that taught me something. At Boston Garden for a practice, the Bruins skated through two-on-ones, three-on-twos, the usual drills, while a small group of onlookers sipped coffee and chatted. In those days, there wasn't the huge gulf in salaries between players and reporters. Hockey was still a game played by overgrown kids, and the camaraderie extended beyond the ice.

When practice ended, the players headed for the Bruins' dressing room, filing off the ice one by one, saying hi to the few media people. Orr, in his yellow practice jersey, sweat pouring from his forehead, nodded in my direction. "How's it going?"

"Not so good today."

Orr paused a second — "See me inside before you go" — and continued toward the dressing room. The sportswriters, notebooks and pens in hand, went into the dressing room for off-day stories and conversations with various players and the coach, Tom Johnson. Half an hour later Orr appeared from the trainer's room, went to the spot where his civvies were hung, and prepared to leave.

"You wanted to see me about something?"

"What happened?" he said. "How come you're having a bad day?"

A long night at work; a car that wouldn't start; a silly argument with a girlfriend; a plane ticket fouled up — I went through my litany of irritants. It was a Murphy's Law kind of day.

"What are you doing now, Russ? Anything special?"

"Don't think so. Why?"

"You're coming with me," he said. "Frosty!" he called to the trainer, John Forristall. "Where's that box?"

Forristall brought Orr a box full of programs, pennants, pucks, pictures, assorted Bruins memorabilia. Orr picked up a handful of sticks and said, "Could you carry the box?"

We went to his car, parked in the old exhibition hall where the Zamboni was stored in the building next to the Garden. Orr opened the trunk, loaded the box and the sticks, and said, "Come on, let's go."

I had no idea where we were going, and he had no intention of telling me. He headed down Storrow Drive, taking the Kenmore–Back Bay exit near Fenway Park. Just before we reached our destination, he glanced over and said, "Just stay with me. And not a word in your newspaper, understand?"

Unloading the box and sticks, we walked into Boston Children's Hospital and got on the elevator. The door opened and Orr went to the nurse's station. He chatted and joked with the nurses, then turned and said, "Come on, let's start in this room down here."

For well over an hour we went from room to room, Orr popping in, unannounced, to visit the kids. Some couldn't believe their eyes; sick as they were, they laughed in astonishment and delight. Bobby Orr! He talked and joked with every one of them, asking names, rubbing heads, giving everybody a little present from the box, leaving a stick, autographing everything in sight. These youngsters were undergoing treatment for cancer, leukemia, cerebral palsy, kidney disease — terrible stuff. Yet nearly all of them, with their teddy bears and stuffed animals, managed big smiles.

When we finished making the rounds on one floor, Orr took the elevator up to the next. He repeated, "Not a word in the paper, understand?" Finally, when he'd given out all the souvenirs, we headed out. Orr didn't say anything on the way back to his car. He climbed in, started the engine, then turned to me.

"So," he said. "How's your day now?"

IN THE TWENTY YEARS I'D KNOWN ORR, never once did he break a commitment that I knew about. His involvement with charity fund raisers, like Johnny Bucyk's, was beyond compare among Boston athletes. I'd seen them both go out of their way to fulfill a commitment. If Orr said he was going to do something, he did it. That's why I knew something about the clinic story was out of whack.

I called Orr, who invited me to his office in South Boston. He was angry and shaken by the *Globe and Mail* story. He said it had been Eagleson who made the clinic commitment, using his name; he had never even heard of it until Eagleson brought it up in a phone conversation back when Orr was still living in Chicago.

"I was in tax trouble up to my ears at the time," he recalled. "Al knew that. We had a big fight over him making a pledge for ninety grand when I couldn't afford it. He'd already done it. He said, 'Don't worry about it. All you have to do is a couple of appearances.' This is a perfect case of Al using my name, mismanaging my finances. Now they drag me through the mud, saying I stiffed them, and the damned reporter doesn't even give my side."

Orr felt embarrassed by the story. People were phoning him about it. I told him I wanted his version and would question people at the clinic. He thought he had some correspondence and promised to dig it up. Meanwhile, he said, it might be helpful to call Eagleson's pal, Dr. Charles Bull. He said Bull was in charge of the clinic. (Bull, of course, was the doctor who confided to Eagleson in 1978 that Jim Harrison's playing career might have been jeopardized by a back operation without giving the same information to Harrison.)

I called Bull. He wouldn't have anything to do with me, saying this was past history. I called Marty York, the writer. York said he stood by his story — Orr had turned his back on a pledge to the clinic. I asked how he knew that. Did he have records proving Orr had made a pledge? York said his sources had verified the story and so had people at the clinic. I asked why he hadn't interviewed Orr. He said he'd tried to, making a call to Orr's office the day before the story ran, leaving a message.

"You made one call to get Orr's side of the story, and because he isn't in you go with it anyway?"

York said he had no choice, it was a good story and he didn't want to get beat on it. He intended to call Orr again, he said, to get Bobby's reaction.

Orr's files, I found, supported his claim that he'd known nothing about the pledge. In 1978, while he was mired in debt after his playing career, Eagleson had made a $90,000 pledge to the clinic at York University, operated by Bull. The clinic would be named the Bobby Orr Sports Injury Clinic, in recognition of Orr's contribution. The president of the university was H. Ian Macdonald, a long-time Conservative and deputy treasurer in the provincial government who later became chairman of the board of Hockey Canada, which Eagleson controlled.

One letter in Orr's file was written by Eagleson to Macdonald in early September 1979. "Young Mr. Orr is having several problems concerning his future....For that reason it may well be necessary to change the name of the clinic on the basis that if everything else runs smoothly the only thing that would change would be the name and a commitment would continue from the writer."

I asked Orr who had made the commitment.

"Al did. I never knew about it, not until he called me one night and said he'd promised York University I'd donate $90,000 for a new clinic they were building for people with knee problems. I said, 'You had no right doing that! I'll do some appearances to help raise money but that's it, understand?' I was ticked. He knew I was in money trouble."

Orr made some appearances, raising more than $20,000 through various fund raisers, including a golf tournament and TV commentary on "Hockey Night in Canada." In 1979, Eagleson wrote Macdonald again, assuring him the pledge would be honored. But in 1980, Orr cut his ties to Eagleson. He was almost broke and refused to pay off what he considered Eagleson's pledge.

On February 20, 1985, York's new president, H. W. Arthurs, wrote Orr asking for a meeting to talk about the $63,531 left unpaid on the $90,000 pledge for the Bobby Orr Sports Injuries Clinic. Orr replied that he "was unaware of the money that Mr. Eagleson, who represented [him] at the time, had pledged in [his] behalf." Arthurs wrote back in June, insisting "York University continues to regard you as responsible for the full amount of the pledge."

In July, Eagleson wrote Arthurs: "I am disappointed to learn that Mr. Orr has decided not to honor the commitment with which he was in full agreement at the time it was made. For Mr. Orr to suggest otherwise at this late date does not speak well for him or his memory."

That prompted this blunt handwritten response by Orr: "Dear Mr. Eagleson, You are the last person that should be talking about anyone having a poor memory."

In October 1986, Eagleson again wrote Arthurs, insisting "Mr. Orr is bound to honor the balance of the pledge since I was his authorized agent, and since he made a part performance on the pledge." Eagleson offered to pay off the pledge himself "if you do not wish to take legal steps against him." He added one condition: "that the name of Mr. Orr be removed from the clinic and replaced by some other name acceptable to York University and to me."

In 1990, the clinic was renamed the R. Alan Eagleson Sports Medicine Clinic.

EXACTLY WHAT HAD HAPPENED in 1980, when Orr severed ties with Eagleson, was a piece of the Eagleson puzzle that had never quite fallen into place. Orr had refused my requests for a detailed interview in 1984, after the *Sports Illustrated* piece about Eagleson, and when I approached him in 1991 he demurred again. I reminded him he'd already done an interview with Ellie Tesher the previous summer in the *Toronto Star*. It was about Orr's shaky financial position in 1980 and detailed some business dealings Eagleson had put him in, his embarrassment over the pledge to the clinic, and his tax problems.

Orr knew I was working on this project but did not want to be part of it. We argued, politely; again he said no. I reminded him, like it or not, that his relationship with Eagleson had played a big part in lending Eagleson credibility and developing his power.

"Don't you think I know that?" he snapped. "I'm embarrassed, that's why I don't want to be involved with your story. I didn't pay attention. I trusted him about everything.

"I've been out of the game since 1979, 1980. I don't have all my records. I have to live with this the rest of my life. The less I think about him, the better I feel. These other players are the ones I feel sorry for. Look, I appreciate what you're doing, just like anybody else who cares about the game. But we should care about the people who make the game what it is."

Orr also reasoned that Eagleson would blame him for anything I wrote. (Eagleson ended up doing just that, before realizing Orr didn't know most of what I'd discovered. Orr was gone from the game when most loans were made from NHLPA funds and when the pension rules were changed. He had never heard of an NHL-owned insurance company called ICE, knew nothing about the disability insurance problems I'd uncovered, had no idea what Crawley Warren was or that Bernie Warren and Eagleson were in bed together.)

I took another run at him: "There are so many others who are helping me along — current and former players, coaches, managers, executives, lawyers, agents. All I want to do is add your story — you and Eagleson, right from the start. It's a part of the puzzle."

I could tell by his sigh he was thinking about it.

THE SON OF IMMIGRANTS from Northern Ireland, Alan Eagleson was born in St. Catharines, Ontario, in 1933, the only boy in a family with three girls. The Eaglesons moved to New Toronto, and Alan turned into a smart, scrawny kid with the aggressive personality of the little man. School was a breeze, but sports weren't. Undersized for his age, unable to win recognition as an athlete, he developed into a fast-talking wheeler-dealer.

In his last year at Humberside Collegiate, Eagleson went through a growth spurt. Now he was as big as his peers, and twice as aggressive. At the University of Toronto, where he obtained a B.A. in 1954, he was a fiercely competitive athlete who flattened opponents on the basketball court and got into fist fights at stoplights. In their book *Net Worth*, David Cruise and Alison Griffiths report that Eagleson befriended ushers at Varsity Stadium to get into football games for nothing and parked free at Exhibition Stadium by telling the guard the president of the CNE had given him permission. He was not short on nerve. While his sister was honeymooning, he unwrapped her wedding presents and prominently displayed them as prizes at a carnival booth where he was guessing weights and ages. To the side were the cheap prizes he actually gave out. At the end of the day, he rewrapped the wedding gifts and returned them.

A lacrosse player like his friend Bob Pulford, Eagleson helped coach youngsters. Tom McKeam, now a Thornhill, Ontario, dentist, recalls a lacrosse practice to which Eagleson brought handbills. "He had them in his car. He was running for election at the time. He called three or four of us over and said, 'Go pass all these out. I'll meet you at five o'clock at the Dairy Queen and you can eat and drink all you want.' We took them and went door to door, handing them out, every one of them, too. At five o'clock, we were at the ice cream stand waiting for him. He never showed up. I never forgot that."

After graduating from U of T law school, Eagleson was called to the bar in 1959. The next year he joined Blaney, Pasternak, Luck and Smela, opening an office in Etobicoke. In the early 1960s, through Pulford, by now a left winger with the Maple Leafs, Eagleson began cementing relationships with other Leaf players of the day — Billy Harris, Bobby Baun, Carl Brewer. But his launching pad to fame and fortune in the hockey world was unquestionably the teenaged, crewcut defenseman from Parry Sound, Ontario, who was then skating circles around kids three and four years his senior with the Oshawa team of the Ontario Hockey League.

Bobby Orr's father, Doug, first talked to Eagleson about his phenomenal son in 1963. Eagleson had come to a baseball banquet at MacTier, near Parry Sound. Orr played first base on the junior league's championship team. While the trophies were being presented, Orr's dad, learning Eagleson was friendly with several of the Maple Leafs, asked if he could possibly help his son, who had been spotted by Lynn Patrick, Boston's general manager. Boston had already secured Orr's NHL rights for a $2,000 advance, which included a stucco job on the Orr family home.

To play in the NHL, the Bruins offered Orr just over $10,000. Eagleson, representing him, cited Joe Namath's rookie contract — a three-year, $400,000 deal with the New York Jets of the American Football League — arguing that Orr was worth as much to hockey as Namath was to football. He threatened that Orr would go back to junior hockey, or play for Canada's national team. Boston, starved for a winner after missing the Stanley Cup playoffs for seven straight seasons, upped the ante, and a landmark deal was struck: a $25,000 signing bonus, $25,000 for Orr's rookie season, $30,000 for his second year.

When Orr was first in Boston, Eagleson was his best friend. They talked on the phone every day. Orr allowed his name to be used by Eagleson at will.

When Eagleson formed the NHL Players' Association in 1967, he named Orr vice president to lend it credibility. At Eagleson's request, Orr recommended him as an agent to dozens of other players. Orr endorsed products and did commercials when Eagleson asked him to. Eagleson said he was going to set up a business, Bobby Orr Enterprises Ltd., with the two of them and some of Eagleson's friends as directors. Orr, still in his teens, said fine.

Orr in those days was a precociously confident, gifted player who was changing the way defense was played. Nobody I've watched — including Howe, Gretzky, and Lemieux — has ever directed the pace and tenor of a game the way Orr did. Off the ice, he was shy and self-effacing, barely able to string two sentences together in public. Eagleson was as fast on his feet as anyone you'll meet. Orr was a great commodity, and Eagleson did well with him. Orr became the first NHL player to earn $100,000 a season and led the Bruins to two Stanley Cup championships in three years. By 1974–75, he was making $200,000 and won his record eighth consecutive Norris Trophy as the NHL's top defenseman. He also led the league in scoring, a feat no defenseman has achieved before or since.

Eagleson had also flourished, parlaying his success with Orr into the largest player-agent business in hockey and one of the largest in professional sport. He became well known in the late 1960s, representing many NHL stars, gaining prominence as the head of the NHL Players' Association, and becoming a household name with the dramatic Team Canada–Soviet Series of 1972, which he organized on behalf of Hockey Canada. His influence was now international, and not much of consequence happened in the hockey world without his knowledge, if not his blessing.

Eagleson had also developed important contacts in the Progressive Con-servative Party. In 1963, at age thirty, he'd been elected to Ontario's provincial legislature. Four years later, working on Davie Fulton's unsuccessful federal leadership campaign, he befriended two future prime ministers, Joe Clark and Brian Mulroney. In 1969 Eagleson himself was elected president of the Ontario Progressive Conservative Association.

After the 1975–76 NHL season, Bobby Orr was up for a new contract. Eagleson began talks with the Bruins late in 1975. Orr had missed seventy games that 1975–76 season because of a fourth knee surgery; he knew his next contract might well be his last. He wanted security, and he wanted to finish out his career in Boston. As always, he left the negotiating to Eagleson.

The first hint that he might leave Boston came not from him or Eagleson, but from Tom Johnson. In his office one morning after practice, Johnson said that Orr's time may be near. "You mean you're going to trade him?" I asked, astonished. You had to live in New England to understand how shocking that notion was. Like Larry Bird and Ted Williams, Orr was a local deity, revered not just for his incomparable talents — Howe still calls him, in this age of Gretzky and Lemieux, the greatest player in NHL history — but also for his tireless work on behalf of local causes.

Johnson said the Bruins didn't want to trade him but might have no alternative if Eagleson didn't agree to a new contract. It would be better to get players in return than let Orr go to another team without compensation. Puffing on his ever-present cigar, Johnson said personally he'd hate to see it happen, but nobody was untouchable — even the prolific Phil Esposito had been dealt by the Bruins to the Rangers earlier that season. Johnson told me the Bruins had made a great offer but Eagleson had rejected it, discouraging the Bruins' brass and the new owner of the club, Jeremy Jacobs. How was the team going to contend, I wondered, with Esposito gone and the possibility of Orr leaving next?

I made a beeline to a pay phone at North Station, under the Garden, and phoned Orr. He lived in a high-rise near the Prudential Building in the Back Bay section of Boston at the time. I told him I'd learned there was a possibility he would be traded. I planned to do a column in the *Eagle-Tribune* and wanted his reaction.

Rather than talk on the phone, he suggested we meet at Pall's Mall, a watering hole on Boylston Street. That's where I learned the seriousness of his contract problems. He was convinced, he said, that the Bruins had no intention of keeping him. The trade rumor didn't surprise him. I asked why he felt the Bruins didn't want him. Quietly, he explained that he wanted to stay in Boston, had been a Bruin since day one, and had given everything he had to the team. He cherished the Stanley Cups the Bruins had won and all the good times, on and off the ice. He said he had told Eagleson to get a deal done so he'd play out his career in Boston. Eagleson had been trying to do so, but after Orr's knee flared up again in November, the Bruins lost interest. I asked how he knew that. He said Eagleson had told him Boston wasn't anywhere near as interested as other clubs.

"What are Sinden and Mooney saying to you?"

Orr said he had not personally been part of the talks because he was afraid he'd lose his temper. Eagleson had always been able to get him the best deal; Orr had trusted him to look after all his affairs since he broke into the NHL. Besides, why should he have to beg the Bruins for a new deal when other teams were eager to sign him? His own participation in the talks would be an insult to Eagleson. Boston would try to divide them, hoping he'd agree to something Eagleson had already nixed. "That's why players have agents. To stay out of that crap."

"Maybe you don't need an agent. Look at the Chief."

Whenever contract time rolled around, Johnny Bucyk — the Bruins' all-time leading scorer, nicknamed by Bronco Horvath because of his habit of ordering teammates around on the ice — would ask close friends for opinions and advice. When it came time to go to the front office, Bucyk represented himself. He usually signed one-season deals with perks and bonuses. He never had trouble coming to terms.

"Chief doesn't understand," said Orr. "The old days are gone. He figures whatever they offer is the best he's going to get. He trusts everybody and he's got nobody looking out for his best interests. I told him to get Al a long time ago but he wouldn't listen."

Orr told me to go ahead and write that I'd learned he may be traded and that his talks with the Bruins were going poorly. And if I didn't believe Boston didn't want to keep him, Eagleson would tell me himself.

I asked where he thought he might end up. Orr tightened his lips, gritting his teeth. I wondered if he'd heard me. "Where do you think you'd go?"

"The Bruins, damn it! I don't want to go anywhere else! I want to stay here!"

He apologized for blowing up. He'd told Eagleson over and over he wanted to stay in Boston. But if the Bruins weren't keen, hell, he had no choice but to go elsewhere. Where? Possibly the WHA, he said, but more likely Chicago or St. Louis. Why did he think so? He swore me to secrecy.

Because, he said, they had already been in touch with Eagleson about signing him. Eagleson had told him Chicago was willing to give him a guaranteed multi-million-dollar contract. Somebody from the Hawks had already contacted him personally to say he didn't have to worry about his future in hockey. Unlike the Bruins, said Orr, the Blackhawks were interested in making him the best offer in hockey history.

When Orr walked out of Pall's Mall, limping distinctly, I had a feeling trouble was brewing. The feeling was reinforced by a phone call not long afterward from Eagleson. Bobby had told him we'd met. Eagleson didn't want to be quoted, just wanted to confirm that the Bruins weren't interested in signing Bobby. Unless their attitude changed, he said, Bobby would be heading elsewhere.

Eagleson was interested in Tom Johnson's mention of a trade, asking if any teams had been mentioned. I said no, though I thought every team in the league would be interested in Orr. Eagleson said I was wrong. One team wasn't: the Bruins.

"Why not?"

"Because," said Eagleson, "they see Bobby as a pig in a poke, damaged goods." He said the new Bruins owners didn't want Orr with his bad knee, whereas other teams were prepared to guarantee extended deals. What teams? He wasn't going to get into that, just wanted me to know about the problems with the Bruins. He said I shouldn't be afraid to write that Bobby might be leaving Boston because it was true.

WHEN MY STORY CAME OUT, the Bruins denied that Orr would be traded. Harry Sinden claimed that contract negotiations were moving ahead and he was confident Orr would stay in Boston.

In April, during the playoffs, I asked Sinden if he could update me on Orr's contract negotiations. We met in a bar at the Marriott Century Boulevard in Los Angeles, where the team was staying, on an off-day during the Bruins' playoff series against the Kings.

Sinden, whose emotions are written all over his face, was clearly distressed. He thought the prospects of keeping Orr looked dim and admitted the matter was out of his control. For the life of him, he said, he couldn't understand what more the Bruins could do. I asked what he meant. He said the Bruins had made Orr a significant offer, which had been rejected by Eagleson. The Bruins had gone as far as they could go, but evidently it wasn't far enough. He sensed that something underhanded was going on — possibly other teams were undermining the Bruins. If he found that was true, he said, he'd insist the offending club be punished for violating tampering rules.

I told him my information was that the Bruins hadn't made a decent offer. Sinden went ballistic, pounding his fist on the bar. "Stop saying that! That's not so!" He said the Bruins had made Orr probably the best offer in hockey history, maybe in Boston pro sports history, but Eagleson had thumbed his nose at it.

I asked Sinden if he had discussed it with Orr. He said they spoke often, but not about negotiations because Orr insisted it was between Eagleson and Paul Mooney, Bruins' lawyer Charlie Mulcahy, and Jeremy Jacobs. Sinden said the affair had put a great strain on his friendship with Orr.

Just before the end of the season, Orr and Mooney, in his first season as the Bruins' president after Jeremy Jacobs bought the team from Storer Broadcasting, had a heated argument at Boston Garden. Orr accused Mooney of trying to "drive a wedge" between player and agent. Orr refused to discuss the contract negotiations with Mooney: "Alan Eagleson's my friend!" he shouted. "Don't you ever try to divide him and me again, understand that?" He stormed off.

Later that spring, a story broke that the Bruins were ready to deal Orr to Chicago for three players. Though roundly denied, it was another indication that Orr was indeed targeted for Chicago. I knew Orr was at his hockey camp in Ontario and phoned to ask about the rumor. Orr didn't think it was true, but he saw it as another indication that the Bruins weren't interested in keeping him.

Shortly after the Bruins were eliminated from the playoffs, I flew to Toronto. Orr had me driven up to Orillia to visit for a couple of days. I knew the contract story would be heating up and wanted to stay on top of it. While I was in Orillia, Orr called Sinden and reiterated that he wanted to stay with the Bruins. But he cautioned Sinden not to put his job in jeopardy, to keep his nose out of it, since Jacobs had put Mooney in charge of dealing with Eagleson.

By late spring, Sinden was openly suspicious of Chicago. At a press conference following Boston's May 26 trade of Ken Hodge to the Rangers for Rick Middleton, the questions shifted to Orr's future with the Bruins. Sinden said he would request the NHL to order Bill Wirtz to take a lie-detector test because he thought Chicago had violated NHL tampering rules and had already offered Orr a long-term deal before his Bruins contract ran out. Lie-detector tests, he pointed out, were permitted in similar circumstances in the National Football League.

In June 1976, Orr signed an NHL contract with Chicago. It was a sad day in New England, where the Bruins' popularity — thanks largely to Orr — had fueled a hockey arena construction boom. Hockey programs were blossoming all over the six-state region. With Orr's exit, Boston fans felt as if a loved one had disappeared. Jacobs, Mooney, and Sinden were the focus of blistering attacks from media members and fans alike.

The move was also something Orr and his wife, Peggy, soon regretted. They realized they'd made a mistake moving to Chicago, where Orr never really felt at home. In Boston, he was comfortable among the blue-collar fans — one of his best friends is Pat Considine, a now-retired longshoreman — while in Chicago he was flaunted like a jewel by Wirtz among the city's moneyed set. That just wasn't Bobby Orr.

THE BACKGROUND TO ORR'S departure had always been incomplete — people in Boston had long sensed there was more to it than had been reported — which was another reason I persisted in my efforts to get him to come forward with his story. I wanted to bring into the open the tight relationship between Wirtz and Eagleson that had been so detrimental to the players over the years.

"You're on the right track," Orr said. "I've had to live with it. My family's had to live with it, but we've come back. But it's the other players that are the story, the people who made this game, the ones who have been affected by the greed. The NHL and the Players' Association just can't be allowed to operate that way anymore."

I said that's why his side of the story was such an important part of the big picture: Eagleson and Wirtz had pulled off some shenanigans, and nowhere was this more evident than in Orr's Chicago deal.

"You know that's true," Orr said. "You were there when Wirtz flew to Boston with me from Bermuda. You heard him. Al had already struck the deal with the Blackhawks, and I was still under contract with the Bruins. He's the reason I left. You heard what Wirtz said that day — I was going to Chicago. I believed Al. I trusted him. I kept telling him I wanted to stay with the Bruins and he kept saying, 'Bobby, Chicago's the one that's guaranteeing you $3 million. Boston hasn't made anywhere near that kind of offer.'"

Back in 1976, I'd spent more than an hour with Orr and Wirtz at Logan Airport. Orr and Wirtz — known as W.W.W. in hockey circles — had been in Bermuda. Orr had called me from the Princess Hotel and asked if I'd pick him up at the airport. Wirtz had some time to kill before his flight to Chicago, so the three of us had a drink in an airport lounge. Wirtz was elated that Bobby was going to Chicago. His father had always wanted revenge on the Bruins, he said, because Milt Schmidt had taken advantage of Tommy Ivan in 1967, acquiring Phil Esposito, Ken Hodge, and Fred Stanfield for Pit Martin, Jack Norris, and Gil Marotte — one of the most lopsided trades in NHL history. This, Wirtz bragged, was the best revenge of all, and Boston would get nothing in return. Wirtz ragged all over the new owners of the Bruins, saying it was outrageous they weren't interested in keeping Orr. Wirtz, on the other hand, was more than willing to pay the best hockey player in the NHL what he deserved. Eagleson, he said, really looked after players he represented. This was going to be such a big deal in Chicago that the mayor would show up.

"But that drink at the airport was after June 1," I said, "after your contract had expired."

"I'd already signed an agreement with Wirtz down in Connecticut long before that. Eagleson was right there."

I was stunned. Orr had already signed an agreement with Wirtz — chairman of the board of governors — while Eagleson, the union director, was there? That would have violated the NHL's tampering rule, which forbids teams from talking to any player under contract with another team. Violators can be fined $500,000 by the league.

I asked Orr if he had any records. He doubted it, he said, because Eagleson had kept many of his records. Perhaps his new Ontario lawyer, Harvey Strosberg, had some material. I asked him to get me whatever he could.

Orr's files turned out to be a gold mine. Among his papers was the agreement he'd signed with Chicago. It was executed at the New Canaan, Connecticut, home of Ross Johnson — a friend of Eagleson's, the president of Standard Brands, and later a principal in the RJR Nabisco takeover chronicled in the best-selling business book *Barbarians at the Gate*. The deal was indeed struck in May 1976, well before Wirtz and Orr got together in Bermuda. Attending the meeting at Johnson's home were Orr, Eagleson, Wirtz, Johnson, and a friend of both Johnson's and Eagleson's, Quebec businessman Roger Baikie.

Baikie had started doing business with Eagleson in the early 1970s, when Eagleson became his corporate attorney and negotiated the buy-out of a holding company from Ed Lumley, who ended up trade and commerce minister in the government of Pierre Trudeau. Baikie owned a chemical company, a fruit company, and some Coca-Cola franchises. "I introduced Eagleson to Coca-Cola," he recalled, noting that Eagleson subsequently picked up legal work from him.

Baikie had been invited to meet with Orr to talk about marketing a new skate blade he had developed. Baikie learned that day that Orr was leaving the Bruins. Eagleson told him that "the Bruins were being very tough on Bobby and very demanding," that "Boston's attitude was not in Bobby's best interest."

Baikie, a long-time friend of Johnson's, arrived at Johnson's home first that day. Eagleson, Wirtz, and Johnson showed up later, together. I asked Baikie if he had records from the trip, and he dug up a flight ticket and a travel agency bill. The meeting was held May 17 and 18, 1976, two weeks before Orr's contract with the Bruins expired. An agreement was struck and signed on the spot, on Standard Brands letterhead:

"We agree to a 3 year contract guaranteed commencing June 1/76 through May 31/79 at $500,000 per annum.

"In addition Chicago will have options annually for a further 7 years on Orr's services at $500,000 per annum.

"The contract registered with the NHL will be 10 x $300,000. The contract will be for services in hockey and other business activities."

The agreement was signed by William W. Wirtz and Robert G. Orr, and witnessed by F. Ross Johnson.

Orr's files contained other fascinating material about Eagleson. During an April 8, 1981, deposition for a delinquent tax case against Orr by the Canadian government, Eagleson swore under oath: "I'm not an agent. I've never been an agent for any hockey player or any individual. I'm a lawyer and I've acted in that capacity." Asked what he did for Orr, Eagleson replied: "As a lawyer for Mr. Orr, I negotiated contracts with the Boston Bruins...recommended the agreement to Mr. Orr, and Mr. Orr executed the agreements on the basis of that advice."

Further in the same deposition, Eagleson claimed: "I certainly don't qualify as an investment advisor...." Knowing of his myriad transactions with money that belonged to players he represented, I smiled at the irony. If he didn't qualify as an investment adviser, why was he investing the players' money? As for his claim that he had never been an agent for a hockey player, I'd bet it would have been news to a great many owners and general managers around the NHL. And if he "recommended" hockey contracts to Orr, who signed agreements based on his advice, how would he explain the letter he wrote to Paul Mooney on January 29, 1976?

AT THE MONTREAL PRESS CONFERENCE announcing that Orr was leaving Boston for Chicago on June 9, 1976, Eagleson bragged that "Bobby [would] be a millionaire by the time he [was] thirty." He claimed that Orr had signed a "guaranteed" $3-million Blackhawks' contract and explained that "the Bruins effectively stopped negotiating with Bobby Orr on December 10, 1975, when he reinjured his knee."

The truth was that Boston had tried to sign Orr as late as the night before the official announcement, and that Eagleson had declined a stunning offer from Boston in that January 29, 1976, letter to Mooney. In the letter,

Eagleson confirmed — and rejected — the Bruins' latest offer. (The letter also mentioned an earlier rejected offer from the previous team owner, Storer Broadcasting.) Eagleson wrote: "As you are well aware, Bobby is anxious to finalize his agreement with you. I am sure your records will indicate that our last offer from you was as follows:

"Salary: $295,000 a year for five (5) years, plus a payment of $925,000 on June 1st, 1980, or 18.5% of the hockey club in lieu thereof.

"You are also no doubt aware that Storer Broadcasting offered the sum of $335,000 per year for a five (5) year contract commencing on the 1st day of September, 1975.

"These offers were both declined by me and my client."

Orr had been offered 18.5 percent ownership of the Bruins? God Almighty, I thought, and he never told me? I soon discovered why. "I never knew," Orr said. "There's no way I was given the details of that kind of offer. I think anyone would remember if he was offered a piece of a National Hockey League club."

After I revealed the ownership offer in the *Eagle-Tribune*, Eagleson denied withholding the information from Orr, using the lame assertion that Orr knew about the offer because a reference to it had been made in the newspaper. That reference, however, appeared five days *after* the announcement that Orr was leaving Boston and three weeks *after* he had signed the Chicago deal at Ross Johnson's home. At the time of the newspaper reference — in a story about Orr's knee — Orr was in Toronto General Hospital for more arthroscopic work on the knee. "Then I went back to the camp in Orillia," he recalled. "It was over with. I was going to Chicago and that was it. I didn't want to dwell on it. Nobody came up to me and said, 'Why did you turn down eighteen and a half percent ownership of the Bruins?' and I never read it in the paper. You would think it was the responsibility of my lawyer to notify me of that offer in writing. That didn't happen."

Besides, how would Eagleson explain his claim to Mooney in the January 29 letter that both he and his client had rejected the ownership offer?

I feel certain Orr would have told me about the offer had he known. Harry Sinden was also certain that Orr never knew of the offer. So were several other people who believe Orr would have told them about it. "During that time," recalled Wayne Cashman, the former Bruins winger, "when Bobby was laid up and he was up for contract in Boston, he didn't bring up an ownership offer or anything remotely close to that with me, and I'll bet we talked a hundred times. If he knew, he wouldn't have kept it to himself."

"Bobby was close to me," said Don Cherry, his coach at the time. "Don't you think if he knew, he would have said, 'Geez, they've made me a decent offer here, part ownership in the team'? At least it would have given him the satisfaction of knowing the Bruins were trying to keep him. He never told me, and Eagle never told me either. Then again, Eagle knew I thought the world of Bobby."

Bill Watters, the former agent, recalled: "I worked for Al during that time at Sports Management and ran the [Orr-Walton] camp those summers. Bobby and I were tight. He used to tell me everything. He told me what he was getting with the Blackhawks. And when he went to Chicago, he would have told me the Bruins' offer if he'd known. He sure didn't tell me he'd turned down eighteen and a half percent or whatever it was."

Paul Mooney said that was precisely why he wanted to talk with Orr the day of their argument. He never got that far because Bobby refused to listen. "We could not comprehend Eagleson writing that letter," Mooney said. "I tried to make it clear to Bobby — 'You know what you're doing?'

"I went a long way to help him but he wouldn't listen. He yelled at me, 'You're trying to drive a wedge between me and my friend!' I was dumbfounded. Looking back at it now, I thought he knew. But I can't say that I told him there was eighteen and a half percent. No, the conversation never got that far."

Mooney is regarded as a man of integrity whose no-nonsense approach streamlined the old Boston Garden into a highly successful moneymaker for Jeremy Jacobs. For all the flak he took over Orr's departure, he remained loyal to the Bruins during those years. He even tried to get Orr back, or at least get compensation from the Blackhawks, by challenging the Blackhawks in federal court to block the move. The case was dismissed by a judge in Chicago.

"I'm comfortable, knowing we tried," Mooney said. "You can see now, after all these years, that there was a clique going and it was very inappropriate. I think Eagleson knew exactly what he was doing. Why wouldn't he want Bobby to have eighteen and a half percent against almost a million? Clearly the Bruins had tried. Eagleson was jerking us around and maybe this was a part of his grand plan. Eagle was a two-bit hustler.

"Eagleson and Ross Johnson were close, and he knew we weren't going to be doing business with Johnson's company [Standard Brands]. Maybe that's why he took Orr to Chicago — because he could do business with Wirtz, and get all that Standard Brands sponsorship for international hockey. I thought Eagleson was telling Bobby — I just assumed that. For them to turn down that kind of offer made no sense.

"In the end," Mooney pointed out, "Jeremy Jacobs is the winner. He saved eighteen and a half percent of his team."

According to a *Financial World* evaluation of the major-league sports franchises, the Bruins in 1994 were worth $86 million U.S. Had Orr accepted the Bruins' offer, his share of the team would have been worth about $16 million U.S.

When his bad knee forced him to retire in 1978, Bobby Orr learned he was in financial trouble. Eagleson had set up a corporation to handle Orr's money — the team paid Orr's salary to the company, and the company paid Orr — but the arrangement was disallowed by both Revenue Canada and the Internal Revenue Service. Orr's accountant, Lyman MacInnis of Toronto, said he warned Eagleson that the scheme was risky and that Orr should be informed. Eagleson, he said, overruled him. As for the "guaranteed" contract Eagleson had bragged about, Orr ended up having to take the Blackhawks and Bill Wirtz to court.

Orr officially severed relations with Eagleson on April 1, 1980, signing a statement that his "affairs were handled in a responsible and competent way" and that he was satisfied with Eagleson's services. "I was clenching my fists that day, ready to explode," he recalled. "I signed it because all I wanted to do was get away from him."

In July 1980, Orr's assets totaled $456,604. His taxes and legal and accounting bills alone amounted to $469,546. By then he had moved Peggy and their two sons, Darren and Brent, back to the Boston area from North-brook, Illinois. It was the most trying time of Orr's life. "I didn't know if we were going to make it or not, financially," Peggy Orr recalled. "Things were scary there for a while."

As part of the Orr-Eagleson "divorce," Eagleson in trust agreed to buy nearly $620,000 in Bobby Orr Enterprises assets. Of that, $330,000 was for the Orr-Walton hockey camp in Orillia, which owed $285,000 in loans, some to Eagleson's friend Irving Ungerman. Another $150,000 was for Orr's investment in seven acres of land near Collingwood; $100,000 was for the car wash Eagleson had arranged for Orr to buy; $40,000 was for Orr's interest in Marty's, a Toronto clothing store Eagleson got him involved in. Because $450,000 was owed in bank loans, however, the $620,000 Orr was getting from Eagleson in trust evaporated on paper. (Eagleson later sold the Orr-Walton camp for $500,000. When the new owners defaulted on their payments, Eagleson repossessed it, subsequently reselling it for $900,000.)

Orr, meanwhile, awaiting the outcome of his dispute with the Black-hawks and the resolution of his tax problems, lived primarily on a $200,000 deferred payment from his playing days in Boston and a personal-services contract with Standard Brands. In 1983, he finally settled with Chicago — for $450,000, less than a third of the supposedly guaranteed portion of the contract. Of that, $200,000 went to taxes and legal fees. Why did he settle? "Because," he said, "I was just about broke."

Orr eventually got back on his feet, but the memory of that dark time still angers him. Today, with a long-time friend, Tom Kelly, and businessman Paul Shanley, he operates a business, Can-Am Enterprises, which handles his many endorsements, including his lucrative association with BayBank, one of New England's biggest banks. He does public relations and personal pro-motions for major companies in Canada and the United States, and works for various charities. He has a big home in suburban Boston, a condominium in an exclusive section of Cape Cod, and a winter home on a South Florida golf course.

His experiences with Eagleson taught him some hard lessons. "Whenever I was in Toronto, Al or Marvin Goldblatt would have a fist full of papers and say, 'Sign here, sign here.' I'd just sign them. I never read any of the papers. I trusted them. I was foolish. If anybody needs an example of why you should read before you sign off on something, I'm it. But it's no excuse to abuse trust, and that's what Al did with me."

8

IN WHOSE INTEREST?

"The player's contract was more or less downgraded in terms of money, and the difference was paid to Alan Eagleson. It was a helluva deal for St. Louis, and a helluva deal for Eagleson, but not so good for the player."
LOU ANGOTTI

ALAN EAGLESON'S DELIVERY of Bobby Orr to Chicago — like his support of the exemption removing player representation from the NHL Pension Society — was one of the more egregious examples of his failure to keep his various roles separate, but there were many others. A letter Eagleson wrote to Blackhawks owner Bill Wirtz a couple of years after Orr's move, in November 1978, shows Eagleson changing hats at will. First, as Orr's agent, he discusses Orr's contract: "This will confirm our discussion concerning Bobby Orr....Our original agreement was that Bobby would be guaranteed three of his six years at $500,000 per year, which amount would have been paid over that three-year period." Eagleson confirmed that Orr, now facing retirement because of his bad left knee, would be working for the Blackhawks for ten years at $150,000 per year. "It is understood, of course, that the ten-year agreement will be on a non-cancelable basis and that the money will be paid to Bobby even if the Wirtz Corporation or the Blackhawks decide that Bobby is not needed in either organization."

In the same letter Eagleson then, as Bob Pulford's agent, discusses the contract of the team's general manager and coach: "When you and I spoke

at an earlier time it had been my suggestion that on the basis of the performance of the Chicago Black Hawks during the 1977/78 season that Bob Pulford
should be considered for bonus purposes. The bonus I suggested was the
sum of $7,500.00 since I feel that Bob Pulford has been instrumental in the
improved playing of the Black Hawks. I know he gives every ounce of his
endeavor to the club.

"I would also inquire on behalf of Bob Pulford if you would be interested
in extending his contract for an additional three years on the basis of the performance he has had to date.

"I don't want to delay Bob Pulford's contract negotiation into the summer of 1979 because I do not think it would be beneficial for him, the Black
Hawks or Bobby Orr."

Acting for a player and for a member of management in the same letter
— well, at least Eagleson saved himself a stamp. Whether such conflicts are
ethical is a question he usually answered by claiming that a conflict's not a
conflict if it's disclosed to all concerned. In October 1991, with Orr's permission, I sent Bruce Dowbiggin, the CBC sportscaster, a copy of that letter to
Wirtz, knowing that Chicago coach and general manager Mike Keenan also
was an Eagleson client. Dowbiggin raised the matter with Eagleson (who
had repeatedly refused my interview requests).

"There are allegations that I'm sure you've heard in the past," Dowbiggin
said, "that you represent Mike Keenan in management and you also represented players. And you can't do an effective job for both people."

"You can be sure," Eagleson replied, "as soon as I act for a manager, I never
act for a player in negotiations with that manager if he's still a client. I acted
for Bob Pulford when he was a player. I negotiated his contract with the
Chicago Blackhawks as a manager. The minute he became a manager, I told
him he should get another lawyer."

This was untrue, plain and simple. The letter to Wirtz was written long
after Pulford became general manager and coach. Eagleson also denied representing Keenan.

"Mike's really not your client?" Dowbiggin asked.

"Nope," Eagleson replied. "But if he decides he's looking for another contract a couple of years hence, who knows?"

One night when the Blackhawks were in Boston I sought out Keenan at the Garden. In the course of chatting, I asked who his agent was.

"Alan Eagleson," he said.

"Was he your agent when you became general manager of the Blackhawks in 1990?"

"He sure was," Keenan replied. "Still is."

Eagleson's ties to Wirtz and the Blackhawks sometimes expressed themselves in more subtle ways. Back in 1979, when Pulford had begun devoting himself to managerial duties, the Hawks had hired Eddie Johnston as coach. Around the same time, Bill Watters, the Eagleson employee who lined up many of Eagleson's new clients, started his own agency business. Johnston had been represented by Eagleson but decided to go with Watters.

Toward the end of the 1979–80 season, Orr officially severed ties with Eagleson. During that 1979–80 season, Johnston — Orr's close friend from their Bruin days together — coached the Blackhawks to a solid 34-27-19 record as Smythe Division champions before losing in the Stanley Cup quarter-finals. In the previous two seasons, Pulford had posted records of 32-29-19 and 29-36-15, getting knocked out of the playoffs in the first round each year. Johnston's Blackhawks had posted the best Chicago record in six seasons, yet he was replaced by Keith Magnuson.

"They gassed me," Johnston told me after losing the job and moving on to Pittsburgh. "It wouldn't have happened if Eagle was still my agent and Bobby wasn't my friend. It was a power play."

Years later, in 1988, Eagleson continued to haunt Johnston. Eagleson urged Pittsburgh chairman Ed DeBartolo to dump Johnston as the Penguins' general manager in favor of Tony Esposito — his long-time NHLPA yes-man. It was a move that, in Mario Lemieux's view, nearly ruined the Penguins. "Tony Esposito is no Eddie Johnston," Lemieux told me in 1992. "E.J. knows how to handle players, how to treat people. I don't know how Esposito got here, what qualified him to be a GM, but we sure missed Eddie."

MANY PLAYERS KNEW from personal experience that Eagleson could be vindictive toward anyone who decided to change agents. Many others said, as

Don Awrey had at the Bruins reunion, that Eagleson would not return their phone calls if they weren't his clients. Still others expressed chagrin at the way Eagleson treated them and handled their affairs.

"I'll tell you how much interest he had in the players he represented," said Bruin winger Cam Neely, an Eagleson client in 1986. "When I got traded from Vancouver to Boston, Eagleson was my agent. When we finally talked, he told me how much I was going to love Philadelphia. I thought he was kidding. When he said it again, I said, 'Al, what's Philadelphia got to do with it?' He says, 'Philly's a great city, you'll love it there.' He was my agent, supposedly looking after my best interests, and he had no idea. I says, 'Eagle, they traded me to Boston.' He just sort of shook it off. 'Oh, well, you'll like Boston, too.' That's when I realized I'd better get a new agent."

In 1989, goaltender Ron Hextall also decided to get a new agent, a decision that drew Eagleson's ire. Eagleson represented Hextall from 1982 to 1989; when Hextall decided to go with Edmonton lawyer Rich Winter instead, Eagleson sought to discredit Winter. First, Philadelphia Flyers executives suggested to Hextall that he break off his relationship with Winter. Then, in the summer of 1989, they showed him photocopies of two letters originally sent to Eagleson. One was from then-Los Angeles King forward Luc Robitaille, the other from Rich Winter to Edmonton goaltender Grant Fuhr. The letters, unrelated to Hextall's contract negotiations, were meant to disparage Winter.

Rich Winter wondered how letters from Eagleson's files had ended up in the hands of Philadelphia management at a sensitive moment. On September 19, 1989, he wrote Sam Simpson, director of operations for the NHLPA, saying that "the NHLPA has provided confidential correspondence from NHLPA files to the Philadelphia Flyers," and complaining about the mysterious manner in which the letters had shown up in Philadelphia.

Eagleson replied to Winter by fax on October 10, 1989, on Players' Association stationery: "You state some 'confidential correspondence' from NHLPA files was sent to the Philadelphia Flyers. In fact, the letters to which you refer, sent by you and Mr. Robitaille, were both sent to me personally, not the NHLPA....Neither letter can be deemed 'confidential' as you suggest."

Winter was astonished that Eagleson did not deny forwarding the letters to Philadelphia management. Having lost a valuable client in Hextall, he was actively undermining both Hextall and Winter and not even bothering to pretend otherwise. Winter replied the same day: "When you forwarded these letters to the Flyers, were you acting as Executive Director of the NHLPA, [Hextall's] former lawyer or in some other capacity? If the latter is the case, please advise me of the capacity in which you were delivering these letters."

Eagleson didn't reply, but he did write Hextall at the height of the 1989 summer player coup: "I was disappointed to learn that you had not told me of your new representative when I called. You told me you felt that because I was probably going to stop representing players you should consider terminating our relationship. I suggested you wait until the NHLPA August meetings were over and that in any event you should wait before you choose another representative...."

Eagleson reminded Hextall that he and his employee, Marvin Goldblatt, had worked with him since 1982. "Our record speaks for itself," he said, noting Hextall had received a $50,000 signing bonus in 1984 and a $1-million, five-year contract in the 1986-87 season.

"Our agreed fee was $8,000 (4%) for each of the five seasons....With four years left on that contract I renegotiated it with the Flyers. I finalized an 8 year deal commencing in 1987/88...at $500,000.00 per year payable 20 years at $200,000 per year."

Eagleson said he would "refresh" Hextall's memory, claiming the goalie had paid Eagleson $10,000 in fees — "by your suggestion, you owe an additional $50,000.00 in fees. By my suggestion you owe an additional $60,000.00 in fees. I am prepared to split the difference and agree to a further payment of $55,000."

Rich Winter was negotiating a new contract for Hextall, yet Eagleson was seeking $55,000 from the one that would no longer be in force. (He had used the same ploy on Rick Middleton after Middleton left Eagleson for another agent, Anthony Turco, a Massachusetts lawyer, in the early 1980s. When Turco negotiated a new contract between Middleton and the Bruins, Eagleson still wanted to be paid for the previous contract, now null and void.)

Eagleson also sought to smear Winter in an issue of *Goals*. The newsletter, which was sent to all players, claimed that Luc Robitaille was enraged at Winter's business practices. Eagleson reprinted a personal letter from Robitaille in which Robitaille stated: "Mr. Winters [sic] is not my legal representative and is not authorized to represent me...."

When his letter appeared in the newsletter, Robitaille was shocked. He wrote Eagleson: "I was surprised to read my June 2 letter in the first edition of *Goals*. When I wrote this letter I did not expect it to be publicized and nobody asked my permission to use this letter, and I would not have agreed to do so. My agent called the NHLPA to express my concern after the letter was published. Despite this, my letter was referred to again in the second edition of *Goals*, and again my agent called the NHLPA to say that this time I was really upset and that this should not happen again for any reason.

"In order to clear up this whole matter I would like this letter to be published as soon as possible in *Goals* since my first letter was used without my permission."

This Robitaille letter was never published. "That proved to me once and for all Eagleson was a conniver, a manipulator," said Robitaille, who now plays for the Rangers. "He purposely used my letter to discredit the guy and never used my other letter. Eagle didn't care about anybody except himself. Misleading everybody, holding back information — he was out for himself. He was a bum."

ONE OF THE MOST REMARKABLE STORIES I heard was told to me by Lou Angotti, a 1962 graduate of Michigan Tech who had a successful eleven-season career with the Rangers, Chicago, Philadelphia, St. Louis, and the Chicago Cougars of the WHA, and a brief subsequent career in management. He now lives in Pompano, Florida, where he still plays recreational hockey. He's a friend of Rosaire Paiement, and we met one night at Paiement's bar, The Penalty Box, in Fort Lauderdale.

Angotti served briefly in 1974 as the St. Louis acting general manager. Eagleson at the time represented Gord Buynak, a third-round St. Louis draft pick. Angotti participated in the negotiations that led to the signing of

Buynak. "The way it went, we had budgeted so much money for each player," Angotti remembered. "Eagleson said, 'I can deliver him for another fifty.' It was to be paid to Eagleson, and we'd make arrangements later on how it would be paid."

"You mean Eagleson was basically on the St. Louis payroll?"

Angotti nodded. He said that Eagleson agreed to deliver Buynak in return for $50,000 for himself. The payments were to be made in $10,000 installments. Sid Solomon Jr., one of the Blues' owners at the time, agreed to the arrangement, said Angotti, because Eagleson was delivering Buynak for less than what St. Louis had budgeted.

"He made it clear that he could sign this player for x dollars. He could save St. Louis some money and everybody would be happy." The Blues had budgeted $400,000. "The player's contract was more or less downgraded in terms of money, and the difference was paid to Alan Eagleson. It was a helluva deal for St. Louis, and a helluva deal for Eagleson, but not so good for the player."

How was Eagleson compensated? Angotti said he personally delivered the first $10,000 installment, a check from the St. Louis Blues. "I went to Toronto. I delivered it right to his house. To him." Did Angotti see anything wrong with that? "Well, sure I did," he said. It was "very uncomfortable," he said, to realize the team was paying Eagleson "to more or less induce" Buynak into signing with the Blues. "I got the impression it may have been done before. Eagleson suggested that he be compensated himself, or in his wife's name."

It was agreed that the $10,000 installments would be paid to Eagleson himself. Angotti said he personally never knew if further checks were issued because he lost his general manager's job early in the 1974–75 season.

I tried to reach Gord Buynak through his father, a Detroit policeman. The father said that the son was away; he'd pass along my request that he call. Not long afterward Gord Buynak called from a pay phone in Iowa. He described himself as "a struggling electrician." In 1974 he had signed a five-year contract, he said, negotiated by Eagleson and Bill Watters, for approximately $300,000, including a $50,000 signing bonus. Buynak said he never paid Eagleson for negotiating the contract but knew St. Louis had paid

Eagleson directly. At the time, Buynak was unaware of how players paid agents. "I just assumed this is how things were done."

Lou Angotti's relationship with Eagleson went back to Angotti's days as a player representative and an NHLPA vice president. He sat on the Owner-Player Council when Eagleson suggested it would be a good idea to allow NHL owners to run the pension. Angotti could never understand why, but Eagleson insisted it was in the players' best interests. "He's a pretty intelligent man," said Angotti. "It wasn't easy for anybody to question whatever he was doing. If you did try, he'd put you down to the point where it was almost embarrassing. Al wasn't the kind of guy that explained something to you. He could be very harsh with his words."

Angotti also recalled going to Eagleson with the idea of the Players' Association entering the business of product endorsements. He thought the union could profit by running its own line of endorsements and merchandising. But Eagleson's friend, former Maple Leaf trainer Bobby Haggert, had started an endorsement company of his own, Sports Representatives Ltd., and Eagleson was sending his clients to Haggert.

When I spoke to Haggert, now a hockey product licensing agent, he mentioned to me that he had represented former Bruin and Ranger winger Rick Middleton. I raised it with Middleton, who seemed surprised: "Why would I want Haggert to be my representative when I was already paying Eagleson to be my agent?" Middleton's records revealed that he had indeed paid Haggert 10 to 15 percent on endorsements, something he had never realized until I reviewed his files.

Middleton, now an executive with a hair-products company in New Hampshire, was furious: "Eagleson was charging me for representing me and handling my financial affairs. Haggert was taking a hunk of my endorsement fees for the kind of sticks I was using, charging my business, which was operated by Eagleson. I never knew that and wouldn't have allowed it if I had. The checks went out of Eagleson's office."

"The project was going through Haggert's new company," Lou Angotti recalled, "and the Players' Association was going to be paid a percentage. I couldn't understand why we would go through another company. Why wouldn't we just do it ourselves?" Eagleson hit the roof at Angotti's suggestion.

"He was very upset and said I didn't know what I was talking about. He jumped all over me."

No wonder Eagleson didn't welcome the suggestion. He had a good thing going. He was directing his own players, the ones he represented, to Haggert, who charged them for setting up their endorsements. Haggert, a client of Eagleson's, paid him in the form of legal fees. It was a cushy deal for Haggert and Eagleson, but — as Angotti said of the Buynak deal — not so great for the players.

St. Louis wasn't the only team that found creative ways to remunerate Eagleson for delivering one of his clients. When Rick Green signed with the Canadiens in 1988, he didn't pay Eagleson an agent's cut. Instead, a $25,000 check went directly from the Canadiens to Eagleson's office. The check indicated that the payment was for international hockey expenses.

BACK IN 1976, WHEN RICK SMITH, a smart, hard-working, journeyman defenseman, returned to the NHL after a stint in the WHA, Ron Roberts — the head of the WHA Players' Association — acted as his agent and "handled the legal end of the St. Louis contract for [him]." Roberts had torn a page out of Eagleson's book — another players' association director acting as agent for some of the union's members.

Smith had got to know Roberts a couple of years earlier and became involved in a Texas land deal. "It was farm land just outside Greensville, Texas — approximately 260 acres," Smith recalled. "I invested with Roberts. I was holding 10 percent of a $300,000 mortgage." Smith put about $30,000 into the deal. Years later, after returning to the NHL, he discovered that Roberts had also represented the general majority partner. He was furious over the apparent conflict and took the matter up with Eagleson in the late 1970s.

Why Eagleson? "Because I was back in the NHL, and I thought he should be made aware of a player agent who seemed to be pulling a shaky deal. I thought it was right to notify the executive director of our Players' Association, who could check into things about agents and at least keep players updated about agents and their goings-on. There had been a couple of agents around that time who had been in trouble for swindling players' money. I went to the Players' Association expressing concern. At first Eagleson was receptive. Then, later, he said he wouldn't touch it, or Roberts. The laws in Texas were too loose."

Smith told Ron Roberts he had gone to Eagleson. "That's when it really got strange," Smith recalled. "First it was a $1-million lawsuit threat. Roberts said he was going to sue me for libel, slander, defamation of character, all this stuff. Something very much like the letter John Ziegler sent out to NHL players in May [1991] about Bobby Orr and Dave Forbes."

"I felt terrible," Ron Roberts told me. "The general partner tried to go south with the money and a lot of people took bigger losses than Rick Smith. He started saying nasty things about me so I sent him a letter, threatening to sue him. But it all blew over."

Smith eventually got back $13,000 of his $30,000 from Roberts. He wrote the rest off as a bad investment, believing a lawsuit in the United States would be time-consuming and expensive. What he found odd was that Eagleson never brought up the subject again. "I could never figure that out. Here's Alan Eagleson, supposedly looking out for the best interests of players in the union, tipped off about an agent involved in a land deal with a player's money. You'd think he'd at least look into it. But nothing ever happened."

Eagleson was the only one of four major-league sports-union leaders who had failed to attend a U.S. Congressional inquiry into sports agents back in the mid-1970s. The U.S. National Labor Relations Board had ruled that union officials could not represent athletes in the same professional sport in which they acted as a union official. Why would Eagleson go out of his way to look into the business dealings of a U.S. lawyer and union leader who was also an agent? It was a land mine that could have blown up in his face. What if his own business practices had come under scrutiny? Besides, Rick Smith hadn't been an Eagleson client, and Eagleson had always been selective about which union members deserved his attention.

EAGLESON'S COOPERATION WITH NHL owners was evident in the fact that, under his leadership, the NHLPA — unlike the players' unions in basketball, baseball, and football — had never challenged the league on antitrust or collusion issues. Pro basketball players had been successful in the 1970s in delaying the ABA-NBA merger until improved player benefits were negotiated, and major-league baseball players were awarded more than $280 million in 1990 in their collusion case against the owners, ending an almost five-year legal battle. Asked why, under his stewardship, the NHLPA had never mounted such a challenge, Eagleson replied, "We looked at antitrust. The same lawyer, Jim Quinn, who's acting for us this time [in 1991], recommended against it in '86 because of the circumstances. We didn't have that type of money."

I called Quinn, the New York antitrust lawyer who later successfully led a court challenge for pro football players against the National Football League. "Eagleson says I recommended against antitrust action by the NHLPA in '86?" Quinn said with a laugh. "Totally false. I didn't have a thing to do with NHLPA collective bargaining in 1986. I never recommended for or against anything they did then because I wasn't associated with the NHLPA or Eagleson." Quinn said he did not become involved with legal advice to the NHLPA until the 1990s.

Salary disclosure is another important practice that came late to the NHL, again because the owners didn't want it and Eagleson was not prepared to take them on. When salary disclosure finally was approved, Eagleson claimed it had been his idea all along. He told the CBC's Bruce Dowbiggin that he had told the players, "The best thing to do is get the salaries out on the table. The votes were 20-1 against from every player rep. Then we went to the membership. As recently as 1988–89, 25 percent only were in favor of salary disclosure. We got it up to about 45 percent in '89 and on the basis of that I said, 'Let's take a chance and force the issue with the players.' And that was the first time we had a positive vote. Even in the '89 meeting, there were five player reps who were adamantly opposed to it. Bobby Smith and Bryan Trottier are two I remember, and there were three others."

Eagleson was revising history. Most players had long been urging that salaries be disclosed. "We wanted it," emphasized Pat Verbeek, a player rep at the time. "For every player against it, there were ten for it, maybe more. He's the one that kept saying we shouldn't have it."

Andy Moog, the former Bruins player rep who now plays for Dallas, told me the same thing. "We asked, 'Why shouldn't salaries be disclosed?' We knew it would help players and agents establish fair market values, and Eagleson kept saying it wouldn't help us."

Wouldn't help the players, or wouldn't help Alan Eagleson? Clearly, salary disclosure would set market standards; one player could gauge his value by seeing what an equivalent player was being paid by another team. NHL management, of course, was adamantly opposed to the idea. "We didn't want it, not one bit," the Bruins' Harry Sinden admitted. "We knew it'd have an immediate escalation effect, throw everything out of whack."

By resisting salary disclosure, not only was Eagleson scoring points with the owners, he was also serving his own self-interest as an agent. Eagleson represented many players individually; so long as salaries were not disclosed, he had an unfair advantage over competing agents. After all, he had knowledge of more salaries than anybody else.

Dowbiggin asked Eagleson about his standards and practices as union boss. Eagleson said, "It's not my job to make decisions for the players. The players have to make decisions for themselves." Not his job to make decisions for the players? What was he doing when he decided, say, to seek the Pension Society exemption without even informing them?

Asked about his record, his legacy in hockey history, Eagleson replied: "You really have to take credit for the success. You have to take the blame for any failures. If there's any degree of failure and people want to describe it in that fashion, that's their opinion and they're entitled to it. The interesting part is that the players who have been around the longest time have no complaints about Al Eagleson."

In fact, Eagleson's role in the pension dispute was widely known by this time, and scores of players who'd been around for decades — including Gordie Howe, Ted Lindsay, Norm Ullman, Bobby Baun, Allan Stanley, Andy Bathgate, Eddie Shack, Eddie Westfall, Ken Dryden, Rod Gilbert, Frank Mahovlich, Jean Béliveau, Bobby Hull, Walt Tkaczuk, Jean Ratelle, Brad Park, Ralph Backstrom, Dallas Smith, Doug Mohns, and Red Berenson — had plenty of complaints about Al Eagleson.

"If you take a look at the executive [committee] of the Players' Association from the time we started," Eagleson told Dowbiggin, "they were all all-stars. And that's the biggest difference in this players' association from any other. We had the commitment of the stars and the superstars. We always added what we called one of the schmucks, a player like Craig Ramsay, like Freddy Barrett — you have to have that type of input. Now we always put a player like that on the management committee of the Players' Association."

"Put" was an interesting verb, considering that the management committee was supposedly elected. And as for Craig Ramsay being a schmuck, Ramsay played fourteen seasons and 1,159 games for Buffalo between 1971 and 1985, the epitome of consistency, unselfishness, and dedication. Eagleson clearly had no grasp of what it takes to absorb all the bruises and stitches Ramsay incurred while playing a Sabres club record 776 consecutive games between 1973 and 1983, distinguishing himself as a brilliant penalty killer and defensive forward. A schmuck, because he didn't score 50 goals a season? That remark — like the "bunch of losers" comment used to characterize some of the game's greatest stars — speaks volumes.

Critics of Eagleson had long pointed to the NHL's restrictive free-agency system as further evidence of his unwillingness to show real leadership in the areas most important to NHLPA members. As Dallas Smith had realized back in 1976, and Ray Bourque had complained in 1990, hockey players labored under the most restrictive free agency in major professional sport.

Not long after the Bruins' 1990 reunion, the issue again came to widespread attention when St. Louis signed Washington defenseman Scott Stevens as a free agent, contracting to pay him $4 million over four years. Under NHL rules, the Blues had to compensate Washington for the loss of Stevens, even though his contract had expired. The price for Stevens, one of the league's top defensemen, was five first-round draft picks — an exorbitant price, and a strong disincentive to sign free agents.

A year later, active in the free-agent market again, the Blues signed Brendan Shanahan of the New Jersey Devils for $1.6 million over two years. The price this time: Scott Stevens, the free agent the Blues had signed a year earlier. It was as if the league was emphasizing the point that you signed a free agent at your peril. League rules prevented players from cashing in on free agency in their prime by punishing teams that signed them.

The decision in the Shanahan case angered many players. They had viewed Shanahan's signing as an indication that the free-agent market might finally be opening up — but only until Stevens was awarded to New Jersey in return, under the arbitration system negotiated by Eagleson.

"The message is clear. Don't sign free agents," Brett Hull said at the time. "The league wants to punish the Blues."

"It's just not fair and they can't possibly say it's fair," said Wayne Gretzky.

For many younger players, the Stevens and Shanahan signings were their first direct experience of the league's restrictive free agency. In fact, Brian Smith, a Detroit lawyer, had fought the same battle years earlier, and because of him the NHL had had to sidestep what had been its biggest threat to the system until the 1990s. Smith had represented former player Dale McCourt in a challenge to the NHL's system in the late 1970s. McCourt had been a member of the Detroit Red Wings when he was awarded to the Los Angeles Kings in August 1978 as compensation for Detroit's signing of free-agent goaltender Rogie Vachon.

McCourt wanted to stay in Detroit, having signed a contract with the Red Wings in good faith to stay with the team unless he was traded. He didn't see this as a trade. Brian Smith knew that the World Hockey Association had filed an antitrust suit against the NHL in 1973, accusing the league of unfair business practices in controlling the careers of pro hockey players, and had settled out of court. (The NHL paid WHA owners $1 million to drop the suit.) On McCourt's behalf, Smith obtained a U.S. federal court order blocking the move. McCourt remained with the Red Wings for the full 1978–79 season while Smith and the NHL battled.

The NHL ultimately won; a judge ordered McCourt sent to Los Angeles. Hockey trading-card companies used an air brush to put him in a Los Angeles uniform for their 1979–80 series of cards, extinguishing the identifiable red and white Detroit colors. But a funny thing happened, making those airbrushed cards a collector's item. McCourt never wore the Kings' purple and gold. Smith threatened to appeal the case — and the entire NHL system of free agency and compensation — under U.S. antitrust laws: "I was going to the Supreme Court and they knew it."

The NHL escaped a showdown in Supreme Court when the Kings traded McCourt's rights back to Detroit; the two teams agreed on another player and two draft picks as compensation for Vachon. McCourt was traded to

Buffalo in 1981. "I'd represented my client's best interests, keeping him in Detroit as he wanted during the Los Angeles fiasco," said Smith. "It was pretty obvious that the NHL didn't want a Supreme Court challenge on antitrust.

"The interesting thing to realize here was that Alan Eagleson refused to help us. It was remarkable to see the head of a union cozy up to management's position, given the opportunity to break through the free agency and compensation barriers."

IN THE SUMMER OF 1991, at about the time the Brendan Shanahan signing was again heating up the free-agency issue, two Edmonton players, Craig Muni and Esa Tikkanen, charged collusion between the league and Eagleson as head of the NHLPA. In a forty-one–page complaint filed with the Alberta Labor Relations Board, their lawyer-agent, Rich Winter, alleged that Eagleson had a conflict of interest and asked the board to throw out the 1986 collective bargaining agreement between the NHL and NHLPA. This would allow the two Oilers to become free agents.

Winter argued that the 1986 agreement, which restricted free agency and limited the chance of competitive bidding for a player's services, was compromised because the union chief also represented some NHL management employees and was beholden to the NHL for his position as international hockey organizer. Winter claimed that "Eagleson, his family and various firms or corporations in which he or his family have an interest" had earned millions of dollars from international hockey in the form of profits from the sale of TV rights, free travel, and other items. He charged that Eagleson "colluded with the NHL to influence the NHLPA" by misrepresenting certain terms of the league's contract offer.

"Eagleson, the NHLPA — which he's operated like his own private domain — and the NHL have their own exclusive little club going with no checks and balances," Winter said. "They've got away with it for years, operating outside anybody's law but their own.

"Because of Eagleson's conflicts of interest, the NHLPA has been nothing but an employer-dominated union and the players have suffered because of it. The trouble is most of them are so young and naive, Eagleson either fast-talked them to death or intimidated them whenever they asked questions."

In a thirteen-page reply, the NHL argued that the Alberta provincial labor board "has no jurisdiction to deal with this matter." Which struck me as odd, since two NHL teams, Edmonton and Calgary, carried on business in Alberta. The NHLPA avoided laws governing U.S. unions by professing to be regulated by Canadian law — Eagleson had explained this to the players — and now the NHL was arguing that the union wasn't subject to Canadian labor laws either.

Eagleson, clearly, used whatever means necessary to wriggle out of labor law scrutiny in either country. I spoke to U.S. Department of Labor counsel Dennis Paquette in Washington, D.C. If Alberta labor law didn't apply to collective bargaining agreements with Canadian players, I asked, who had jurisdiction over the union representing these players? Canada or the United States? I told Paquette that if I didn't get an answer from him I'd go to the U.S. Secretary of Labor. Paquette said he'd get back to me.

Meanwhile, Winter was also seeking answers to various questions from the U.S. government. (Besides being a Canadian lawyer, he's licensed as a California attorney.) Robert M. Guttman, assistant secretary for labor-management standards, referred Winter's complaint — that the NHLPA violated U.S. pension reporting requirements — to another Labor Department agency. Guttman also said a copy of Winter's complaint had been forwarded to the U.S. Department of Justice, as Winter had requested.

Guttman noted that the NHLPA, despite ties to the United States, was "domiciled" in Canada and that U.S. reporting laws were "generally limited to the activities of persons or organizations within the territorial jurisdiction of the United States." By whose labor laws, then, were players on U.S. teams protected? Players paying U.S. taxes and working for U.S.-based corporations, whose union dues were deducted from employee paychecks, might well have wondered which laws they were subject to.

As far as I could see, both current and retired players were falling through the cracks. Given the NHL's position in the Muni and Tikkanen complaint in Alberta, Dennis Paquette now appreciated the situation. "We don't pretend to control Canadian labor law, but if fourteen of twenty-one teams are U.S., there's enough there to realize U.S. labor law should apply even if the union is based in Toronto," he replied to my questions, suggesting it might be a good idea to have an NHL player file complaints with the U.S. Justice Department and the Labor Department.

Paquette acknowledged that, in 1989, he had not had full disclosure of how the NHLPA operated. Without that information, he had written an opinion that the players' union did not have to file annual reports in the United States. To Paquette, it was now clear that the NHLPA was made up of more U.S. citizens, or Canadian citizens living in the United States, than Canadian citizens on Canadian teams, and that the NHL used that work force to generate the vast majority of its income in the United States.

Which had been precisely Brian Smith's basis for threatening a U.S. Supreme Court antitrust action against the NHL and NHLPA in the Dale McCourt compensation issue: the fact that the NHL was more a U.S. business than a Canadian one. "I feel that over the years the bulk of the players are playing south of the border, and they aren't getting the full benefit of the labor laws in this country," Smith told me. "When something is challenged in Canada, the NHL's position — and Eagleson's position as union leader — is that there's no jurisdiction there. If something is challenged in the United States, the position is that there's no jurisdiction because the NHLPA's a Canadian union. For God's sakes, who's watching after the players? What kind of business practices have they been allowed to operate under for all these years?"

9

THE MILLION-DOLLAR CARROT

"I wouldn't have taken the deal, because on his end,
he was wearing two hats. Personally, I wouldn't permit
myself to get in that position, but it wasn't my call."
PETER KARMANOS

A TRIM, DAPPER LITTLE MAN with Mediterranean features, a graying mustache, and a balding head, Peter Karmanos doesn't look like the chief executive officer of a major corporation. But the company he and two partners founded in 1973, Compuware, based in Farmington Hills, Michigan, has had considerable success selling software used to test and debug large computers. In 1989, Karmanos was named Entrepreneur of the Year by the Institute of American Entrepreneurs.

Karmanos grew up in Detroit as a Red Wings fan. In 1974, Compuware began to sponsor youth hockey in the Detroit area. Between 1974 and 1986, Compuware teams won fifteen state championships and six national championships. By 1987, Karmanos had bought part ownership of the Windsor Spitfires of the Ontario Hockey League; in 1988, the team won the OHL championship and went on to the Memorial Cup finals. In 1989, the OHL granted Karmanos the first American franchise in the junior league's history. The Windsor Spitfires were sold, and the Detroit Junior Red Wings began play in 1990.

Karmanos's hockey ambitions didn't end there. He had his heart set on an NHL franchise. Compuware made its first inquiries about buying an NHL team through Bob Goodenow, the Detroit lawyer and sports agent who eventually succeeded Alan Eagleson as head of the NHL Players' Association. But Goodenow "didn't have much of a relationship with people in the league," Karmanos recalled, "and I finally got frustrated." Jim Rutherford, a former NHL goaltender who had become Compuware's hockey adviser, recommended his former agent, Eagleson, for the job of searching out a team. Any sale of a franchise would require the approval of league governors and owners, and Karmanos knew that Eagleson was a good friend of both NHL president John Ziegler and board of governors chairman and Chicago Blackhawks owner Bill Wirtz.

"Alan knew everybody inside the NHL and knew what was going on, or at least had ways of finding out," said Karmanos. "The objective was for us to use his influence, his connections, and his intelligence — he's not stupid — to get us a team. And if he did, he stood to make a sizable amount."

Wanting to do "something dramatic," Karmanos offered Eagleson a $1-million broker's fee, with incentives that could have doubled it. Rutherford met with Eagleson in Toronto on September 13, 1988. A week later, Eagleson wrote to Karmanos, "I have now reviewed the discussions I had with Jim Rutherford alone and with Jim and you last week. I am satisfied that I can work with you and not have any conflict with my position as Executive Director of the National Hockey League Players' Association. I would suggest a retainer of $10,000 (U.S.) against an hourly rate of $300.00 (U.S.). The hourly fee would be charged for all travel time as well....A fee of 5% on the purchase price would apply if purchase is concluded....In the interval, I have made preliminary inquiries on your behalf."

In October 1988, Karmanos and Eagleson signed an agreement. Compuware would indeed pay Eagleson $300 an hour, against the $10,000 retainer he had by then been paid, plus travel expenses. The agreement called for a brokerage fee of $1 million "upon the completion of the purchase of an NHL franchise." Compuware also agreed to pay Eagleson an extra $200,000 for each $1 million the purchase price was below established value. The agreement listed specific values for each club. Major-market teams like Montreal, Toronto, Boston, and Los Angeles were listed in Group A, at $40 million each. If Eagleson landed a Group A team for $35 million, in other words, $5 million below its established value, he would get an additional $1 million (5 x $200,000) along with his $1-million brokerage fee. The fee was to be paid in U.S. dollars for U.S. teams and Canadian dollars for Canadian clubs.

Karmanos said Eagleson's mandate was to contact NHL owners and representatives, find out which teams were for sale, obtain and verify financial information about the teams, and introduce Karmanos and Rutherford to NHL owners and league representatives.

"Our two best allies will be Bill Wirtz and John Ziegler," Eagleson wrote to Karmanos. "I would recommend meeting with them separately or together as quickly as possible. John Ziegler is well aware of Compuware and their contribution to minor hockey. I have already discussed some possibilities with him. I am meeting with him for a golf date in New York on September 29th and will pursue matters further at that time."

In October 1988, Eagleson told Karmanos he had talked to Ziegler about the St. Louis franchise. "Ziegler thinks they are in sound financial shape and that the team and crowds are improving. Others tell me the owners are sensitive to cash flow." In February 1989, he wrote to Karmanos, "I may go to Chicago on Thursday evening to meet with Bill Wirtz to get clarification and-or assurances related to some information I have received. Bill should be able to tell me whether it is correct or not."

In another letter to Karmanos, on February 22, 1989, Eagleson revealed confidential information about Marcel Aubut, president of the Quebec team, who headed the group that purchased the Nordiques from Carling O'Keefe Breweries in November 1988. "I was able to help Aubut and he can be a major ally in our endeavors....The Nordiques were purchased by Marcel Aubut and a group of Quebec companies. Price was $14.8 [million] Canadian. Aubut received 5 percent for negotiating the deal but has no money in it. He is the spokesman, Governor, and limited partner. Their contract with Carling O'Keefe...for advertising rights almost guarantees a positive cash flow of .750 million per year. Playoff participation adds to this figure. I expect Quebec to sell or trade some of their high priced players (Goulet, Stastny)."

Aubut later told me he was surprised by Eagleson's comments. He said Eagleson did not assist in the purchase of the Nordiques. "Maybe he gave me one element when he gave me encouragement. I cannot recall any time that he played a role in my transaction." Aubut was also shocked to learn that Eagleson had revealed financial details behind the purchase. "It's all confidential documents! How could he?" Aubut shouted. "Nobody knows about those numbers. The only place they are is in Carling O'Keefe, they are here, and they are with the league and the president's office.

"They're not the right numbers," Aubut added, furious that such information had been released. (Whether or not the numbers were right, Eagleson wasn't entirely off the mark. By the trading deadline of the 1989–90 season, Quebec had indeed traded away both Peter Stastny and Michel Goulet.) Aubut, a member of the NHL's board of governors, said he was not aware Eagleson worked as a broker for Karmanos or Compuware: "I've never heard about it before you just told me now."

Aubut wasn't the only owner Eagleson offended by providing privileged information. He spread fact and gossip about the private lives of several NHL owners — financial details, personal lives, family troubles, it was all grist for his mill. In a confidential rundown on every NHL club and its owners sent to Karmanos shortly after they'd struck their deal, Eagleson said of Edmonton owner Peter Pocklington, "Can be an asset if handled properly....He will be a valuable source of information. Peter and I have been friends for 15 years through business affiliations and politics. We have come to know each other very well over the past 10 years because of hockey.

"Peter insists the Oilers are not for sale. The fact that he sold Gretzky to Los Angeles suggests otherwise."

Pocklington later told me Eagleson had indeed phoned to inquire whether the Oilers were for sale: "I said no." Asked if he was aware Eagleson was providing reports about him and other owners to Karmanos, Pocklington said, "No, I sure wasn't."

Regarding New York Islanders owner John Pickett, Eagleson informed Karmanos: "He is a very wealthy man. He is married to Robin, his second wife. They are a great couple. Their home in Palm Beach is 3 miles (and 5 million dollars) north of our villa in Manalapan, Florida. We see them socially each time we are in Palm Beach.

"They love a winner and the Islanders are in the rebuilding process. They stay all winter in Florida for tax reasons. They spend 3 months in Long Island every summer. They do not see Islander games in person more than 3 or 4 times a year.

"Conclusion — Wealthy owner. Probably has a loser for the next three years. May become bored and wish to sell. John wishes Pocklington had talked to him about Gretzky."

On New Jersey Devils owner John McMullen: "Is sole owner. He has an intense dislike for Ziegler. Wants me to be NHL president or Commissioner (he must think I am crazy).

"Spent 32 million for franchise and TV and cable rights (paid to Flyers, Rangers and Islanders). He has complained to anyone who will listen that the NHL owners screwed him on the deal. He still owes money to NHL and is a slow and reluctant payer."

On the Washington Capitals: "Abe Polin is the major shareholder and Dick Patrick is the spokesman for the club. Abe has suffered some personal family tragedies and has been somewhat reclusive with respect to hockey meetings.

"The team has never won more than one round in the playoffs but has a core of good, reasonably young players. Conclusion: Worth watching. Owner may say he has had enough. I suspect that Dick Patrick would try to head a group of purchasers."

On the Buffalo Sabres: "The Knox brothers still have the partnership guiding authority. There have been rumbles of dissatisfaction from the other partners. The partnership agreement is apparently subject to adjustment or review in the summer of 1989. Bob Swados is a minor partner who is Alternate Governor. He will be a good source of information. At the moment Seymour Knox is still the head man...."

On Winnipeg Jets co-owner Barry Shenkarow: "He has reduced annual losses from 2 million dollars to about $500,000. He is rich enough to afford those types of losses. Conclusion: Team is probably available at the right price. Should be our first or second target (along with St. Louis)."

On the Vancouver Canucks: "Vancouver is owned by Western Broadcasting which may be the subject of a takeover bid. It is a public company. If this were to happen, I think Griffiths would pull the team out of the deal and give it to one of his sons as a toy (either son would wreck the toy)."

Eagleson closed his letter, written on Sports Management Limited letter-head, by promising to tap his sources for more information before meeting Karmanos in November 1988. He added that a fee statement for his work would be forwarded.

One of Eagleson's suggestions to Karmanos was that they go after the Toronto Maple Leafs. One of the league's original six teams, the Leafs had been a Toronto institution since 1926. They continued to draw sellout crowds although they had not won the Stanley Cup since 1967. Eagleson's idea was to buy the franchise and move it to Hamilton, thirty miles west. In a letter to Karmanos, he concluded the Leafs "would be an excellent value, even at an exorbitant price." The move would have enraged Toronto fans, and it's questionable whether the league would have allowed it, but Eagleson's logic was impeccable. He spelled out the reasons "we must seriously consider Toronto" in a follow-up letter:

"(a) The team makes money with bad management and a bad team.

"(b) Toronto controls the Hamilton franchise. One could buy Toronto and sell-off the rights to the Hamilton market.

"(c) Buy Toronto and move Toronto to Hamilton and keep Toronto area rights."

Not wanting the letter to fall into the wrong hands, Eagleson did not mail it to Karmanos in Michigan. Instead, he forwarded it to Jim Rutherford, on the Canadian side of the border. To Karmanos he wrote, "I have sent this material to Jim in Windsor on a 'Personal and Confidential' basis in care of the Windsor Spitfires, in order to avoid any customs problems."

Karmanos told me he never took the Toronto idea seriously because there was "no way an American" would be allowed to buy and move a Canadian institution like the Toronto Maple Leafs. But if anyone had a chance of pulling it off, it was Eagleson, who had strong ties to Harold Ballard, the owner of the Leafs. In his 1992 memoirs, Eagleson recalled meeting Ballard at Maple Leaf Gardens in 1989, the year before Ballard's death, while Eagleson was quietly working for Karmanos and Compuware. Eagleson's book does not mention whether he raised the subject of a possible purchase of the team. According to Eagleson, Ballard tried to hire him, offering "whatever goddamn job you want — Leafs' general manager, coach, president, trainer — take all of them."

At the time he suggested the Leafs to Karmanos, Eagleson had also recently made good connections in Hamilton. That city's Copps Coliseum had been the site of 1987 Canada Cup Tournament games promoted by Eagleson. And in an interview with Don Cherry, Eagleson mentioned that one NHL team, St. Louis, had been looking into the possibility of moving to Hamilton.

In another letter to Karmanos, Eagleson wrote of Ballard and the Leafs, "Owner froze estate in 1967 by creating a family trust of 51% of the common shares (non-voting). When the family was closely-knit, Ballard decided to avoid estate taxes. This decision has come back to haunt him. He is presently alienated from 1, or 2, or all three of his children. This varies from day to day. He refers to one son as a hippie, to the second son as a lazy lout, and to his daughter as a drifter.

"The three Ballard children have made public statements which confirm their 51% of non-voting shares....In the event of any sale, the three children will reap the greatest financial reward."

Of Ballard's long-time companion Yolanda McMillan Ballard, Eagleson noted, "She has apparently co-habited with Ballard for a 3 to 5 year period. Ballard has an apartment in the Maple Leaf Gardens building and Yolanda stays overnight more often than not. She and her daughter have both officially changed their names to 'Ballard.' This causes the Ballard children no end of anguish.

"Yolanda is a convicted felon and served more than a year in jail for conspiracy to defraud." (In fact, Ms. McMillan served less than four months of a three-year sentence.)

After I disclosed Eagleson's relationship with Karmanos and Compuware in the *Eagle-Tribune*, Eagleson claimed to have made the Maple Leafs suggestion as a joke. But why, in another letter, would he have written to Karmanos: "Ziegler worries about Buffalo's future if Hamilton gets a franchise"? And who'd bother routing a sensitive letter via Windsor, to avoid customs, if he didn't mean business? Eagleson evidently thought that, with Ballard near the end of his life, a deal for the Leafs could possibly be cut.

By February 1989, Eagleson had zeroed in on St. Louis as the team to buy. He sought to arrange a meeting between Jim Rutherford and St. Louis chairman Mike Shanahan and president Jack Quinn during the NHL All-Star break in Edmonton on February 7. But a week before the game Eagleson told Rutherford the St. Louis officials "[preferred] not to meet with [us] in Edmonton" because of a concern with "possible misinterpretations." Eagleson told Rutherford he was still welcome to come to the dinner and game as his guest, but not to discuss their relationship with anyone. He instructed Rutherford in writing: "If anyone asks, the answer is, 'Al used to look after me when I was a player. He is helping us with our hockey operations in Compuware as they relate to the international scene.'"

Rutherford did not go to Edmonton. Instead, a meeting took place in St. Louis a couple of weeks after the All-Star game, a trip, incidentally, for which the NHL Players' Association helped pay Eagleson's expenses. On February 24, Eagleson and Karmanos met in St. Louis with Mike Shanahan to discuss a possible purchase of the team. A bill from a Toronto travel agency shows that the union paid $1,346 for Eagleson's airfare. A notation on the statement reads: "New York, St. Louis, Chicago re: Mtgs with Wirtz."

Karmanos was under the impression that Eagleson indeed conducted union business on the St. Louis trip. He thought Eagleson met with the St. Louis team. In fact, the Blues were playing in Calgary, Alberta, on the day of the Karmanos-Shanahan-Eagleson meeting. Shanahan, too, believed Eagleson had other business in St. Louis; he thought Eagleson met with Jack Quinn about a Blues player, Jeff Brown, who was an Eagleson client. (Brown, in fact, played for Quebec at the time.) If so, why would the players' union get a $300 bill for expenses, taxis, tips, meals, and drinks for meetings in "Chicago & St. Louis" February 23–24?

In the end, the St. Louis deal never got off the ground. In late 1989, the NHL announced expansion plans, setting a $50-million price on the new franchises. Karmanos thought the price ridiculously high. That valuation would have an inflationary effect on all franchises; he dropped his effort to buy an established team. Instead, he made a bid to put a new franchise in St. Petersburg, Florida. Eagleson, he said, was not involved in that project. Their relationship ended a couple of months before the 1990 NHL expansion. "We ended it on a very amicable basis," Karmanos said. "He did what we thought he was supposed to do for the money he got."

Compuware had paid Eagleson's firm, Sports Management Limited, a total of $37,800 U.S.

Eagleson's work for Karmanos represented a potential conflict of interest. Ziegler and Wirtz — their "allies" — sat across the negotiating table from Eagleson at contract time, when the owners were naturally interested in holding down player salaries and benefits and restricting free agency. Karmanos would have needed their approval for any purchase of an existing franchise; Eagleson would have needed that approval to collect his $1 million plus. How, then, could he represent the NHLPA members effectively?

"I wouldn't have taken the deal," Karmanos said candidly of his arrangement with Eagleson, "because on his end, he was wearing two hats. Personally, I wouldn't permit myself to get in that position, but it wasn't my call. It was Alan's, and he assured us he was acting with approval from the Players' Association."

Eagleson maintained there was no real conflict because the conflict was disclosed. In fact, said Karmanos, Eagleson himself raised the issue. "He's the one that said, 'Before I could do that, I'd have to get permission from the players. He told us he had gotten permission from whoever the player reps were, I think Bryan Trottier and somebody else."

Trottier, the former New York Islanders star and NHLPA president between 1985 and 1992, was widely viewed as an Eagleson yes-man. He declined to talk to me, saying he felt uncomfortable answering a question that had been asked of him as a witness testifying before the U.S. grand jury in Boston. (By this time Eagleson was being investigated by the FBI.) Jim Rutherford said that the "somebody else" was Mike Liut, then an NHL goaltender and one of the NHLPA vice presidents. Liut didn't know about Eagleson's work for Karmanos.

Despite Eagleson's reassurances to Karmanos, a great many other NHL players told me they had no knowledge of the Compuware-Eagleson connection, including several team representatives. (Eagleson claimed that all Players' Association decisions were made by the NHLPA executive board, made up of team representatives.) The player reps and executive board members

I spoke to — Hartford's Pat Verbeek, Boston's Andy Moog, Los Angeles's Marty McSorley, the Rangers' Mike Gartner, and San Jose's Doug Wilson — all said they knew nothing of Eagleson's attempts to land Karmanos an NHL team.

Eagleson missed several opportunities to disclose his work for Karmanos to the NHLPA — at the annual Players' Association meeting in 1989, for instance, when Ed Garvey's report drew attention to some of his other conflicts. Nor is there any reference to Karmanos or Compuware in Eagleson's memoirs. Nor did Eagleson mention it in a letter to former Bruins star Phil Esposito in 1990.

Esposito, who was spearheading the bid to put a franchise in Tampa, had heard that Eagleson was involved with Karmanos's St. Petersburg bid, as he mentioned at the 1970 Bruins' twenty-year reunion. In October 1990, Eagleson wrote Esposito, "I am still the Executive Director of the NHLPA, and have no present intention of being involved in any ownership of any NHL club. (I will not use the word 'never', because 'never' is a long time)."

Gil Stein was an NHL vice president and general counsel when Eagleson represented Compuware. In answer to written questions I submitted to him through Boston lawyer Ken Felter, Stein said he, too, was unaware that Eagleson had been paid to represent a potential buyer of an NHL club while head of the NHLPA. Asked if he considered it a conflict of interest, Stein said he wanted to know "all the relevant facts" before drawing a conclusion. He did say that "it would have been appropriate that there be full disclosure to the Board of Governors of the league and to the NHLPA were such arrangement made."

No disclosure was made to the union, and none was made to the NHL board of governors. This was confirmed by Oilers owner Pocklington, a member of the board. Pocklington was aware of the Karmanos-Eagleson relationship personally, he said, because of Eagleson's inquiries about whether the Oilers might be for sale. But, he says, the relationship was never disclosed to the board.

"It's pretty tough to row your boat in two rivers at the same time without disclosure," Pocklington said. "While serving as the director of the union, that's pretty tough. Unless he made disclosure and had no one on the other side minding either way, that's a little different."

"I never knew he was representing Karmanos and Compuware," said Harry Sinden after our *Eagle-Tribune* report of February 1993 disclosed the arrangement. "He should have told the board of governors, told the players, told everybody involved. There's no question he put himself in a deep hole on this one."

THE LONG-TERM NHL EXPANSION PLAN announced by John Ziegler in 1989 was called "A Vision of the '90s." The plan called for the twenty-one NHL teams to grow to twenty-eight by the year 2000. Peter Karmanos had another description for the "vision" — he called it "a scheme." He said, "It just became apparent a lot of the owners were going to try to build value in their teams by inflating the price of expansion."

Competing for two new NHL franchises were groups from Ottawa, Hamilton, Miami, Tampa, and St. Petersburg. Bidders made their pitch at a meeting of the NHL board of governors in December 1990, at the Breakers Hotel, in Palm Beach, Florida. "We went down and tried to make a reasonable bid and plea for some sanity on how they should handle expansion," Karmanos said. He offered $29 million, with an additional payout from profits over a period of seven years to meet the $50-million figure. Instead of the $5-million nonrefundable down payment demanded by the NHL, he suggested he would spend $5 million to $10 million for marketing and promotion to build season ticket sales for the 20,000-seat St. Petersburg Sun Dome. To secure his bid, Karmanos took a lease for hockey games in the building.

Karmanos argued that it would only hurt the NHL in the long run to go for the quick score. (Four shaky expansion teams had gone under in the 1970s, hurting the league's credibility.) But the owners, he said, refused to listen. "Instead of trying to build value through really running a business properly, they were going to hustle some value by saying, 'Well, geez, the expansion team's worth $50 million, so therefore my team has to be worth more.'"

Karmanos called the scheme "sheer lunacy," citing the sale of the Hartford Whalers in September 1988, for $32 million, and the sale of the Stanley Cup champion Pittsburgh Penguins in 1991 for about the same amount —

and those teams already had players, a staff, and an arena rental agreement. For the privilege of paying $50 million, an expansion team would be starting from scratch.

Karmanos recalled asking John Ziegler about the $50-million price. He said Ziegler jumped to his feet, yelling, and refused to discuss the matter: "He was almost irrational." Karmanos also recalled questioning Bill Wirtz, the Blackhawks owner and chairman of the NHL's board of governors, about the $5-million down payment. Karmanos argued that a new team would be better off spending the money on marketing and promotion. Marketing, after all, is what had helped Compuware's junior team draw a record 17,773 people to a game in 1993. But Wirtz did not see the point.

"He said, 'You know what I spend a year on season ticket promotion? A quarter million dollars.' His answer blew me away. I said, 'We're talking about an expansion team here, not a traditional original-six hockey team with a history back into the 1920s.' The real problems in hockey are with Mr. Ziegler and Mr. Wirtz."

The NHL chose Ottawa and Tampa — in Peter Karmanos's view, the least qualified bidders, but the only ones willing to meet the demand for $50 million, including the $5-million nonrefundable down payment, with the rest payable in one year. The league and the owners split the money. Esposito — with no building to meet the NHL's seating capacity requirement — ended up stuck with a 10,400-seat hall at the Tampa Fairgrounds. The NHL may not have adhered to its own rules, but it got its money in the end.

PETER KARMANOS, MEANWHILE, continued on as owner of Compuware's junior team, the Detroit Junior Wings, and a youth team, the Compuware Ambassadors, before finally landing an NHL team. He came back for another kick at the can only after Ziegler's administration had been replaced in 1992. He bought the Hartford Whalers in 1994 for a reported $38 million under a restriction that the team must remain in Hartford for at least three seasons unless permitted to leave by the NHL board of governors.

Karmanos called his quest to land a team through Eagleson, and then through expansion, "one of the strangest business exercises I've been through." As it turns out, he was not the first would-be NHL owner who had looked to Eagleson for help. In his memoirs, Eagleson said that in the early 1970s he was offered $2 million by Jim Pattison, owner of the World Hockey Association's Vancouver Blazers, to "swing a merger" between the NHL and the rival WHA. Eagleson said he turned Pattison down flat because a merger would have hurt the players.

Eagleson also said he was later offered $1 million by Peter Pocklington (whose Oilers were then in the WHA), and his general manager, Glen Sather, to help arrange a merger. Eagleson said he told them he could not support a merger as long as the WHA was healthy.

In 1979 Eagleson did help orchestrate the merger, of course, and Edmonton was one of four WHA teams absorbed into the NHL. Pocklington confirmed that he'd sought Eagleson's help — "Sure, I offered him the money. A million bucks would have been cheap to get into the NHL back then" — but said he never did pay Eagleson "because he had nothing to do with the merger."

10

EVERYBODY'S BANKER

"I have made my money mostly by fortuitous investments
in real estate. There has not been one speck of impropriety."
ALAN EAGLESON

BACK IN NOVEMBER 1981, Alan Eagleson hosted
a luncheon at Le Rendez-Vous in Toronto. The luncheon was held in honor
of two couples who were getting married: then Toronto mayor Art Eggleton
to Brenda Clune; and Howard Ungerman, an employee of Eagleson's law
firm, to Judi Blady. Among those attending were former Toronto Maple Leafs
captain Darryl Sittler and his wife; Metro Toronto Chief of Police John Ackroyd; Metro Toronto Chairman and future *Toronto Sun* publisher Paul Godfrey; lawyer Julian Porter, chairman of the Toronto Transit Commission, and
his wife, publisher Anna Porter; Air Canada vice president Jack Callen; Marvin Goldblatt of Rae-Con Consultants, an Eagleson business; Tom Wells,
Ontario Minister of Intergovernmental Affairs; Arthur Harnett of Harnett
Consultants; D. Scott McCann of Teledyne Canada (a company on whose
board Eagleson sat); Gordon Canning (an Eagleson pal) of Blue Mountain
Resorts in Collingwood; and one Norman Donaldson, whose name showed
up in Zena Cherry's social column in the Toronto *Globe and Mail* as being
associated with "Doneagle Construction Ltd."

In his memoirs, Eagleson mentions the doubles championship he won
in the summer of 1980 at the Toronto Lawn Tennis Club with Norman

Donaldson. What Eagleson didn't mention was that his tennis partner was also a long-time business partner, or that the NHL Players' Association, under Eagleson's direction, was helping to fund several Donaldson ventures.

At the time of the luncheon, two companies linked to Donaldson had borrowed more than a half-million dollars from the NHLPA for real estate developments. Eagleson, paid by the players to administer the NHLPA and its money, was loaning union money to his friend and business associate without their knowledge.

In February 1981, New Leaf Florists Limited borrowed $275,000 from the NHLPA for townhouses being built in Toronto's Cabbagetown area. It was an interest-only loan. The loan agreement was signed by Donaldson's wife, Marie, the president of New Leaf; Norman Donaldson was listed as the guarantor. In the Toronto phone book I found the Donaldsons listed at 9 May Street. In a brief telephone conversation, Marie Donaldson told me she knew little of the matter and referred questions to her husband. He, however, refused to talk. Although Donaldson could claim that the business was headed by his wife, she evidently thought otherwise; and Players' Association correspondence about the loans was addressed not to her, but to him.

In October 1981, a second firm, Tesson Developments, borrowed $300,000 from the NHLPA for five residential lots in Scarborough, Ontario. Donaldson was secretary-treasurer of Tesson; the president was William Wilson, a construction contractor and friend of Donaldson's. This, too, was an interest-only loan.

Both the New Leaf and Tesson loans appeared trouble-free at the start; the borrowers began paying interest, as well as some principal. Then they started missing payments altogether. By July 1983, no interest had been paid on the New Leaf loan since the previous August. Tesson interest payments were also "consistently late," according to Players' Association documents. The NHLPA files I reviewed contained numerous reminders to Donaldson and Tesson president Wilson that they were behind on their payments.

At the same time that the NHLPA was dunning Donaldson for payment of the New Leaf loan, he was in business with Eagleson on another real estate project. In 1976 Eagleson had bought a house in the Rosedale area of

Toronto, at 30 Rosedale Road, for $350,000, borrowing money from two of his hockey clients, Bobby Orr and Marcel Dionne, to finance it.

In 1981, after Orr had severed ties with Eagleson, Eagleson took out a $600,000 mortgage on the property from the Canadian Imperial Bank of Commerce. In 1982 Norman Donaldson took ownership of the house. With the CIBC mortgage still in place, Donaldson took out a second mortgage, from Eagleson himself, of $1.25 million. Donaldson also obtained a $1.15-million construction loan from Harcom Consultants Limited, operated by Arthur Harnett, who had managed Eagleson's successful effort to become president of the Ontario Progressive Conservative Association in 1968 and who subsequently did advertising and TV work for Eagleson during the Canada Cup tournaments. (One of Eagleson's first acts as Ontario Tory president was to create a new full-time position, making Harnett executive director of the association.) The plan was to convert the large single-family home into "not more than" five apartment units. It is unclear what happened to the plan, but the property was sold in 1983 for $1.09 million. The mortgages were lifted from the property, though it's not clear how Eagleson recouped his personally held second mortgage.

Despite the history of late payments on the Donaldson company loans, the Players' Association repeatedly extended them. The New Leaf loan, originally due in February 1982, was renewed for another year in 1982, "restructured" in April 1983 (even though no interest had been paid since the previous August), then "extended" in January 1984, with a reminder to Donaldson to pay back taxes. In November 1984, the loan again came due. Nine months later, in August 1985, it remained unpaid, and more than $10,000 in late interest payments had accumulated.

Try not paying your mortgage for nine months and see how your bank reacts. What did the Players' Association do? It retroactively amended the loan to Donaldson, extending it to November 1986. Eagleson was playing fast and loose with union money.

NHLPA records indicate Donaldson never had to pay late penalties. His original loan agreement did not specify any such penalties. Instead, it allowed Sam Simpson — the union's director of operations — to "take such action" as he deemed "advisable in the best interest of all participants."

Simpson, of course, answered to Eagleson. As he himself later told me, he was "stuck between a rock and a hard place."

In early 1985, Donaldson obtained yet another loan, this time from Simpson, despite the trouble Simpson was having in collecting on the other loans. This loan, issued by Simpson as a trustee, was for $80,000 and secured by Donaldson's Collingwood property. Records did not indicate the source of the money — there's nothing to show that it came from the NHLPA.

While Donaldson's firms were granted grace periods and loan renewals, the union's money was clearly at risk. In August 1983, for example, New Leaf owed more than $22,000 in taxes, water, and sewer charges on the Cabbagetown property. That meant trouble for the union since tax payments take precedence over a mortgage. There was even more serious trouble with the loan to Tesson for the five lots in Scarborough. In February 1985, with Tesson owing approximately $290,000 in principal and interest, the Players' Association executed its power of sale. Two of the lots were sold to a company operated by a Toronto businessman, Nick Bigioni. That deal, too, was financed by the NHLPA, which gave Bigioni a $230,000 mortgage.

Bigioni, of Bigioni Management Services Ltd., bailed out Donaldson's company and the NHLPA again in March 1985, agreeing to buy the remaining house lots. The Players' Association finally recouped its investment, but the holder of a second mortgage was left holding the bag for "a significant sum." NHLPA documents did not identify who got burned.

The Players' Association finally closed the books on the New Leaf loans in 1986 when a Toronto lawyer, Roman Maksymiw, one of the original guarantors of the loan, paid off the mortgage. In the end, the New Leaf loan had taken five years to repay, the Tesson loan almost four years. Both were originally supposed to run for one year. Over that time, a total of $395,000 was loaned to Tesson and $380,000 to New Leaf.

Who authorized the loans? They were granted by Simpson, the director of operations, as trustee for the players. But the agreement of trust, authorizing him to loan the money, was signed "per RA Eagleson." To complete the cozy arrangement, Eagleson's employee, Howard Ungerman, handled much of the correspondence and paperwork for the loans. (When I sought to interview Ungerman, he asked for my questions in writing, then refused to answer them, citing solicitor-client privilege and suggesting I was "fishing.")

Whatever Simpson's role, Alan Eagleson — Donaldson's solicitor, business partner, tennis partner, and friend — took a direct interest in the loans to the companies associated with Donaldson. Indeed, he helped get the loans extended. In a March 1983 memo about the Tesson mortgage, Simpson wrote to Eagleson: "In response to your request about refinancing the above mortgage, I have now spoken to the Investment Committee who has agreed to redo the mortgage." The same memo asked Eagleson to see if the new terms of the loans were satisfactory to the borrower — "let me know so I can make the necessary arrangements for the funds."

In January 1985, Eagleson intervened to buy time for Donaldson on the New Leaf loan. A letter to Donaldson from Howard Ungerman noted the loan had been due in full the previous November, but added, "Mr. Eagleson has indicated that you may need some time in this regard so Mr. Simpson is prepared to give you a few months if necessary to rearrange funds." More than six months later, the loan was extended.

Players I interviewed for our *Eagle-Tribune* reports, including many player reps and executive board members — Andy Moog, Jim Peplinski, Dave Barr, Mike Gartner, Pat Verbeek, Peter Taglianetti, Steve Kasper, Ryan Walter, Mike O'Connell, Tony Esposito — had no idea their union's money was being loaned to Eagleson associates. The "investment committee" mentioned by Simpson was a complete mystery to them.

"Investment committee? We didn't have any investment committee," said Mike Milbury, the Bruins' player representative until 1982 and an early critic of Eagleson. "If I had known about loans or any of that stuff, an investment committee or Eagle using our money to loan to his friends, you know darn well I would have asked questions."

There's good reason why Milbury never heard of the investment committee. Simpson himself later admitted it didn't exist.

I asked several mortgage experts to comment on the Donaldson loans. After reviewing them, John Leeson — whose career in mortgages spanned more than forty years, including a stint with Bank of America's Canadian division — commented: "I do not see how any rational lender could hit serious delinquency, power of sale even, and then not only renew (and increase the loan), but also reduce the rate and, on unfavorable terms such as agreeing to allow a new first to be registered, without prepayment of your existing mortgage. Talk about giving the shop away!" Of Eagleson, Leeson said, "The loans appear to have been made as if they were his own money. When loaning your funds out, you do not have to consider the decisions you are making. The losses, if any, are yours alone. However, when you are a solicitor, or mortgage company, etc., loaning on behalf of some other person or group, then it is incumbent upon you to take precautions to ensure the funds are invested wisely. He should know these things. This is Alan Eagleson we're talking about. Alan Eagleson, Q.C. We're not talking about Mary from Milwaukee."

Lorraine Mahoney, a benefit and pension adviser, was also astounded by the loan of union funds to firms associated with Donaldson. "Why would you not take great diligence in investing into guaranteed returns? Why not seek a stellar investment vehicle? Why were these funds helping friends of Mr. Eagleson? Why were they mucking about with these loans when better avenues were available for the players? As a friend of mine put it, this appears to be an example of when blue chips turn into cow chips." (Eagleson had referred to the mortgages made by the Players' Association as being "blue chip" loans.)

Mahoney noted that interest-only loans — the sort granted to New Leaf and Tesson — are normally granted only when "both the security and borrower are of exceptional quality." One of the NHLPA loans was initially a second mortgage, which meant another lender had first claim on the secured property. "Second mortgages are not considered wise investments."

Bill Dermody, the Hamilton lawyer hired by the players in 1989 to review later NHLPA loans, said of the New Leaf and Tesson loans (of which he was unaware at the time of his review), "The players [Eagleson and Donaldson] knew one another, had business back and forth. There is a connection of friendship, characterized again later in the 1987–88 loans by Eagleson. These files clearly show why private mortgage investments with escrow funds are unsatisfactory and undesirable. The funds — players' money invested in these loans — were put at a real risk. When it is other people's money you are responsible for managing, you have to use a higher standard of care in handling those funds."

Bob Allan, a veteran of twenty-two years in the mortgage business, also questioned the repeated renewals of the loans and the lack of penalties for late payment. "They seemed to be directed back into the same deal again and again and again. They were tied up for many, many months beyond the term of the mortgage and there was no opportunity to move those funds into other investment vehicles which could have proven to be safer. There were no penalties involved. In fact, there were some very generous terms to the borrowers in terms of allowing them to prepay and open up the mortgages.

"Those New Leaf and Tesson loans are not at arm's length. Eagleson is Donaldson's business partner at the time. That fact should have been disclosed in a formal statement to the association. This isn't just a guy touting money out of trust funds. This is very clearly a conflict."

Safer and more profitable investments were certainly available when the NHLPA put money into Donaldson's projects. On the New Leaf loan, the interest rate was 17 percent, and the final return for the players' fund just under $114,000. Interest of 17 percent and a return of $114,000 may sound high by today's standards, but bank and government investments offered substantially higher returns at the time. If the NHLPA had simply invested the $275,000 in T-bills for a full five years, it would have earned interest of almost $250,000.

I discovered two other loans made from players' union money in the early 1980s. Both borrowers had ties to Eagleson. Malcolm Gray, a former *Globe and Mail* reporter whose father-in-law was friendly with Eagleson, obtained a mortgage on his house through Eagleson. In 1983, Gray and his wife borrowed $87,000 from a trust headed by Marvin Goldblatt to buy a house in Toronto when they moved from Vancouver. Of that, $27,000 came from the Players' Association.

When I located Gray, he had moved to Moscow, where he worked for *Maclean's* magazine. He said he knew Eagleson from covering "big sports stories." He said he told Eagleson of his move from Vancouver in 1983, and Eagleson "mentioned there were investment monies available, money that active and formerly active NHL players had put up." Gray added that

Eagleson was friendly with his wife's father, Arnie Patterson, a Halifax radio announcer.

Another loan, apparently made in 1981, involved more than $400,000 and went to a firm connected to Irving Ungerman. This loan was made by Eagleson himself, acting as trustee for the players. It was made to Martin Tauber and Irving Ungerman Limited. Ungerman, known as "The Chicken Man" because of his chicken-processing plant in Toronto, is the father of Howard Ungerman, Eagleson's law partner, and the former manager of George Chuvalo, the boxer. Ungerman also ran All Canada Sports, the company involved, as we'll see, with a Canada Cup rink-board advertising scam in 1991.

The Ungerman loan showed up on a union statement for the 1982 fiscal year, at which time the balance was $399,666. An accompanying note said that the mortgage was "originally $436,000." The loan was a first mortgage on a small industrial building at 480 Tapscott Road in Scarborough, just east of Toronto. I located Martin Tauber, who explained, "I knew Irving Ungerman personally. I gave him an opportunity to buy 25 percent of the building. Irving helped me. When I bought this building, we took a mortgage with Al Eagleson's office. Where he got those funds, I didn't know."

IN AUGUST 1991, IN PREPARATION FOR an upcoming Canada Cup Tournament organized by Alan Eagleson, Team Canada held a five-day training camp at Blue Mountain Resort in Collingwood. Wayne Gretzky, Mario Lemieux, and Eric Lindros were among the hockey stars who came to Blue Mountain that summer. Many players also teed up for a charity golf tournament at the resort's new Monterra Golf Course. Eagleson, the promoter of the Canada Cup, explained that the resort was chosen as the site of the training camp after a chance meeting with Collingwood mayor Joe Sheffer.

"I bumped into Mayor Sheffer a couple of weeks ago and he told me Collingwood would love to be a part of the Labatt Canada Cup," Eagleson said in a February 19, 1991, press release. "I called Mike Keenan and he thought it was a great idea. Since our main training camp will be in Southern Ontario and most of our games will be in Ontario, we decided to have a resort camp in the Georgian Bay area."

The press release did not mention that Eagleson had a considerable personal stake in the area, or that Collingwood intertwined many of his political connections, business associates, family members, and friends.

A scenic resort area on Georgian Bay, about 100 miles northwest of Toronto, Collingwood offers skiing in winter and fishing, boating, and tennis in summer. Blue Mountain at Collingwood is Ontario's largest ski resort. It was founded by Jozo Weider in 1941. After his death in a car accident in 1971, his son George and his brother-in-law Gordon Canning took over the resort. An $800,000 lodge was opened in 1978, along with a motel.

In 1980, Canning announced a $21-million, seven-year expansion. Blue Mountain Resorts Ltd. bought the nearby Georgian Peaks ski resort. In early 1981, the Ontario Ministry of Industry and Tourism, in the Conservative government of Bill Davis, to whom Eagleson had close ties, announced a $12-million grant to the Craigleith–Blue Mountain Ski Resort areas of the Collingwood region. It was part of the Tories' $1.5-billion Board of Industrial Leadership and Development program, in which the government provided matching grants to cities and towns for historic rebuilding and the encouragement of tourism. Blue Mountain was off and running. By January 1982, the new $5-million Blue Mountain Inn was open, a 103-room hotel at the base of the mountain. It was built for year-round activity, and included an indoor pool, squash courts, games room, a gym, and lighted tennis courts. It also had a 125-seat disco and a large bar.

Eagleson told the *Financial Times of Canada* that in 1980 he had teamed up with an unnamed Collingwood area developer on a property deal in Blue Mountain and said, "I've done very well." Back in 1979, before Canning announced the expansion and before the government began pumping money into the area, Eagleson's tennis and business partner, Donaldson, and another company — Karnco Limited, operated by Donald W. Karn — had bought about five acres of land in Collingwood Township, just north of Collingwood, for $176,000. It was evidently a good deal. Less than seven months later, Blue Mountain Resorts bought an adjacent lot of similar size for more than double the price, $375,000.

Doneagle Investments Inc. was incorporated September 22, 1980, with Eagleson as president and Donaldson as secretary. The corporation was dissolved in 1984. Corporation papers authorized Eagleson and Donaldson to borrow money and to mortgage any "currently owned or subsequently acquired property."

In 1984, Donaldson listed Eagleson as a partner when he transferred a portion of the five acres — 34,000 square feet, or just under an acre — to Eagleson for a token $2. Eagleson's employee, Howard Ungerman, prepared the sale documents. On them, Donaldson listed Eagleson as a "partner" and beneficial owner of the land as well as his solicitor. Two years later, Eagleson built a $120,000 cottage on the waterfront lot (next door to a home that belonged to Donaldson). Listed on the building permit was Ernie Rowley, who operated Sandhill Construction, which, as we'll see, was later involved in the transfer of Canada Cup rink-board advertising money by Irving Ungerman's company, All Canada Sports. (In early 1993, while a U.S. grand jury was hearing testimony to decide whether criminal charges ought to be brought against Eagleson, the cottage was put on the market for $695,000. His real estate agent, Flora Wendling of Lush Realtors, described the vendor as "flexible.")

By 1987, the Ontario government had approved a thirteen-story hotel-condominium development at the top of Blue Mountain at an estimated value of $80 million. Adjacent to the ski hills, the seventy-two–acre site was to house 290 condos, 215 hotel rooms, a convention center, swimming pool, and tennis courts. The Tory government supported the development; the Liberals opposed it.

Others close to Eagleson were also investing in Collingwood Township. Eagleson's son, Trevor Allen, and daughter, Jill Anne, purchased a nearby piece of land for $90,000, with financing from their father. They weren't the only ones plowing money into the region. By 1987, according to Erv Brewda, a Canadian mortgage expert, Collingwood was "one of the hottest areas in the country" for real estate speculation and was attracting the interest of such investors as Nelson Skalbania, the Vancouver entrepreneur, and Len Gaudet, disgraced head of the now-defunct Osler brokerage firm in Toronto.

That year, 1987, the NHLPA loaned $500,000 toward the purchase of fifty acres in Collingwood Township to Eagleson's law partner, Ungerman, acting as trustee for his father's company, Irving Investments Limited.

Through another company, Irving Ungerman, of course, had previously borrowed players' union money for the Tapscott Road building. Eagleson also invested $100,000 in the deal from a trust fund for his daughter, Jill. Her money was later withdrawn and replaced by money from another investor whom he declined to name (it turned out to be Hockey Canada, which for all practical purposes he ran). Twenty-one months later, a company called Monterra Properties bought the land back from the Ungerman trust for just over $1.9 million. On paper, Irving Investments made a profit of $848,000 on the original purchase price.

That same day — August 30, 1989 — seven firms and individuals associated with Eagleson purchased property in Collingwood Township from Monterra, in separate transactions totaling $900,000. The buyers and purchase prices were: Sam Simpson, the NHLPA director of operations, and his wife, $135,000; HUD Holdings, named for Howard Ungerman, $125,000; Marvin Goldblatt, Eagleson's employee and the NHLPA accountant, $125,000; Jialson Holdings, an Eagleson family business, $140,000; Kingsmar Holdings Limited, an Eagleson business, two parcels at $125,000 and $115,000; and James Bull, brother of Eagleson's long-time friend Dr. Charles Bull, $125,000. No mortgages were listed in the transactions. It's unclear whether the purchases were cash.

Another company headed by Howard Ungerman also invested in the area that year, 1989, buying a Collingwood tire company for $1.58 million.

On February 22, 1991, Eagleson guaranteed a $750,000 private loan from Monty Beber, a Toronto businessman, to Monterra Properties for land in Collingwood Township. The president of Monterra was Eagleson's friend, John Kadwell; its directors included another Eagleson friend, Gordon Canning, and the son of the founder of Blue Mountain, George Weider. Canning and Weider were the president and chief executive officer, respectively, of Blue Mountain Resorts Limited, which ran both the Blue Mountain Resort ski area and the Monterra Golf and Tennis Club.

At the time of the 1991 Canada Cup training camp in Collingwood — which, you'll recall, came about because of the chance encounter between Alan Eagleson and the mayor — not only did Eagleson have a home nearby, not only did he have friends and associates who had invested in the area, and not only had he helped fuel the boom by loaning out NHLPA funds on favorable terms to his friends and associates without the knowledge of the union members to whom the money belonged, but he himself had a piece of the action at Blue Mountain. He personally held a 12.5 percent interest in Monterra Properties; add in the holdings of other family members, and the Eaglesons owned a quarter of the company.

I HAD BEEN INTRIGUED BY THE NHLPA loan to the Cleveland Barons ever since Rosaire Paiement had told me about it and Wilf Paiement had confirmed that some of his own money, managed by Eagleson, had gone into the loan. By going through NHLPA documents, as well as through Wilf Paiement's files, I learned that on February 23, 1977, the NHLPA loaned $600,000 to the NHL "to ensure that the Cleveland Barons [then an NHL team] would remain in existence" until the conclusion of the 1976–77 season. On the surface, it was an admirable attempt to save the jobs of some hockey players, but at another level, a highly questionable move that invited questions. For starters, why didn't the NHL owners make the loan?

"Because they wouldn't do it," recalled former Bruins president Paul Mooney, an NHL governor at the time. "They were arguing among themselves. We were talking $40,000 a team and no way some teams — Washington was one — were going to pitch in to save Cleveland. That's how the loan came about. Ziegler turned to Eagleson and said, 'Fork up the dough.'"

Fifteen days later, the Players' Association and the NHL struck a deal — a $600,000 loan that would yield up to 11 percent interest. Wearing his hat as union boss, Eagleson had obligated NHLPA money to the NHL. Off came his NHLPA hat and on went his lawyer's hat, which he wore when forming a trust fund held by Marvin Goldblatt and Sam Simpson — his agency business employee and his hand-picked union employee, respectively — to front the loan.

Off went the lawyer's hat, on went his agent's hat. He made an investment for some of the players represented by his agency business, involving their funds in the loan through the Goldblatt-Simpson trust.

Wilf Paiement, for example, represented by Eagleson from his rookie year, 1974, until he went with Bill Watters in 1979, had $20,000 of his money invested in the Cleveland loan. Paiement, whose finances were administered by Eagleson's Sports Management Limited, said he was asked permission by Graeme Clark — who worked for Sports Management — to use his money in the loan "late in the [1976–77] season, maybe with two or three weeks to go." When Paiement got his money back, early the next season, Clark sent him a letter informing him that a check for $21,147.85 "which is repayment in full of your loan to the NHLPA" had been deposited in his account. Clark added this handwritten postscript: "This is the loan you made to the NHLPA so that the NHLPA could support the Cleveland Barons."

To many players, the Cleveland loan symbolized Eagleson's conflict of interest as both union head and player agent. "He never gave me the opportunity to be a part of that loan and make a profit on interest," said former NHLPA vice president Brad Park. "You'd think the responsibility of the Players' Association executive director would be to be fair to all players. Every player deserved the chance to decide whether or not he'd be a part of that loan individually."

Park said he never knew that clients of Eagleson's player management business had been involved in the Cleveland loan. In fact, the players never even knew that union funds were being used until after the bail-out loan had been made. The minutes of the 1977 owner-player council meetings list Park, Terry O'Reilly, and Ed Westfall among the player reps who "unanimously" voted approval of the Cleveland loan repayment (as well as the new one-third buy-out of player contracts).

"Cleveland loan?" said Westfall, then a player rep for the New York Islanders and now a color commentator for the Islanders. "What Cleveland loan? I don't remember anything about a loan to the Cleveland Barons. I also never knew Eagleson had mixed our Players' Association money into a loan with players he represented so his players could make money. This is all new to me."

O'Reilly was even more adamant. "My name's listed on those minutes as being there at the meeting, unanimously approving those things?" He was furious, asking to see the minutes for himself. I delivered a copy to his home in Georgetown, north of Boston. After reading it, he was even more insistent. "Those minutes say it was a unanimous vote to approve, but that's totally untrue! I did not vote to approve any of that. As far as a loan to Cleveland, this is the first I've heard about $600,000 of Players' Association money going to Cleveland or the NHL. I didn't vote on any of this."

Ken Dryden, the former Canadiens goaltender, was also listed as having been at that meeting. "That's kind of bizarre," he said, when I reached him in Toronto. "My first reaction is — a $600,000 loan to Cleveland? Why couldn't the owner partners come up with $600,000?

"It's important to remember we were outsiders," Dryden explained. "The players were really a collection of junior partners in the owner-player meetings. Only one person was a real insider. Only one person had an extensive insight from our perspective. That's where the power was: Alan Eagleson."

In his memoirs, Eagleson remembered the loan this way: "The NHL put up $800,000 and the NHLPA put up $800,000, on a note guaranteed by the NHL. The NHLPA in effect loaned $800,000 to the NHL owners, who loaned it to Cleveland to get them through the year, which was their last." Eagleson called the loan "something the NHLPA can be proud of, done strictly in the interests of the game."

Eagleson's recollection doesn't square with NHLPA records or the accounts of former players and NHL executives. Why wouldn't he have revealed the loan to the players before making it? As the union director who also operated a player agency and management business, the loan put him in the position of giving players he represented an unfair advantage over players he didn't. And since Eagleson had many clients on the Cleveland team, it was in his interest to keep those players solvent so that they could continue to pay him.

IN THE COURSE OF HIS WORK with Ed Garvey, Bill Dermody, the Hamilton lawyer hired by the players to review loans made by the NHLPA in the late 1980s, scrutinized three loans. One was a $320,000 loan to a friend of Eagleson's, David Baker Sr., a car dealer, for the purchase of property in Richmond Hill, Ontario. One was the aforementioned $500,000 loan to a trust operated by Howard Ungerman on behalf of Irving Ungerman, to purchase land in Collingwood, the deal that yielded an $848,000 profit. And the last was a $1.2 million loan to Eagleson's friend, Marvin Teperman, for a shopping mall in Burlington, Ontario.

In a letter sent to NHLPA members after the 1989 Garvey investigation, Eagleson claimed that all three loans made more money than conventional investments. The $320,000 Baker loan was for three years at 12 percent interest. A three-year certificate from the Royal Bank of Canada, Eagleson said, earned 7 percent. The players would make an extra $48,000 in interest. The $500,000 loan to Ungerman also paid 12 percent, rising to 13 percent after the first year. The $1.2 million loan to Teperman returned 11 percent interest.

I asked mortgage experts for their opinions of the three loans. All agreed to review them, on the understanding they were speaking as individuals, not as representatives of their companies. All raised red flags about the loans.

"The big clicker is that they are interest payments only and they're not open — the loans may be renegotiated," said Tony Giovinazzo, a commercial mortgage underwriter.

John Leeson also cited the interest-only terms. "What that does is minimize the investor's outlay while increasing the mortgagee's risk. If anything happens to the real estate, or mortgagor, the principal balance is right where it started."

Erv Brewda, who had been in the mortgage loan business for nineteen years, noted that the Baker loan was for $320,000 on a $370,000 purchase price. "It's a good deal for the guy borrowing the money. With no payments to make, except interest, that's a fabulous deal. There was nothing but $50,000 into the deal. He walked away with 320 Gs." Brewda dismissed Baker's statement to Eagleson that his own real estate agent appraised the property at more than $750,000. "The appraisal is worth absolutely nothing," said Brewda. "An appraisal by a sales rep — that blows me away."

Leeson, who visited and photographed the Richmond Hill site, said setting a value higher than the purchase price on the Baker land "would be speculation." He said the property was zoned rural-residential and that would be hard to change because of a zoning freeze at the time in Richmond Hill.

Paul Morris, a commercial mortgage expert, scoffed at Eagleson's assertion that Baker had supplied a net worth statement of $2.5 million. "Net worth and 60 cents might get you a cup of coffee," said Morris. "I wouldn't have made the loan on 86 percent — 320 versus 370 — of purchase price. No way."

Brewda was also skeptical of the $500,000 loan for land in Collingwood made to the company controlled by Irving Ungerman. "To put a mortgage on that I would have to see the subdivision plan. And I would have done an appraisal from an outside accredited appraiser." As for Eagleson's claim that Ungerman had a net worth in excess of $25 million, Brewda said, "Somebody could be worth $25 million in real estate value. Cash flow is another thing. A lot of the big boys are taking the big plunge. Look at Donald Trump."

Al Bond, who'd been in the lending business for two decades, said the Ungerman loan favored the borrower. "Interest only quarterly helped with cash flow. Very reasonable for the borrower. The person lending could have done better. The borrower probably saved a half to one point (in interest) on the loan plus a fee."

The experts were less skeptical of the $1.2 million loan to Teperman for his Mount Royal Plaza. Said Brewda, "If the numbers are right, it's not a bad mortgage. I'd have to know how many units there are in the shopping plaza, what the income is, what's the cost, how much rent it is receiving, and what it would sell for."

John Leeson called Teperman's plaza "a mid-sized neighborhood shopping plaza, doing reasonably well at present with low vacancy." Eagleson had claimed the site was worth $4.5 million. Leeson said, "A value of over $4 million is excessive for what is strictly a neighborhood shopping center." He pointed out that "the area is not the best," with welfare housing opposite the site. Leeson also said the 11 percent interest rate on the Teperman loan was low. He said rates were substantially higher at the time the mortgage was issued.

After the June 1989 player meetings at which these three NHLPA loans became an issue, Marvin Teperman wrote to Eagleson (who no doubt solicited the letter): "As I recall, I could have obtained as good or better terms from the trust companies which offered to lend me the money." Al Bond did not buy Teperman's claim. "That's an absurd statement — he could make better loans elsewhere. Why didn't he?"

Of all three loans, Brewda said, "If I had two million bucks kicking around, I certainly wouldn't be giving it to one lawyer or one person to invest as he saw fit. I'd want to know what was going on with it through direct contact or monthly statements."

Leeson had these comments on the three loans: "One thing I notice — the solicitors appear to be acting for mortgagee and mortgagor. Any normal commercial mortgage transactions should be backed by a competent full appraisal of value (not 'I visited the site and it was worth, etc.')."

Bill Dermody did not get to look into the earlier loans (to New Leaf, Tesson, Malcolm Gray, and Martin Tauber and Irving Ungerman Ltd.) when he did his review in 1989: "Those were the ground rules agreed upon by Eagleson and the players." His review covered only the David Baker, Ungerman trust, and Marvin Teperman loans. Dermody concluded, as I did, that the players "didn't know a thing about mortgages made using their money. They had never been informed."

Eagleson later claimed in a letter to NHLPA members to have been cleared by Dermody's report. Dermody takes a different view. "He read the text of my report before it was even issued," he said of Eagleson. "I did that as a courtesy. What he read and agreed to in that report was that there was a perception of his benefit by position. He could call that whatever he wants, but that point was explicitly clear. It was certainly not condoning or clearing him of his past involvement with allowing escrow funds to be issued to his personal friends or clients."

11

FAST AND LOOSE

"Everybody who knows me knows I'm careful with not
only my own money but my clients' money and with
the association money."
ALAN EAGLESON

N HIS 1989 REPORT, written at the time Alan
Eagleson was facing discontent among NHLPA members, Ed Garvey also
raised the issue of Eagleson's spending habits. "Any player who has seen
Alan at international events can confirm that Alan does, indeed, go first
class," Garvey wrote. "There are no limits on his travel expenses and he has
refused to allow us to examine his expense records. We are not really looking
for a dinner here or there, we were trying to find out if you, his employer,
are able to review his records. The answer is no....

"He works part-time, and he determines how much he does and when
he does it," Garvey wrote. "Specifically, the contract says he 'shall devote
approximately 60–65% of his working time annually to Association matters.'
He is his own boss."

Aware of the players' growing dissatisfaction, Eagleson sent a letter to all
NHLPA members boasting of his thrift. "The NHLPA has always kept a very
low budget for operations," he wrote. "I am very cost-conscious and our 22-
year history shows that we manage reasonably well on a tight budget." In a
1989 *Goals* newsletter distributed to the players, he elaborated the theme.
He said that his $175,000 salary and $10,000 office expense allowance

covered "all office expenses, secretarial staff, executive assistant fees and rent." Once those costs were taken into account, he said, his own salary was "about $90,000." As he did so often, Eagleson was brazening through, saying what needed to be said to quell the discontent. But the figures he cited did not begin to tell the real story.

At the inception of the NHLPA, in 1967, members paid annual dues of $1,000. By 1989 annual dues had risen to $3,000. For the 1995–96 season, dues will be $4,800 U.S. per player. NHLPA dues are deducted by NHL teams at source, meaning they are subtracted from player paychecks. During most of Eagleson's tenure, dues accounted for about 75 percent of the union's income; the balance came from royalties and interest.

NHLPA financial statements I obtained showed that union expenses totaled $4.7 million for the 1986–90 fiscal years, an average of more than $1 million a year. The $4.7 million included $1.6 million for professional fees; $861,560 for meetings; $552,718 for employee salaries and benefits; $273,168 for promotion, gifts, and awards; and $177,901 for career counseling.

Eagleson's own contracted NHLPA salary between July 1, 1987, and June 30, 1991, totaled $768,400 U.S. (for "60–65 percent of his time"). Under his revised contract, signed in February 1990, Eagleson also received up to $20,000 U.S. for his secretary, as well as reimbursement of all other "reasonable expenses." He also received a $25,000 bonus in any year the NHLPA made a profit of $600,000 on the international hockey events he organized, and he was scheduled to receive $100,000 U.S. a year until 1993 for his work in international hockey after he stepped down in late 1991.

Although Eagleson claimed that the money paid to him covered all office expenses and rent, the financial statements showed that the association paid an additional $229,250 for office and general expenses and $160,076 for "occupancy" fees during the 1986–90 fiscal years. From mid-1988 to early 1992, the rent went to the Eagleson family firm that owned Maitland House. The statements also list a $111,000 commitment toward Eagleson's annual pension of $50,000 U.S. at age sixty-five, and expenditures of $80,697 for automobiles, including Eagleson's car.

A DETAILED BREAKDOWN OF NHLPA financial statements for the fiscal years 1987, 1988, and 1989 showed that the union paid almost $1 million in fees and expenses to Eagleson or firms tied to him. Other union expenses, in part attributable to him, consumed a further $900,000. The bottom line was at least $1.85 million in expenses during the three-year period. Here is a break-down of payments made by the NHLPA to various Eagleson firms during that three-year period:

- $730,384 to the law firm of Eagleson Ungerman, which includes fees for Eagleson's services as head of the NHLPA;
- $24,000 in rent to Jialson Holdings, an Eagleson family trust, which owned the building where the NHLPA offices were housed, at 37 Maitland Street in Toronto;
- $15,000 to Rae-Con, the Eagleson consulting firm, for renovation and moving expenses connected to the move to 37 Maitland;
- $5,842 to Sports Management Limited, Eagleson's agency, for benefit payments made on behalf of NHLPA employees;
- $3,974 to Sports Management Limited for telecommunication.

Various other expenses attributed to Eagleson and reimbursed by the NHLPA from 1987 to 1989 include:

- $52,342 for promotion, gifts, and awards;
- $30,728 for special meetings;
- $24,584 for international hockey expenses;
- $8,430 for players' meetings;
- $7,722 for telecommunication expenses incurred by Eagleson or his law firm;
- $32,648 for automobile lease payments;
- $17,180 for miscellaneous ("business lunch, coffee, sugar, pop, film processing");
- $8,853 for gas, parking, and other expenses;
- $7,500 to Canada Life for Eagleson's pension;
- $2,276 allocation of salary for Shayne Kukulowicz (the son of Aggie Kukulowicz of Air Canada);
- $1,600 allocation for Jill Eagleson, Eagleson's daughter;
- $336 for Co-op Taxi service.

Other expenses paid by the players' union during those years include:

- $238,940 for airline tickets under two accounts (players' meetings and special meetings);
- $183,664 for hotels under three different accounts (players' meetings, special meetings, and promotion, gifts, and awards);
- $101,841 in office and general expenses (includes a $15,000 payment to Rae-Con, the Eagleson company);
- $60,104 in charitable donations;
- $59,245 for game tickets;
- $43,370 for promotion of Rendezvous '87, a series between the NHL and the Soviets;
- $41,840 for telecommunication;
- $36,917 for gifts;
- $26,687 for meals under two accounts (players' meetings and promotion, gifts, and awards);
- $24,000 to Fieldhaus Ltd. for an apartment in London, England, in 1987 and 1988 (before Eagleson purchased the Pimlico lease with Bernard Warren's help);
- $19,274 for golf and tennis club dues and expenses;
- $14,776 for limo, taxi, and car rental;
- $13,209 for International Hockey airline tickets, hotels, and meals;
- $9,323 for life insurance for Eagleson and five other employees;
- $2,130 for YMCA memberships for Eagleson and NHLPA director of operations Sam Simpson.

This list of expenses is by no means exhaustive. The NHLPA picked up the tab for many other things along the way. Eagleson billed the union $1,560 U.S. during a July 1987 trip to London, England, for eight meals; the union also paid for theater tickets for his insurance pals, and Wimbledon tickets. The union also paid for Wimbledon tickets for two of Eagleson's Conservative Party cronies and a sportswriter pal. In August 1987, Eagleson billed the NHLPA $1,000 U.S. for the tickets, including two for Roy McMurtry, one for Tom Wells, and one for George Gross of the *Toronto Sun*. He also charged the players $100 U.S. for a Wimbledon ticket for "E. Gross" in 1988. Gross, corporate sports editor of the *Toronto Sun* and Eagleson's friend since the mid-1960s, told me he and his wife, Elizabeth, may have received tickets from Eagleson but he was surprised to learn the tickets were charged to the NHLPA. Gross said he did not pay for them but understood them to be exchanges for tickets he gave Eagleson.

Gross remembered seeing Roy McMurtry, Canada's high commissioner in London at the time, at Wimbledon; also Tom Wells, then agent general for the Province of Ontario in the United Kingdom; and an Air Canada official. As high commissioner, McMurtry, the former chairman and chief executive officer of the Canadian Football League, was Canada's ambassador. He got involved with Eagleson's pal Bernard Warren, the London insurance broker, through Voyageur Insurance Company of Canada. Warren's insurance business, of course, made out handsomely after the Mulroney government granted Voyageur the exclusive right to sell travel insurance to passengers of Air Canada. McMurtry wound up on the board of Voyageur.

That same month, August 1987, the players' union was billed $456 for a golf outing at Lambton Country Club in Toronto with NHL president John Ziegler, Aggie Kukulowicz of Air Canada, Jim Gregory of the NHL officiating staff, Toronto insurance agent William Sutton, and Joe Grant of Licensing Corporation of America. In June 1988, Eagleson submitted a $2,000 bill to the NHLPA for car washes at One-A-Minute Carwash in Toronto. A note indicated the union was to pay half; the other half would be split among the Canada Cup and three Eagleson businesses.

Eagleson billed the special meetings account $545 for meals, tips, and "drinks and snacks with players" on a July 1988 trip to Edmonton and Calgary. He notes that he was in Edmonton for special meetings with "Gretzky & Pocklington (re: Gretzky wedding.)" Gretzky was married on July 16 that year to Janet Jones.

Dinner at Toronto's Sutton Place Hotel in October 1988 cost $4,928 — 80 meals, 156 liquor drinks, 39 bottles of wine, 15 beers, 38 bottles of mineral water, taxes, and tips. The event was listed in NHLPA records as "J. Sopinka Dinner." John Sopinka, Eagleson's friend and former lawyer (he once sent Bobby Orr a stern letter on Eagleson's behalf) was about to replace Willard Estey as a Supreme Court justice. The NHLPA paid one-quarter of the tab while Hockey Canada picked up the rest. Sopinka, thanks to Eagleson, sat on Hockey Canada's board of directors and attended hockey events all over the world at the expense of the nonprofit organization.

A $1,500 bill in November 1988 covered tickets to a Maple Leaf game at Maple Leaf Gardens for "Air Canada personnel" and other Eagleson friends and associates. That same month, the union paid $2,454 to Jutan International Limited for eighty cassette players. Where the cassette players went is not recorded.

According to Bill Dovey's Price Waterhouse review of NHLPA records, lawyers' bills cost the union almost $1 million in the 1987-89 period. Besides the $730,384 paid to Eagleson's law firm, the union also paid $176,709 to the Washington, D.C., firm of Shea Gardner for pension plan and legal services. (Larry Latto of Shea Gardner was the lawyer who presented Eagleson's contract demands to the players in 1986, the same day that negotiations were to begin with NHL owners about a new collective agreement.)

Dovey's review also noted $55,872 in player arbitration fees paid over three years to Greg Britz, the Boston lawyer who had been American Airlines' general manager for Canada until 1980 and had resigned after the internal flap caused by his having given Eagleson free airline passes.

EAGLESON'S HEADQUARTERS — 37 Maitland Street, a two-story brick building with a small parking area to one side — was purchased in May 1988 by Jialson Holdings Limited, an Eagleson family company. Eagleson immediately installed the union as a tenant. Before Ed Garvey's report, most players were unaware the head of their union was also, in effect, their landlord. (The union moved out in 1992, after Eagleson stepped down.)

The union's rental agreement with Eagleson's family company included rental of parking spots. The union paid $29,064 a year for 1,265 square feet of office space, plus $500 a month for parking. From 1988 to 1991, four parking spaces were reserved for the NHLPA. The $500 covered three spaces; the union got the fourth space for free. That space was for Eagleson, whose law offices were also housed in the building. The lease called for free parking for union visitors "as may be available."

I discovered that Hockey Canada's contract with Eagleson's law firm also included a monthly parking agreement. Hockey Canada, like the NHLPA, began renting office space at Maitland House in 1988, paying $1,000 a month. In 1991, the new Hockey Canada agreement upped the rent to $2,400 a month for about 1,250 square feet of space, plus "partial use" of six parking spaces. In all, Hockey Canada and the Players' Association rented a combined 2,500 square feet — about two-thirds of the roughly 3,700-square-foot total — in a building that also housed Eagleson's law firm, his consulting firm, and his agency business.

In 1991, while Eagleson was organizing the 1991 Canada Cup, six parking spots were rented to Hockey Canada for $600 per month. The NHLPA was still renting four. Between the two agreements, Eagleson was renting out ten parking spaces at the building — quite a trick, considering it has only four legal parking spots.

Where did everybody park? Someone who worked in the building laughed when I asked. "We used to park ten or eleven cars out back, jam 'em right in on the driveway. Keys were tossed around all the time to move cars blocked in that had to be moved."

Jim Laughlin was manager of site plan examinations for the Toronto Zoning Examiner's office. He said such "jamming" violates Toronto's parking regulations, which define a parking space as an unobstructed area at least 5.9 meters long and 2.6 meters wide (about 19 by 8 feet) that is "readily accessible at all times, without the necessity of moving another motor vehicle." Laughlin said, "If they were jamming in six, seven, eight, or more cars at a time, they were in violation."

What about renting ten spaces in a four-space lot? Laughlin chuckled. "I don't know what to say about that. I guess it's a situation of buyer beware."

While the union was paying more than $160 for each of its spaces, parking spots were going for $120 a month at an indoor parking garage a block from Eagleson's building.

LIKE HIS HANDLING OF NHLPA FUNDS, Eagleson's management of his clients' finances raised questions. As mentioned, this was one of the main reasons

Bobby Orr terminated his relationship with Eagleson. Jim Dorey, a Maple Leaf defenseman from 1968 until he was traded to the Rangers in 1972, and an Eagleson client from 1968 to 1970, also found himself with tax problems in the late 1970s. At Eagleson's suggestion, Dorey, like Orr, had allowed Eagleson to set him up as a limited company. "You bought property and whatever under Jim Dorey Enterprises to decrease your taxes," said Dorey, who now lives in Kingston, Ontario. "That was the setup." In 1978, Dorey was audited by Revenue Canada. Certain deductions were disallowed, his returns were redone, and he was ordered to pay back taxes. For several years after his retirement he had to make payments. Dorey said it cost "around $80,000" to bail himself out.

Another former Eagleson client, Rick Middleton, agreed to give me access to his files, and with the help of a chartered accountant we discovered some things that left Middleton shaking his head. Middleton had been a first-round draft pick of the New York Rangers in 1973. As a wide-eyed teenager fresh out of junior hockey in Oshawa, he wanted Eagleson as his agent — "He was Bobby's agent. It was well known around hockey that he was the one who had all the connections, all the pull."

Eagleson got him a three-year contract worth $242,500, including a $100,000 signing bonus. In 1976 Middleton was traded to Boston, where he developed into a polished right winger whose pretty goals often made the highlight reels. Like Orr and so many young players of the day, Middleton concentrated on hockey while Eagleson handled everything else, including his money. "I never bothered looking at the details of how he managed my affairs," Middleton recalled. "I just trusted him and went along with whatever they said. That's why I was paying them."

"Them" included Eagleson employees Marvin Goldblatt and Graeme Clark, who helped manage the finances of players represented by Eagleson. Eagleson's company set up a corporation, Rick Middleton Enterprises, invested the player's money in interest-paying term deposits, kept financial records, issued checks to pay various bills, issued annual reports, and filed tax returns. In return, Middleton paid Sports Management Consultants and Sports Management Limited $109,025 U.S. from March 1974 to March 1982.

If Middleton had looked at the details of his finances, he would have found a loan he didn't know about to an Eagleson family company; so many other loans to Eagleson clients that Middleton would end up taking out a loan himself; repeated overdrafts; and errors in math that a Grade 9 student wouldn't make.

On April 9, 1974, $5,000 was withdrawn from Middleton's account and paid to Nanjill Investments. Middleton's checkbook bore the notation: "re Pony." Nanjill Investments was another Eagleson family business (named for his wife, Nancy, and his daughter, Jill). Pony Sporting Goods was a Markham, Ontario-based sports equipment company and a subsidiary of Campbell Manufacturing Co. Ltd. The president of Pony was Chris Lang, long-time accountant for the international hockey events promoted by Eagleson and, later, treasurer and a director of Hockey Canada. Eagleson himself was a director of Pony.

A demand note in Middleton's file, also dated April 9, 1974, from Nanjill Investments Ltd. and signed "R.A. Eagleson," promised to pay Rick Middleton Enterprises $5,000 "together with simple interest at 7 1/2 percent per annum." Middleton said he did not recall the $5,000 payment, had never heard of Nanjill, and was unaware of its connection to Eagleson.

Middleton's records reveal that no interest was paid to Rick Middleton Enterprises while the loan remained outstanding. When Nanjill finally repaid the $5,000 principal almost four years later, on March 7, 1978, no interest was paid then, either. Graeme Clark, who handled Middleton's finances, told me no interest was paid because the investment went bad. Clark, in fact, gave Eagleson credit for repaying the original $5,000.

The $5,000 Nanjill loan was one of many made from Middleton's money, most of them mortgage loans to fellow players who were also Eagleson clients, including John Garrett, Paul Henderson, Butch Goring, and Mike Walton. Loans of Middleton's money totaled $123,000 in less than a year. Though Middleton was earning a good salary, so much of his money had been loaned out that on December 29, 1974, he took out a loan of $55,000 from the Royal Bank to purchase a $100,000 life insurance annuity through Eagleson's management business. Middleton recalled that loan but never realized he'd had to take it because so much of his own money had been loaned out.

"I never would have agreed to that if I had known what was going on," he said. "I was getting paid by the Rangers. My salary was going to Toronto, to Al's office. I didn't know what they were doing with it, which I know sounds foolish, except my job was playing hockey and theirs was to effectively manage my finances."

Middleton was also unaware of checkbook and bank account problems. Overdrafts showed up on seventeen of his monthly bank statements between September 21, 1973, and May 18, 1982. Checks from his account were returned because they were postdated or not signed. One deposit in Middleton's business account included the notation that it had been deposited to another player's account in error.

And that $5,000 interest-free Nanjill loan, the bad investment in Pony? Eagleson mentions Pony in his memoirs. Saying he'd been part of the group that organized Pony Sporting Goods, Eagleson wrote, "Pony became a strong shoe company internationally, eventually taken over by the Japanese." Which contradicted Graeme Clark's assertion that the Pony loan had gone bad, and raised a question in Rick Middleton's mind that's gone unanswered to this day: "If Pony was so good, why didn't I make a penny on it?"

EAGLESON'S CLAIM THAT HE WAS CAREFUL with the association's money sounded hollow to many players and hockey associates who had seen him in action all over the world. Outside hockey circles, he was also well known for his largesse. Hugh Murphy, vice president and manager of La Coquille Club Villas in Manalapan, Florida — where Eagleson had a home — recalled that Eagleson and his family would "bring me souvenirs all the time" from Canada Cup tournaments and other events.

Manalapan is an affluent town just south of Palm Beach, on Florida's Atlantic Coast. La Coquille Club Villas is an exclusive development secured by white fencing, an electronic gate, and a monitored security system. Eagleson purchased his villa, at 103 West Evans Drive, from Ontario Justice Richard Holland and his wife, Nancy, for $200,000 on April 3, 1980, through Lloyd R. Ludwig of Full House Inc.

Back at the time of the sale to Eagleson, the Hollands gave a reception at their Toronto home to celebrate their daughter's call to the bar. Guests included then-Chief Justice of Ontario William G. C. Howland, two former chief justices, George A. Gale and Dalton C. Wells, and five Supreme Court of Ontario judges — J. David Cromarty, W. David Griffiths, J. M. Labrosse, Robert F. Reid, and Robert C. Rutherford. Also at the Hollands' party were J. Peter Rickaby, crown attorney for North York, Kenneth Jarvis, secretary of the Law Society of Upper Canada, Aggie Kukulowicz of Air Canada, and Alan Eagleson.

Mr. Justice Holland recognized my name when I called him in Toronto. "You're the one investigating Eagleson," he said. Mrs. Holland recalled that Eagleson had had another place in Florida, a condo at the St. Andrews Club in Delray Beach. Judge Holland recalled that a developer had bought the St. Andrews condo from Eagleson. Eagleson's partner in that condo was F. Ross Johnson, the president of Standard Brands of New York before its merger with Nabisco, at whose Connecticut home Bobby Orr had signed with the Blackhawks before the expiration of his Bruins' contract.

I found the developer, Lloyd Ludwig, living in a Fort Lauderdale condo, Everglades House, formerly owned by Chicago Blackhawks owner Bill Wirtz. "It was an all-cash deal," Ludwig said of his purchase of the Wirtz condo. "My attorney was Al Eagleson." Full House, he said, was a company he operated on behalf of Eagleson and Johnson. Ludwig said he never charged Eagleson a dime in commissions or expenses — "They got a free ride as far as that went." Ludwig had made the down payment for Eagleson's Manalapan condo himself, he said, and Eagleson had reimbursed him.

Back in the late 1960s, Ludwig, a Detroit-born builder of bowling alleys who did business in Toronto before moving to Florida, had been involved with a football team, the Toronto Rifles of the Continental Football League. As chairman of its executive committee, he was looking to move the team from Exhibition Stadium at the CNE. "We couldn't get a stadium and Eagleson had a lot of connections with the government there. He's a big politician. He got us the stadium [Varsity Stadium, owned by the University of Toronto] the city itself would not give to us. The province would not give it to us. But when Eagleson got done negotiating it, we paid less for it than we were willing to pay. We had a good football team for three years."

Bobby Orr hoped to end his career in Boston, but Eagleson orchestrated Orr's move to Chicago. At Eagleson's urging, Orr secretly signed an agreement with Blackhawks owner Bill Wirtz at the Connecticut home of Ross Johnson in May 1976, before his Bruins contract had expired. His "guaranteed" Chicago contract led to a court battle.

When Peter Karmanos hired Eagleson to find him an NHL team, Eagleson failed to disclose the deal.

Former NHL goaltender Jim Rutherford worked for Karmanos and helped in the effort to secure a franchise.

With Harold Ballard in failing health, Eagleson suggested that the Maple Leafs might be purchased and moved.

In the late 1980s, surplus funds in the NHL's Pension Society became the subject of a bitter dispute between the league and the players. To the dismay of Gordie Howe and many other retired players with meager pensions, Alan Eagleson supported the owners' claim that they were entitled to most of the surplus money.

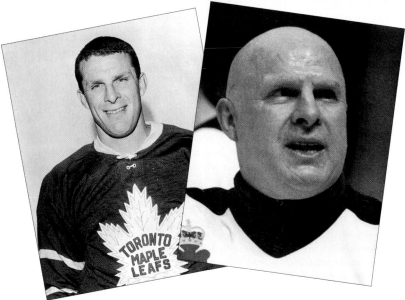

Former Maple Leaf defenseman Carl Brewer (in his playing days and today) — ironically, one of Eagleson's first NHL clients and godfather to Eagleson's daughter — wound up spearheading the drive to expose the union leader. Frustrated by the lack of information he was getting about his own pension, Brewer and his partner, Sue Foster, began organizing other retired players.

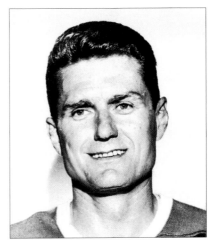

Andy Bathgate, at first reluctant to get involved in what he thought was merely a vendetta against Eagleson, ended up the lead plaintiff in the retirees' suit against the NHL Pension Society.

Allan Stanley joined the battle after being persuaded by his old defense partner, Bobby Baun, that the NHL Pension Society had wrongfully allocated money that belonged to the players.

A jubilant Eddie Shack embraces Toronto lawyer Mark Zigler after the 1994 Supreme Court decision that upheld the awarding of the pension surplus to the players. Zigler, a pension specialist, had earlier represented Dominion Store employees in their dispute with Conrad Black and the other owners of the grocery chain.

Chris Lang was one of several Eagleson associates who signed lucrative agreements with Hockey Canada and the Canada Cup. Lang was also involved with Eagleson in a sports equipment company.

A boyhood pal of Eagleson's, Bob Pulford ended up general manager of the Chicago Blackhawks, whose owner, Bill Wirtz, was chairman of the NHL board of governors and a close friend of Eagleson's.

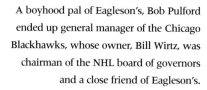

While serving as assistant general manager of the St. Louis Blues, Lou Angotti personally delivered $10,000 to Eagleson's Rosedale home after the Blues signed a player, Gord Buynak, whom Eagleson represented.

Former Bruin and Ranger Rick Middleton, an Eagleson client, discovered irregularities in his financial affairs, which were handled by one of Eagleson's companies, Sports Management Ltd.

As the force behind Hockey Canada and the Canada Cup, Eagleson dominated international hockey. His critics believed that he betrayed NHL players when he negotiated their collective bargaining agreements; Eagleson needed the permission of the NHL owners to use their best players in the Canada Cup tournaments he organized.

Claiming — falsely — that he received nothing for staging international tournaments, Eagleson persuaded players such as Wayne Gretzky, Mark Messier, and Ray Bourque to compete against the world's best for the glory of their country and the benefit of their pension fund. With Eagleson now discredited, the future of the Canada Cup is uncertain.

Eagleson, here with 1987 Team Canada members, assured the players that "neither I, nor any member of my family, nor any company with which I'm associated" had ever got money from an international hockey event. Undisclosed Hockey Canada agreements called for more than $1.5 million in fees, expenses, and bonuses to be paid to companies and people close to him.

Eagleson used Hockey Canada money to help finance the purchase of a 50-acre Collingwood property in which he and a family company, Jialson Holdings, had a significant stake.

Although Hockey Canada is a nonprofit organization partly funded by tax dollars, NHL players were denied access to detailed financial statements.

Eagleson's control of end-board advertising during Team Canada games allowed him to funnel huge sums into accounts at Cambio Valoren Bank in Zurich. In return for an Air Canada rink-board ad, he received travel passes that he and members of his family used for trips to such places as London, Frankfurt, Nice, and Bombay.

Eagleson's friend Irving Ungerman received NHLPA loans and was president of All Canada Sports Promotions, the company through which Eagleson channeled money diverted from the Canada Cup.

Labatt employee John Hudson participated in the 1991 Canada Cup rink-board scheme, backdating agreements at Eagleson's request. After an internal inquiry, Hudson resigned and moved to Arizona.

Highly regarded criminal specialist Brian Greenspan of Toronto explained Eagleson's refusal to surrender to U.S. authorities by saying he wouldn't let his client travel to Boston for a "trial by ambush."

Toronto lawyer Edgar Sexton, who has represented such high-profile clients as former prime minister Brian Mulroney, is part of the "dream team" Eagleson assembled to help fight his legal battles.

John Sopinka acted for Eagleson and served on the board of Hockey Canada before his appointment to the Supreme Court of Canada. Other influential Eagleson friends include former Liberal PM John Turner.

Eagleson has still not been charged in Canada. Author Conway discovered a former Eagleson employee working out of the RCMP office that shared information with the American authorities.

When Ludwig tried to buy Bill Wirtz's Fort Lauderdale condo, he said, Wirtz's brother, with whom Ludwig was dealing, tried to jack up the price on him. He raised the matter with Eagleson. "Al and I were pretty good friends. Al was always involved with real estate. To make a long story short, I had an attorney down here who was just as square as square. My nickname is Rocky. He says, 'Rocky, stop mussing around.' I think Eagleson was handling the Bobby Orr deal at the time. You know, Bobby Orr was going from Boston to Chicago."

Ludwig said he talked to Bill Wirtz about it. "I said, 'I'm down to close this thing. Now you're screwing around.' Everglades House is a quiet condominium. They held too many drunken parties here. It wasn't big enough for him because it wasn't worth a million dollars. In fact, I think I paid him if I remember just under $200,000 cash for the thing. But I gave him a deadline on it and then he decided, you know, to jack the price up."

Ludwig turned to Eagleson. "One call from him closed it up, evidently. Al owed me. It closed in no time. My legal fees with Al Eagleson was absolutely friendship, just like I never charged him anything for the other deals."

Eagleson's neighbors at La Coquille Club Villas made for a fascinating cast of characters. Not long after he purchased his place, in 1980, a villa a few doors away was bought by Howard and Helen Lang, parents of Chris Lang, the long-time Hockey Canada director and former Canada Cup treasurer. On November 11, 1987, a couple of months after the 1987 Canada Cup tournament, the Langs' villa was turned over to their heirs. Others at La Coquille Club Villas included Beland Honderich, then publisher of the *Toronto Star*, and Ralph Wilson, owner of the Buffalo Bills of the NFL.

Eagleson's entry in the *Canadian Who's Who* notes that he was on the board of directors of a company called Teledyne Canada. Since it was a public company, I asked Bruce Dowbiggin to buy one share. Through information available to shareholders, we discovered that Eagleson had been a director from June 19, 1973, to November 5, 1975, and again from May 26, 1977, to the spring of 1993. According to records provided by the corporate controller of the company, Eagleson owned 1,000 shares — the only director with shares. He'd been paid $8,000 in fees the previous year.

Teledyne Canada's businesses include metal fabrication and industrial services. The company produces sod cutters, harvesters, fork-lift trucks, bus bodies, and farming equipment. It also manufactures mobile equipment and machinery for mining and construction. Teledyne Canada's parent company is Teledyne Inc., based in Los Angeles, which in May 1993 owned 76 percent of the Canadian subsidiary.

Teledyne Inc. produced, among other things, shower massages, Apache helicopter bodies, and jet engine metal. The company was charged with defense fraud by the U.S. Justice Department and paid a $4.3-million settlement in 1989. In another fraud case, Teledyne pled guilty on November 9, 1992, to falsifying tests on parts used in weapons and in the space shuttle; bribing foreign officials; and selling zirconium, a metal resembling titanium that turned up in Iraqi cluster bombs. Teledyne was fined $17.6 million, a record sum in a U.S. criminal defense fraud case. As of August 1995, other fraud cases against Teledyne are being litigated.

Why was Eagleson a director of Teledyne Canada? Presumably he brought something more to the company than hockey expertise. He was a global traveler and power broker with international deal-making experience and important political ties, of course, but I was unable to discover exactly how or why he had been appointed to Teledyne Canada's board. I was intrigued to note that another of his neighbors at Manalapan was retired General Alexander Haig, chief of staff to President Richard Nixon during Watergate and President Ronald Reagan in the 1980s.

In the mid- and late 1980s, at the time Eagleson became an officer and then president of La Coquille Club Villas, Eagleson and his wife were close to a woman named Judy Stedman and her husband. The two couples had known each other eight or nine years, Judy Stedman told me when I tracked her down in Naples, Florida. They met playing tennis, and she and Nancy Eagleson became close friends.

"They invited us to the Canada Cup in 1987," she recalled. "My husband went, my former husband. Alan invited several couples." She described Eagleson as "very charming" and was aware that he had been mentioned in the newspapers as being the focus of an FBI investigation. "I'd like to think he was a Robin Hood type of person."

Judy Stedman steered me to her now-estranged husband, Kim Stedman, whose acoustical tile business was based in Deerfield Beach, Florida, and who was living near Houston, Texas. Stedman, originally from Winnipeg, confirmed that he had gone to the 1987 Canada Cup tournament as Eagleson's guest. "I was kind of privileged because I sat between the general manager of the Philadelphia Flyers, Bobby Clarke, and the manager of the Edmonton team, Glen Sather, up in the box. Alan introduced us as guests."

Stedman was a long-time hockey fan. "I was following hockey very closely during that period so Alan and I used to talk hockey. It was always interesting to me when he would offer some of the personals about players and so forth." He recalled staying at the Westin Harbour Castle Hotel in Toronto during his 1987 Canada Cup visit, but did not recall whether he paid for the room. (The Westin Harbour Castle bought end-board advertising in the 1987 tournament through All Canada Sports Promotions, a company run by Eagleson and Irving Ungerman.) Stedman recalled that at least two other couples from Manalapan attended the tournament as Eagleson's guests. "As I see it, it was the spreading of goodwill. I feel that's what Alan was doing — business entertainment."

It wasn't Eagleson's money to throw around. Hockey Canada, the NHLPA, and the NHL were to share in profits from Canada Cup games. Money that went to "business entertainment" was money that didn't make it to the bottom line. And the players, at that time, could not find out what was being spent in the name of Eagleson's expenses.

"I don't think he invited just anybody to those things," Stedman said. "I think he felt there was the possibility that successful business investments for the union may come out of this, and we did talk on occasion on those kind of bases. I was trying to get involved with an acoustical ceiling product with Alan. I didn't know where the investment may be coming from. I made a presentation to Alan, principally. I told him about it, but that was about all. He wasn't much interested, so I dropped the idea. I was really looking for him to invest. Nonetheless, it was a good trip."

Stedman also remembered Eagleson inviting him to a Players' Association summer meeting at the Breakers Hotel in Palm Beach and sitting at

Eagleson's table at dinner. Recalling the players' coup of 1989, Stedman said, "I can tell you the hurt he felt when Gretzky didn't support him, because I was with him — the hurt when some of these top players didn't support him." He added that he believed Eagleson was highly respected — "He was very close friends with the prime minister" — and that there was a side to him most people didn't see. "He does things he doesn't want people to know about," Stedman said, "and he does them really just out of the kindness of his heart."

12

FOREIGN EXCHANGE

"Neither I, nor any member of my family, nor any company with which I am associated, has ever received money directly or indirectly from any international hockey event."
ALAN EAGLESON

NOT LONG AFTER THE Bruins reunion in 1990, at a charity golf tournament, I began asking current and former NHL players if they could dig up any information they had about Canada Cup events. It soon became clear that they were as unclear about Canada Cup financials as they were about NHLPA expenses. "We can't get them," Andy Moog told me, lining up a putt. "Eagleson says they belong to Hockey Canada. There have been reports with one-line income numbers from Canada Cups and international hockey, but never any full breakdowns of revenues and expenses."

Stopping by the Bruins' offices adjacent to the Boston Garden one day, I asked Tom Johnson, the Bruins vice president, if he knew where I could find Canada Cup financials for, say, the 1987 tournament. Johnson hummed and hawed. He assured me that everything had to be on the up-and-up because Hockey Canada was responsible for keeping Canada Cup tournament financial records, and Hockey Canada had nonprofit status from the Canadian government. Undoubtedly the financials were scrutinized closely. He also made the point that player pensions were enriched by money raised at Canada Cup tournaments and international events, including the exhibition tours in which the Soviets played NHL teams. But no, he said, he had never actually seen a Canada Cup tournament financial breakdown. He suggested I ask Harry Sinden, the Bruins president and general manager. Sinden said he had never seen one either. But, he said, the NHL's front office got a financial report. It was up to NHL president John Ziegler to monitor the financial details of Canada Cup events.

Ziegler tap-danced around the question when I interviewed him in Manhattan in 1991. "Are Hockey Canada and Canada Cup financial statements available to NHL players?" I asked.

"I don't know, you'd have to ask Hockey Canada," he replied, a strange answer considering that the NHLPA, like the NHL, had contractual agreements with Hockey Canada. How could business partners not share financial information?

Then again, when former Bruin player rep Dave Forbes had asked Eagleson for Canada Cup financials in late 1990, he'd been turned down cold. "He said that information was none of my business and that these records would not be available to me," Forbes recalled. "He then said that any and all dealings he has had with international hockey have been as a member of the board of Hockey Canada and as a result felt it was none of my business. I said, 'Alan, that's really interesting. Who was there representing the players if you were there representing Hockey Canada?'"

Brad Park, the former NHLPA vice president, told me Canada Cup numbers were "a mystery" when he was a player. "To tell the truth, I don't think we made much of an issue about it. The subject was discussed, how much did our pensions go up because of playing, but Eagle always fluffed that stuff off. He'd say, 'Whatever it is, it is. What the hell. You guys play and you get something out of it. I don't get a dime. I put the Canada Cup together for you guys, not me.'"

Despite assuring the players that he received no benefit from international hockey, Eagleson used his position as NHLPA boss, chief international hockey negotiator for Canada, and de facto head of Hockey Canada to line his own pockets. As long as the owners allowed him to use NHL stars in international exhibitions, and as long as he could persuade the players they owed it to their country and their pension fund to participate, he had what he needed to stage high-profile exhibitions. Some people felt that the owners allowed their players to participate with the expectation that Eagleson would remember the favor when it came time to negotiate a new collective bargaining agreement.

Eagleson, of course, had been the driving force behind international hockey ever since he orchestrated the 1972 series decided by Paul Henderson's famous goal with thirty-two seconds remaining in the final game in Moscow. As chairman of Hockey Canada's International Committee, he organized five Canada Cup tournaments between 1976 and 1991. As far back as 1976, Hockey Canada agreements called for payments to his businesses for secretarial services and office rent.

Several of Eagleson's associates also worked on the 1976 Canada Cup under agreements with Eagleson and his agency business, Sports Management Limited. Under one contract, Eagleson provided Howard Ungerman and two secretaries to Hockey Canada. The agreement called for an unspecified hourly fee for the services of Ungerman, who later became his law partner, as well as half the pay for two secretaries.

Marvin Goldblatt, who helped run Sports Management Limited, was made comptroller of the 1976 Canada Cup under an agreement calling for $20,000 plus "additional compensation." The agreement did not specify whether the payments would be made to Goldblatt or to Sports Management. Hockey Canada also contracted to pay Sports Management for the services of a receptionist and an accountant. The accountant was Sam Simpson, Eagleson's director of operations for the NHLPA. In 1987, Simpson signed a $72,000 agreement to serve as comptroller and "liaison to Team Canada" for the 1987 Canada Cup.

A board of directors, including Canadian political and civic leaders, was supposed to oversee the workings of Hockey Canada, but the board members — who lacked Eagleson's grasp of the hockey world, and who were mainly his friends — were largely content to allow him almost autocratic rule. (Asked in 1991 how to reach Hockey Canada's International Committee, Team Canada publicist Bill Tuele told me: "You write to Alan Eagleson at Eagleson Ungerman. There's no other office.") Before the 1991 tournament, in a joke that contained more than a grain of truth, Eagleson himself was quoted by *The Hockey News* as saying "One of the great things about the Canada Cup is that it's run by a very small committee — me."

My first clue about the dubiousness of Eagleson's claim that he didn't receive money from international hockey turned up in the footnotes in Hockey Canada's 1987 financial report. One note said: "Mr. Eagleson received reimbursement of office expenses under his contract with the Canada Cup 1987," but did not specify the amount. The financial reports also showed that Hockey Canada paid $636,000 between 1990 and 1992 to unnamed "directors and other related parties." The payments were for consulting, management, secretarial, and other office services.

For the four years leading up to the 1991 Canada Cup, Eagleson and his law firm had agreements with Hockey Canada worth $445,000 in fees and expenses. That did not include other expenses he charged Hockey Canada, including travel and promotion. In 1988, he signed a three-year agreement with the Canada Cup of Hockey, an arm of Hockey Canada, calling for payment of office expenses related to his work on international hockey events. The payments included $1,000 a month for rental of office space at 37 Maitland Street.

The 1988 agreement also called for payments to Eagleson of 12 percent of his business taxes, postage, photocopying costs, and phone bills from 1988 through 1990. A separate three-year agreement called for the Canada Cup to pay his law firm $18,000 a year "to retain the services of your secretaries and receptionist in connection with the carrying on of our business of organizing and administering international hockey tournaments."

By the terms of the 1991 agreement, Hockey Canada agreed to rent office space at Maitland House for $2,400 a month, payable to Eagleson Ungerman. The agreement also gave a detailed breakdown of what Hockey Canada was to get for its rent money, including:

- 50 percent of Eagleson's own office space;
- 90 percent of his permanent law secretary's office space and 95 percent of his part-time secretary's space;
- 50 percent of the office space used by his son's secretary;
- 20 percent of the Maitland House basement storage space;
- a third each of the reception and photocopying areas.

Hockey Canada also agreed in 1991 to pay 35 percent of all the law firm's phone bills and postage costs. In addition, Hockey Canada was to pay Eagleson's law firm 15 percent of its 1991 real estate taxes, business taxes, heating and utility costs. All payments were to be made by Hockey Canada on receipt of "a written request" from Eagleson Ungerman.

A separate 1991 agreement between Hockey Canada and Eagleson's law firm called for payment of $18,000 a month — $216,000 for the year — for secretaries, a receptionist, and bookkeeping. Once again, the agreement gave a breakdown of what Hockey Canada was buying:

- 90 percent of the time of Eagleson's personal secretary;
- 95 percent of the time of Eagleson's part-time secretary;
- 50 percent of the time of the secretary for another lawyer in Eaglson's law firm;
- 50 percent of the time of a bookkeeper and a receptionist.

The agreement also required Hockey Canada to pay 95 percent of the estimated $100,000 salary the law firm was paying Eagleson's son, Trevor Allen Eagleson, plus all expenses for the younger Eagleson's services as "Director of Administration for Canada Cup 1991." Hockey Canada also agreed to pay Eagleson's law firm 55 percent of the cost of the salary and benefits of another lawyer in the firm who would attend to Canada Cup matters in July, August, and September, 1991. That Eagleson employee was Timothy J. Lemay.

One of the Hockey Canada agreements specified that Lemay was to spend about 40 percent of his time between July and September in 1991 on Canada Cup business. Hockey Canada, in other words, was paying 55 percent of his salary and benefits in return for 40 percent of his time. Lemay was Trevor Allen Eagleson's brother-in-law (Lemay was married to the sister of Trevor Allen's wife). He was also an employee of Eagleson Ungerman. Hockey Canada was essentially subsidizing Eagleson Ungerman.

Lemay declined to answer my questions about his role at Hockey Canada, though I did learn that one of his duties was to help run a Canada Cup golf tournament. Howard Ungerman, Eagleson's employee, who signed the 1991 Canada Cup agreements on behalf of the firm, also declined requests for an interview.

With Eagleson running the show, international hockey tournaments also led to handsome agreements for three of his associates: Sam Simpson, Chris Lang, and Marvin Goldblatt. Eagleson, his employee Goldblatt, and his long-time associate Lang all contracted with Hockey Canada to help run the international competitions. Each then, acting as an agent of either Hockey Canada or the Canada Cup, contracted the other two.

In 1988, for example, Hockey Canada signed an agreement with Christopher Lang & Associates for Lang's "financial expertise." Lang, also a Hockey Canada director, signed the agreement on behalf of Lang & Associates; Eagleson and Goldblatt signed on behalf of Hockey Canada. The four-year agreement called for Hockey Canada to pay $3,500 a month to Lang's company for three years, then $7,000 a month in 1991, when the tournament took place. Hockey Canada would also pay all "reasonable expenses" on top of the $210,000 in fees.

Lang had been involved with Eagleson in international hockey since 1972; a previous Canada Cup agreement had called for payment of $15,000 for his services as treasurer of the 1976 tournament. He also had agreements to provide financial expertise to other Hockey Canada international teams in the 1980s, and financial services to the 1987 Canada Cup tournament.

Eagleson and Lang also had business and personal ties. Lang, as mentioned, was president of Campbell Manufacturing Company Limited, a sports equipment manufacturer related to Pony Sporting Goods Limited, the company to which Rick Middleton's money was invested. Pony's directors included Alan Eagleson; investors in Pony included an Eagleson family business, Nanjill Investments, and a number of hockey players represented by Eagleson. On the personal side, of course, Eagleson was a neighbor of Lang's parents at La Coquille Club Villas in Florida.

Also in 1988, Lang and Eagleson, on behalf of Hockey Canada, contracted Marvin Goldblatt to provide "accounting services and to supervise the financial staff" for international hockey tournaments. Goldblatt's deal was the same as Lang's: three years at $3,500 per month, a fourth year at $7,000 a month, plus expenses.

Completing the tight circle, Lang and Goldblatt, on behalf of Hockey Canada, signed agreements with Eagleson in 1988 that covered his office expenses as promoter of the 1991 Canada Cup and other international events. Lang and Goldblatt, again on behalf of Hockey Canada, also signed a four-year, $210,000 agreement with NHLPA employee Sam Simpson, hiring him as comptroller for the Canada Cup. At the time, Simpson served under Eagleson as director of operations for the NHLPA. (Simpson maintained that the Players' Association was reimbursed $240,000 for his services and another $100,000 for Eagleson's expenses related to international hockey. A financial statement supplied by Simpson reflects those payments.)

Goldblatt, a long-time employee of one of Eagleson's businesses, was to provide "accounting services and supervise the financial staff" for the 1991 Canada Cup. Goldblatt's original four-year agreement with Hockey Canada was terminated after three years, and a new agreement, to pay Rae-Con for Goldblatt's services, was signed. I could not find the reasons for upgrading the deal, and Goldblatt refused my requests for an interview.

Under the new agreement, Hockey Canada agreed to pay Rae-Con $7,000 a month "plus benefits and expenses" for Goldblatt's services as director of finance for the 1991 Cup. Hockey Canada also agreed to pay all Rae-Con secretarial and office rental expenses. Rae-Con, of course, was also located at 37 Maitland Street, where Hockey Canada was already renting office space. The new deal guaranteed Goldblatt a car and all expenses, "including entertainment and promotional expenses."

The Rae-Con agreement was signed for Hockey Canada by Chris Lang and Hockey Canada chairman H. Ian Macdonald, former president of Toronto's York University, which operates the R. Alan Eagleson Sports Clinic.

Exactly how much money Eagleson and the others actually collected under all these agreements remains a mystery, since Hockey Canada financial statements as of 1992 still gave no breakdown of expenses. The statements do show that office, secretarial, and consulting services cost Hockey Canada close to a million dollars between 1989 and 1992.

Eagleson's 1987 contract with the NHLPA entitled him to a $25,000 bonus in any year the NHLPA's share of international hockey revenues exceeded $600,000, and the 1987 and 1991 Cups both topped that mark. Along with the bonus, the contract called for Eagleson to be paid a $100,000 consulting fee for his work on international hockey in 1992, after he stepped down as head of the union, and for reimbursement of his international hockey expenses.

Eagleson even stood to make money on his secretary. His contract with the players' union called for the NHLPA to pay "60% of the salary, benefits and other costs" of his secretary, to a maximum of $20,000 U.S. a year. His contract to organize the 1991 Canada Cup, meanwhile, required Hockey Canada to pay his law firm $18,000 a month for the services of various staff members. The agreement specified that Eagleson's secretary would devote 90 percent of her time "to service the Canada Cup 1991."

It is not known how much the secretary was actually paid in 1991, or how her workload was apportioned. She, too, declined to be interviewed. From union records, I learned that the secretary, Patti (Wylie) George, born in Scotland, had been making $35,360 a year as of March 1, 1993. If the Players' Association was already paying her up to $20,000 U.S. (about $25,000 Canadian at the time) for 60 percent of her time, why was Hockey Canada paying her to spend 90 percent of her time on 1991 Canada Cup work? You can only work 100 percent of the time, but Eagleson had arranged it so that, between the union and Hockey Canada, his firm was being remunerated as if she were working 150 percent of the time.

After Eagleson's legal problems came to light, Patti George and her husband moved to Trinidad.

THIS NEAT LITTLE TRICK of making money on his employees was not new. Among the first Eagleson employees pressed into service for the 1976 Canada Cup tournament were Bill Watters and Rick Curran. Watters, of course, is now assistant general manager of the Maple Leafs. Curran, once a hockey player at Merrimack College in North Andover, Massachusetts, is now a sports agent based in Philadelphia. In 1976, both were employed by the Eagleson company, Sports Management Limited, while also working at the Orr–Walton Sports Camp.

Eagleson added them both to the Hockey Canada payroll. By 1977, the nonprofit organization was paying Watters as general manager of Canada's international team in the world championship competition, and Curran as travel coordinator for its junior world championship team. Watters said his Hockey Canada salary totaled more than $100,000 between 1977 and 1979. But he said the money was deducted from the salary he was supposed to be paid to operate Sports Management.

"International hockey was paying me to administer not only the tournaments and their responsibilities but Eagleson's company as well," Watters said. Hockey Canada work, he said, took only two or three months. "The Hockey Canada money I was getting, it paid me for my Sports Management job also. That's exactly what Al did. The company saved paying me whatever Hockey Canada paid me. It's that simple. In effect, Hockey Canada was saving money for Sports Management."

Curran, too, said he had to turn over his Hockey Canada pay. When the checks came in from Hockey Canada, he was instructed by Marvin Goldblatt to endorse them and turn them over. "What was happening is Hockey Canada was paying us a salary," Curran explained, "but during that time period we were also doing our own business for Alan." Curran said he did not know if anybody at Hockey Canada, other than Eagleson, knew of the arrangement.

One chartered accounting report, issued to Eagleson concerning the Orr–Walton Sports Camp, noted that Curran was paid $14,000 in 1977 and 1978 for camp business, but that the camp had been paid $19,500 by Hockey Canada "during this period" for Curran's services. Eagleson, of course, was a partner in Bobby Orr Enterprises, the company that owned the camp.

Eagleson did not dispute making money by renting employees to Hockey Canada when the arrangement first came to light in the 1984 *Sports Illustrated* story. "The guy works for me, and if I can put him to work and make a million dollars, it's my million dollars, not his....If I pay my guy 30 (thousand) and rent him for 50, that makes me smart."

Eagleson neatly skipped over some ethical, moral, and legal issues in that explanation. First, Eagleson himself had effective control of Hockey Canada. Second, Hockey Canada should have had to account for its expenses, answering whether services were purchased as efficiently as possible. After all, Hockey Canada benefited from taxpayers' money, and it was offsetting some of Eagleson's private-business payroll. Third, Eagleson did not disclose to the players his hidden interests in Canada Cup events. On the contrary, he claimed neither he, nor his family, nor any company with which he was associated had benefited from any international hockey event, a claim made in letters mailed from Canada to the United States — grounds for mail fraud charges in the States.

Rick Curran had other fascinating experiences in international hockey. He said that in the late 1970s, while in Europe during an international hockey event, he flew with Arthur Harnett, on Eagleson's instructions, carrying a pouch of money to an airport in Zurich. He said he met with an unidentified man to whom he gave the money. Curran said he had no idea what the money was for, but that it came from a hotel room, where it had been counted following a game the night before.

Curran also said that Derek Holmes, the executive director of Hockey Canada from 1974 to 1980, would know about Eagleson's Swiss bank connections, and that Holmes had left Hockey Canada after questioning Eagleson's handling of international hockey business.

Holmes, a meticulous, multilingual, silver-haired man, recalled Eagleson's dominance of the other Hockey Canada directors. "The board from time to time questioned various things within budgets — 'Why was this amount of money necessary?' Al's answer would always be, 'Listen, I raised it. I'll tell you how we're going to spend it.'" Board members were generally well-meaning people, Holmes said, interested in the overall good of hockey. But they never challenged Eagleson. "You might get verbally smacked and frozen out. He always had an answer whether it was adequate or not." Holmes eventually grew dissatisfied, and less susceptible to the verbal bullying. "I suppose at the end I was less intimidated than a lot of people. He was irritated. I was more of a burden. Maybe that's why I was no longer there after 1980."

IN ALL, THE SECRET HOCKEY CANADA agreements covering the five Canada Cup tournaments called for more than $1.5 million in fees, bonuses, and expenses from international hockey for Eagleson and companies and people close to him. Among the players, the reaction was one of stunned outrage. Ray Bourque, the Bruins captain who played in all three Canada Cup tournaments in the 1980s, spoke for many when he learned what had gone on behind the scenes of past Canada Cup tournaments. He remembered Eagleson's pitch when recruiting players: "He always told us he was doing it for the love of hockey, for Canada, for pride in our country, for our pensions — and we should, too. We believed him."

"I never knew about any of those agreements," said the Bruins' Harry Sinden. "It stinks to the high heavens and I'd tell Al the same thing. It's embarrassing to people who care about this game. I don't know if it's illegal, but there's too much smoke coming out of this thing for there not to be a fire somewhere."

Bob Goodenow, the new head of the players' union, said after reading our September 1993 *Eagle-Tribune* report: "The Hockey Canada board lost control of its operation and expenses for Canada Cups to Alan, Marvin Goldblatt, Sam Simpson, and Chris Lang. That's what it shows."

When agents Ron Salcer of Los Angeles and Rich Winter of Edmonton learned of the agreements, they told me I had confirmed the concerns they had raised in 1989. "The people I feel worst for now," Salcer said, "the outrageous part of all of this, are those players of the 1980s who were misled into trusting him, believing they were playing in international hockey events with all profits going to their pensions, while Eagleson kept saying he never benefited."

"I've expected something like this since we first started asking questions," said Winter. "It was obvious something was wrong because we couldn't get answers. Eagleson never thought any of this would see the light of day. It's about time. The documentation we were denied is finally coming out in the open."

When Salcer and Winter had first pressed Eagleson for detailed information on international hockey finances in the late 1980s, Eagleson, in response, had invited all hockey agents to a meeting on May 15, 1989, in Toronto. Eagleson promised the agents would hear "all financial details" of all international hockey series between 1972 and 1987 involving NHL union members.

At that meeting, presentations were made by Chris Lang and Sam Simpson — whose contract with the players' union, incidentally, specifically called for him to answer all questions from players. In a letter to the agents shortly after the meeting, Eagleson claimed that Simpson had, as promised, "presented a full statement on all receipts from international hockey and how the money was spent....Mr. Chris Lang, Treasurer of Hockey Canada, presented Canada Cup statements to the meeting."

According to agents and lawyers who attended, however, no mention was made of the Hockey Canada agreements with Eagleson, Simpson, and Lang. "It's outrageous, that they'd have all these agreements and not disclose them to us," said Mike Barnett, Wayne Gretzky's agent. "Information was the whole point of that meeting and now, just finding out about them tells me they were holding back."

Steve Bartlett, an agent from Rochester, New York, recalled Lang's presentation. "I remember him getting up there, spouting off, assuring us there were no improprieties....I think those agreements would have a little bit to bear on what was going on. Those agreements were pertinent. If you're going to give all financial details of Canada Cup and international hockey events, give all financial details. I mean agreements between Hockey Canada and the executive director of the union, the director of operations of the union, the man giving the presentation himself — they're all pertinent financial details."

"In blind faith, what was presented was accepted," said Rollie Thompson, who attended on behalf of himself and his partner Bob Murray of Boston. "It was a general overview of what was going on. We were never informed of those agreements for payments." Thompson said he left the meeting satisfied with the international hockey accounting. When he learned from the *Eagle-Tribune* of the agreements, he was livid: "I had players in that, players who took part in international hockey events."

Bill Dermody attended with fellow lawyer John Agro, representing players disenchanted with Eagleson's leadership. "I remember it well," Dermody recalled. "Mr. Lang didn't disclose any agreements. Now we've found out why. If they'd stood up there and revealed the information about their agreements, that would have been it. Eagleson had already gone on record with a letter to players saying neither he, nor his family, nor any company he was associated with, had received money directly or indirectly from international hockey."

"That's the first I knew of Hockey Canada agreements with Alan Eagleson, in your articles," said Lou Oppenheim, an agent based in New York. "Canada Cup, and international hockey, was to benefit the players' pensions. That's what he always said. That's the reason they played." Of the May 15 meeting and follow-up letter, Oppenheim said, "They just tried to tell everybody, 'Trust us, trust us, trust us.' They tried to bury everything. It's obvious now why. Had they revealed those agreements, I honestly believe [Eagleson] wouldn't have physically been able to leave that meeting."

Hockey Canada president Ron Robison was caught off guard by our newspaper pieces about international hockey. Reached in Calgary, he said, "I'm quite surprised at the documentation. I'm quite surprised at the depth of it. It's all quite accurate." Robison told me an internal investigation of past business practices, including Eagleson's expenses, would be wrapped up by early October 1993, after review by the board of directors. (He had confirmed Eagleson's resignation from Hockey Canada a few weeks after our February 1993 report, saying that Eagleson would be welcomed back if the internal investigation found no wrongdoing.) Robison had first said the internal investigation would be done in May; then June; then it would be completed by early fall. After further revelations about Eagleson's Canada Cup agreements were published in the *Eagle-Tribune*, however, Hockey Canada suspended its internal investigation altogether, citing high costs.

"These are things we just didn't know," said Murray Costello, the Canadian Amateur Hockey Association president, who added that any future international hockey undertaking by the CAHA would not involve Eagleson. "Eagleson certainly has lost all credibility within the IIHF [International Ice Hockey Federation] community. He was presenting himself as not benefiting from international hockey, when in fact he was. We'll decide on a future Canada Cup with the Players' Association."

The agreements and financial details came as a shock to Costello. "We have never seen those numbers," he said. He shook his head and took a deep breath when asked what he thought of Canada Cup expenses in the 1980s. "All I know," he said, obviously agitated, "is that none of those monies ever came back into the development of the game in Canada through our organization. From our standpoint, that's the shame of it."

IT WASN'T THE FIRST TIME Costello had been let down by Alan Eagleson. Back in 1976, the CAHA had been promised $1 million in return for its support of the first Canada Cup tournament. Hockey Canada needed the CAHA's support to get the IIHF to sanction the event and allow teams from other countries to play in it.

Don Johnson, the CAHA president at the time, struck a "gentleman's agreement" with Eagleson, who was organizing the tournament. "I never saw a written agreement," said Johnson, now retired in St. John's, Newfoundland. "There never was one that I know of, only a handshake. I dealt with honorable people. I trusted Mr. Eagleson."

Johnson said the CAHA was promised $1 million from 1976 Canada Cup revenue for youth hockey programs in Canada. He said he decided not to take the money in a lump sum but to let Hockey Canada bank it and pay the interest to the CAHA. "The reason — get this clear — we did not get the money is not Mr. Eagleson or Hockey Canada," he said. "It is because Don Johnson of Newfoundland wouldn't take it."

Why not? "For two reasons. We got grants from the government, for one. I was afraid to lose the federal money — about $200,000 to $250,000 at the time. Secondly, all I was interested in was getting $100,000 a year in interest from the $1 million in the bank forever. I wanted to leave a legacy for minor hockey development. To help our instruction and development programs with youth hockey players who need to learn the skills of the game. That's quite a legacy, don't you think? A hundred thousand dollars a year to the young people of hockey forever."

Hockey Canada financial records show that a $1-million fund was set up on November 26, 1976, with the notation "interest income on this fund may be contributed from time to time to the Canadian Amateur Hockey Association." CAHA financial records show that the CAHA collected its first interest payment, $108,000, in July 1978. Another $90,000 was paid in January 1979.

In early 1979, Costello succeeded Don Johnson as CAHA president. He had other ideas about the million dollars. He wanted Hockey Canada to turn it over to the CAHA immediately. "We couldn't understand why Hockey Canada should be permitted to hold on to $1 million, which we could be using for our minor hockey development programs." He and Gordon Renwick, another CAHA official, said that when the CAHA tried to claim the money, Eagleson refused to turn it over unless the CAHA agreed to surrender control of all Canadian amateur and international hockey programs, including the Olympics. The CAHA declined. Hockey Canada stopped interest payments on the $1 million. The CAHA sued Hockey Canada and Eagleson. An out-of-court settlement was reached in early 1982. The CAHA finally received its $1 million, plus about $94,000 in interest, in June 1982, almost six years after the 1976 Canada Cup.

Including earlier interest payments, the CAHA received a total of about $1.3 million for its Canada Cup return. Hockey Canada was granted another $246,000 as part of the settlement, bringing the total payout to something over $1.5 million. Costello did not question the figures at the time. "There was considerable pressure being put on by the sport minister of the day, Gerry Regan, to have the feud over these matters between Hockey Canada and the CAHA settled," Costello recalled. "He, in fact, called a meeting where the ultimate agreement was reached on how these monies would be divided. It happened right in his office."

Regan told Kathryn May of the *Ottawa Citizen*, with whom I was collaborating: "We were interested in the fact that the organizations involved in hockey shouldn't be feuding and should get along, so we acted as an honest broker to try and get an agreement between them. Hockey Canada seemed to be moving in and doing all the international hockey, and there needed to be some straightening out of that. So we had some meetings that involved Gordon Renwick and Murray Costello, and Alan Eagleson from Hockey Canada." Regan recalled that Supreme Court Justice Willard Estey, Hockey Canada's chairman and director at the time — and a close friend of Eagleson's — may have attended that meeting.

"I never went to that meeting," Justice Estey told me. "I'm positive I never attended a meeting in Regan's office. I refereed the rows on the board."

When asked about particulars of the settlement, Estey replied: "Chris Lang was secretary-treasurer of Hockey Canada and that fell under him. I wasn't interested in this agreement as long as we got our share. I presume we did it all through the auditor."

How had the million dollars been invested while in the care of Hockey Canada? "Chris Lang should know all about that," said Estey, "how it was invested or where it was invested. I sure don't." (Lang refused my interview requests.)

Court records in the CAHA lawsuit revealed that a $1-million certificate had been invested with Montreal Trust in the name of "The Hockey Canada Trust." It was due to mature January 19, 1983. The eventual payout from the five-year certificate — $1.5 million — is less than would have been earned from simple bank interest and far less than from government of Canada treasury bills.

In 1981, interest rates on T-bills in Canada averaged 20.37 percent. Eagleson was quite aware of the good returns. The bank statements and management records of former Bruin Rick Middleton, whose finances were supervised by Eagleson's management company, show that, as an agent, Eagleson was profitably investing the money of his clients in the higher-paying investment vehicles.

Lorraine Mahoney, the benefit and pension adviser, agreed that the CAHA would have received more money on the $1 million had the investment been wisely managed. "It would make sense and be sound money management to move $1 million from an account returning 9 percent to a savings or T-bill account returning 15 or 16 percent," she said. "That $1 million in 1977 just shrunk with inflation erosion, not to mention serious missed opportunities with better interest rates available in those years."

"Who was watching the investment of $1 million?" said Murray Costello. "That's a good question. Whoever it was certainly did a poor job for our CAHA return. Why would anybody allow that money to be locked up at something like 9 percent for five years when it could have made much more?"

Why indeed? I said I'd look into it, and Costello give me CAHA approval to research the history of the investment with Montreal Trust. The trust company also required the approval of Hockey Canada, however, and Hockey Canada blocked the move. Why? Ron Robison would only say that the information was "confidential."

13

NOWHERE TO HIDE

"Eagleson initiated these actions in an effort to
conceal his unlawful activities from U.S.
and Canadian authorities."
RCMP REPORT

A REVIEW OF FINANCIALS from all five Canada
Cup tournaments between 1976 and 1991 showed that, collectively, they
generated $42.3 million in revenues, primarily through ticket sales and the
sale of TV and advertising rights. Expenses totaled about $29.6 million —
about 70 cents of every dollar taken in.

The percentage of money that went into expenses was lowest for the
first tournament, in 1976. That year, expenses consumed $2.8 million of the
$6.2 million in reported revenue, about 45 cents on the dollar. The figure
climbed to 76 cents on the dollar for the 1981 Canada Cup, 78 cents for the
1984 cup, 72 cents in 1987, and 71 cents in 1991. From all five tournaments, Hockey Canada, the NHL, and the NHLPA shared total profits of
$12.3 million — about 29 cents on the dollar. (The total included a share for
the old World Hockey Association Players' Association in 1976.) The players'
share was approximately 11 cents on the dollar.

Little information is available to explain where all the expense money
went. The Canada Cup financial statement for 1976, for example, lists only
four categories of expenses: series costs ($1.9 million), Team Canada expen-
ses ($386,000), Team USA expenses ($214,000), and prizes ($322,000). The

statements for the tournaments of 1981, 1984, 1987, and 1991 are some-what more detailed. For those four tournaments, management services and office and administrative expenses alone totaled $3.16 million — almost as much as went to the players in those years. Promotional costs totaled anoth-er $881,778 between 1981 and 1991, while expenses for accommodations, meals, and travel were $3.5 million. Expenses for Team Canada and Team USA were $5.7 million for the four tournaments; arena rentals and commis-sions were a little over $3.6 million.

Those figures do not include the expenses of Hockey Canada's Interna-tional Committee, led by Eagleson, which oversaw Canada Cup tournament planning and organization. According to 1987 and 1988 Hockey Canada statements, International Committee expenses for those years totaled $1.9 million, including $795,298 for salaries and benefits, $323,078 for office expenses, $154,368 for accommodations and meals, and $108,836 for insurance and other costs. Prior to the 1991 Canada Cup, the International Committee spent $630,835 on administration, $590,723 on operating costs, and $28,959 on "committee" expenses. The financial statements do not show how the money was spent. Expenses are shown only as one-line categories.

International hockey would not have been a cash cow without the NHL stars, who received nominal pay to play for Team Canada and Team USA. They believed that both the NHL and NHLPA profits from international hockey would enhance player pensions — so they had been told by Eagleson and by former NHL president John Ziegler. In a written response to my questions in 1993, however, former NHL president Gil Stein said he knew of no such agreement involving the league.

The NHLPA, on the other hand, was definitely obligated to pay into the pension fund. As mentioned, under the agreement negotiated by Eagleson the union was required to pay 25 percent of contributions out of its share of international hockey profits. Only if there were no profits did the owners have to pick up the whole tab. I could find no NHL players who were aware of this wrinkle. Critics of Eagleson understandably called this arrangement a bad deal for the players, and further proof that Eagleson was in bed with the NHL bosses.

For the three Canada Cup series of the 1980s — in 1981, 1984, and 1987

— Hockey Canada financials showed total income of just over $24 million. Included was $7.2 million for TV rights, $1.5 million for other advertising, and $13.6 million in gate receipts. Expenses showed nearly $5 million paid to the IIHF, $2.5 million for arena rentals and commissions, $1.4 million for travel, and close to $1 million for accommodations and meals. Promotion cost a collective $674,319; insurance $429,841; office expenses $414,772; officials $316,654; ground transportation $207,128; equipment $47,270. Team Canada's expenses were just over $2 million while Team USA costs were just over $1.4 million.

This blizzard of numbers simply demonstrates that a great deal of money changed hands whenever Eagleson staged an international tournament, money that may never be fully accounted for. Total profit in the Canada Cup tournaments of 1981, 1984, and 1987 was nearly $6 million. Of that, the NHLPA, Hockey Canada, and the NHL each received less than $2 million. The players, in other words, received about 8 percent of reported income. In my car-racing promotion experience, if we'd ever paid out 8 cents on the dollar in purse money to the drivers, we would have been out of business in no time.

EAGLESON SEEMS TO HAVE HAD a finger in every pie, large and small. Marty Alsemgeest, a Toronto clothier, had been both a client and a business partner of Eagleson's (Bobby Orr Enterprises had been a part owner of Marty's in Toronto). In the 1980s, Alsemgeest received Canada Cup and NHLPA business, which was done by gift certificates. What bothered Alsemgeest, he said, was that Eagleson "would use some certificates issued to the Players' Association for his own clothes, or for friends of his he'd send over. He'd call and say, 'Take care of this guy,' and a little while later I'd be fitting a friend of Al's on a certificate.

"I lost the contracts to Natale's," Alsemgeest said of the 1991 Canada Cup. Eagleson, he said, insisted on special treatment. "By the time you're done, you end up with nothing. Everything becomes a big chisel. I don't have to kiss anybody's ass. It's not the end of the world." Despite Alsemgeest's brave talk, losing the Canada Cup and NHLPA business did sting. "I've got a wife and kids to support," he said. "I'm caught between the devil and the blue sea."

The man who picked up the business also found himself in a tricky spot. Cam Natale outfitted the 1991 Team Canada entourage. His late father, Gene Natale, had built a Toronto clothing business, Natale's Clothiers, and developed a relationship with Eagleson. The 1991 order was for more than $100,000 in clothing — blazers, trousers, ties. In Natale's bill, forwarded to Labatt for payment, were additional invoices for tailored suits for Eagleson himself. Labatt, according to Natale, refused to pay the approximately $28,000 for Eagleson's suits (though he later claimed, after admitting he had spoken to Marvin Goldblatt about me, that the Labatt problem had been resolved). In earlier years, Natale said he saw no problem in tossing in extra clothing for Eagleson. He received compensation in the form of Canada Cup tickets and access to a private box at Copps Coliseum in Hamilton, Ontario, to watch the 1987 Canada Cup games.

Natale also said that Eagleson's son received contra deals — clothing in return for game tickets. Of course, there were some perks for Natale, too, handed out by Eagleson. After the 1987 tournament, Natale said, Eagleson gave him a gold-and-diamond championship ring, a trophy, and a gold watch.

Doing business with Air Canada was also fruitful for Eagleson. At least one Air Canada employee, Aggie Kukulowicz, profited from the relationship. Kukulowicz had worked more than thirty years for Air Canada; he was in the airline's sports bureau in Toronto. At the players' expense, he played golf and went to hockey games. Eagleson used him as a translator for international events — Kukulowicz speaks Russian — for which he received pay from the NHLPA. At one point, he had the use of a Players' Association car, a practice stopped when Bob Goodenow took over the union.

Kukulowicz benefited from Hockey Canada as well, receiving more than $12,000 while on the Air Canada payroll. "Any payments to Mr. Kukulowicz were approved by the board," said Louise Hélène Senecal, a lawyer for Air Canada who issued a statement to me on Kukulowicz's behalf. "Any payment or benefit was reflected on his tax return."

Why was Eagleson generous with Kukulowicz? Perhaps because Air Canada fit nicely into his plans. Eagleson's control of Canada Cup tournaments enabled him to use the airline to benefit himself, his family, and his friends, getting free travel passes in exchange for rink-board advertising.

On March 27, 1987, Air Canada agreed to buy $84,000 in rink-board advertising for the 1987 Canada Cup tournament. Rather than issuing a check, however, Air Canada honored twenty-eight flight passes between March 30, 1987, and December 31, 1989, worth an average $3,000 apiece.

In the fall of 1994, following an internal Hockey Canada inquiry, at least $60,000 in Air Canada tickets were determined to have been used from the Canada Cup tournaments. Tickets converted by Eagleson himself between 1989 and 1993 included three flights to London, two to Frankfurt, one to Zurich, one to Vancouver, two to Chicago, one to Nice, one to Paris, and one to Tampa. Between 1988 and 1991, Eagleson's wife used $37,000 in Air Canada travel passes issued in return for Canada Cup advertising. Her travel included London (eight times), Paris (twice), New York, Frankfurt, and Bombay, India. Eagleson's daughter used Air Canada travel passes worth $9,000 between 1989 and 1991 for trips to Vancouver (twice), Paris, New York, and Bombay. His son, Trevor Allen, traveled four times on the freebies between 1988 and 1992, a $6,000 value. Trevor Allen's wife, Yasmine Eagleson, also used $5,000 in Air Canada passes from the Canada Cup, traveling to London, Winnipeg, and Halifax. Howard Ungerman also took a $1,000 trip to Chicago in 1992 using a pass.

The bottom line, of course, is that the passes did not rightfully belong to Eagleson, his family members, or his friends. They were generated by the efforts of NHLPA players who competed on behalf of Hockey Canada in the Canada Cup, having been persuaded that they were doing so for the good of their pension fund, and — like Eagleson — the honor of their country.

NHL PLAYERS AND AGENTS weren't the only ones who took a keen interest in the *Eagle-Tribune* reports that shed light on Canada Cup finances, Eagleson's lucrative agreements with Hockey Canada, and his Swiss banking connections. On November 21, 1991, while in Zurich, Switzerland, Eagleson himself faxed Patti George and Marvin Goldblatt in Toronto:

Please go through the Russ Conway articles and find the reference and statement by Derek Holmes re Swiss-Bank-accounts.

He says in the article something to the effect that Hockey Canada had a Swiss account and that Eagleson and Chris Lang keep details to themselves.

Send it to Werner Schwarz asap.

Thanks,

R. Alan Eagleson.

The fax was on Cambio Valoren Bank stationery; Werner Schwarz was vice president of the Cambio Valoren Bank, in Zurich, where the International Ice Hockey Federation was based. That fax was the start of Eagleson's attempt to cover up a complex diversion of rink-board advertising money from the 1991 Canada Cup tournament.

Labatt Brewing Company sponsored the 1991 tournament, paying $4.2 million to Hockey Canada for all rights to tournament programs, rink-board advertising, and television advertising. Eagleson negotiated the deal with John Hudson, Labatt's director of media properties. Eagleson told Labatt that end boards during Team Canada games and playoff games were excluded from the deal, because the IIHF had retained them. The end boards are the most valuable advertising panels in a hockey rink because they get the most television exposure.

On behalf of Labatt, Eagleson sold European TV and rink-board rights to a Zurich-based advertising agency, CWL Werbung, and its subsidiary, CWL Telesport. The managing director of CWL Telesport was Volker Kosters. Eagleson explained to Kosters that end boards during Team Canada games and playoff games were excluded from the deal because Labatt had retained them. CWL agreed to pay Labatt $725,000 U.S. for these rights.

The deal with CWL also specified that 40 percent of any profit over $750,000 Canadian earned in CWL's resale of European rink-board and television rights would be given to Hockey Canada. Volker Kosters later testified before a Swiss magistrate that any payments to Hockey Canada were to be made to the Cambio Valoren Bank in Zurich, where Eagleson controlled the Hockey Canada accounts.

By withholding the end-board rights in Team Canada and playoff games from both CWL and Labatt, Eagleson retained them for All Canada Sports Promotions. His long-time friend Irving Ungerman — father of his law firm employee and recipient of NHLPA funds for private property deals — was president of All Canada Sports. Because of the agreements Eagleson, on behalf of Hockey Canada, had negotiated with Labatt and, on behalf of Labatt, had negotiated with CWL Telesport, All Canada Sports was free to sell end-board rights during Team Canada games and playoff games and pocket the money. Nobody would be the wiser.

Eagleson retained help in selling the end boards, contracting Rich Bremner of Core Media in Toronto. In a letter dated April 1, 1991, Eagleson told Bremner that, in the sale of end-board advertising, Core Media was acting as an agent for CWL Telesport. He had, of course, already informed CWL that end boards in Team Canada and playoff games were excluded from the deal. Bremner sold end boards for Team Canada games to five companies — Sony, Alan Candy's, Tim Horton Donuts, Gillette, and Boss Man — at $50,000 each. Withholding a 15 percent commission from the $250,000 gross, Bremner sent All Canada Sports $181,900 on August 28, 1991, and $45,475 on September 30, 1991.

Buss Marketing of Toronto also sold end-board advertising for All Canada Sports. Gary Buss sold $125,000 in end-board ads — to such companies as Microsoft and Canon — turning over $113,687 to All Canada Sports (after deducting commission and GST). Buss also arranged a contra deal with Compaq, whereby laptop computers were exchanged for rink-board ads. Although Irving Ungerman was president of All Canada Sports, Buss said that he dealt only with Eagleson, Eagleson's son, and Labatt representative John Hudson.

On November 28, the Westin Harbour Castle Hotel also paid All Canada Sports $69,550 for two end-board ads in the 1991 Canada Cup. Since neither Core Media nor Buss Marketing seems to have been involved in the Westin sale, it appears that Eagleson may have made the sale himself. The Westin check was deposited in Account 1008-108, All Canada Sports, at the Bank of Montreal at Dupont Street and Symington Avenue in Toronto, around the corner from Irving Ungerman's office.

Between October and early December 1991, in other words, more than $400,000 in end-board money — from Core Media, Buss Marketing, and the Westin Harbour Castle — was paid to All Canada Sports.

In Zurich, meanwhile, the bank accounts were also getting fat. Between March and December 1991, $150,000 from CWL was deposited in the All Canada Sports account (289-576-253) at Cambio Valoren Bank, and $750,000 from CWL went into the Hockey Canada account (289-576-261). Eagleson had control of this $900,000, which was collecting interest in Switzerland.

AFTER THE *EAGLE-TRIBUNE* REPORTS of September 1991, Eagleson clearly grew concerned that the end-board scheme might come to light. In the words of someone with detailed knowledge of both Eagleson and Ungerman at the time, "They panicked." If officials from Hockey Canada, or Labatt, or anyone else started breaking down advertising income, sooner or later the question would arise: Where did the end-board money go? Eagleson decided to unload it from the accounts in Toronto and Zurich before anybody discovered what he had done.

Just before Christmas 1991, Irving Ungerman cleaned out the All Canada Sports account in Toronto — the account in which the end-board money had been deposited. He had one check drawn up for $374,500, payable to Hockey Canada. Another, for $53,500, was made payable to Eagleson Ungerman for "legal fees for closed circuit boxing." A third check, for $37,500, was made payable to Sandhill Construction, a company operated by Ernie Rowley, who had built Eagleson's waterfront home in Collingwood.

While attending a Christmas party at Ungerman's office, Eagleson picked up the three checks — to Hockey Canada, Eagleson Ungerman, and Sandhill Construction. He was unusually nice that day, pulling a pen from his pocket and offering it to an employee of Irving Ungerman. "I knew something was up," said the employee. "He wasn't going to buy me for a pen."

The $374,500 check that Eagleson got from Ungerman was deposited in a "Canada Cup 1991" account in Toronto. A handwritten note on All Canada Sports stationery indicated it was "payment on behalf of CWL towards purchase of board advertising and T.V. rights." In fact, the transaction served to forward money from All Canada Sports to Hockey Canada from the sale of end boards that Eagleson had sliced off for himself.

An undated Hockey Canada invoice to Irving Ungerman's attention at All Canada Sports later directed Ungerman to deposit $374,000 from the sale of rink-board advertising into a "Canada Cup 1991" bank account. A Hockey Canada bank statement and deposit slip revealed that the transaction was made on December 19, 1991. But Hockey Canada's general ledger for the fiscal year ending June 30, 1992, revealed that account number 5010 was credited with $350,500 on that December 19, with another $24,500 going to a GST account, number 3050. The 5010 account, according to the RCMP, was "a revenue account established to record the sale of TV and advertising Rights by Hockey Canada to Labatt. This transaction served to reduce the funds receivable due Hockey Canada from Labatt, in the same amount of $374,500, GST included." In other words, Labatt got to keep $374,500 it actually owed Hockey Canada because Eagleson was unloading his dirty money on Hockey Canada.

A few days after the Christmas party, Eagleson instructed an All Canada Sports employee to destroy the original $37,500 Sandhill Construction invoice and replace it with another, which he would send to be typed. The new bill reflected that the check was payment related not to construction but to rink-board advertising. A few months later — after the FBI had announced it was looking into past hockey business practices, including the Players' Association — Eagleson attended a meeting in Ungerman's office. After that meeting, he instructed that a promissory note for $37,500 be issued to Sandhill Construction. The note was to be backdated; it was to replace the second $37,500 bill for rink-board advertising, which he had ordered to replace the original Sandhill bill indicating payment for construction. The backdated invoice in May 1992 turned the $37,500 into a loan, rather than a rink-board advertising expense.

In the meantime, the bookkeeper at All Canada Sports had also been instructed by Irving Ungerman to turn the $53,500 payment to Eagleson Ungerman for legal expenses into a $53,500 loan from All Canada Sports. Sometimes instructions from Ungerman, or from Eagleson's office, specified that letters be typed with a large open margin at the top. Eagleson had access to several different letterheads: Eagleson Ungerman, Canada Cup, All Canada Sports, NHLPA, Hockey Canada, and probably others. Some of the end-board business came directly from Eagleson's 37 Maitland Street office, with copies faxed to Ungerman's All Canada Sports office.

"Several things happened post Canada Cup 1991," stated an RCMP report by Staff Sergeant John K. Beer, signed by Ontario judge Ramez Khawly on November 2, 1994, that "heightened Eagleson's awareness that his unlawful actions might be discovered by U.S. and Canadian authorities. Investigative Reporter Russ Conway of The Eagle-Tribune, Lawrence, Massachusetts, published a five-part series entitled 'Cracking The Ice' during the latter part of September, 1991, wherein it was alleged that Eagleson was involved in questionable business practices as head of the NHLPA, a Director of Hockey Canada, and Chairman and Chief Negotiator of the Canada Cup. In an article on September 24, 1991, Conway makes a reference to a Swiss bank account that was allegedly set up by Hockey Canada to facilitate international hockey tournaments. I believe that this public mention of a Swiss bank account in late September, 1991, may have caused Eagleson some concern, particularly in light of the fact that on or about September 26, 1991, Eagleson had on deposit at the Cambio Valoren Bank approximately $750,000 Cdn. (excluding interest) that he had received from CWL (Telesport) in a transaction, involving fraud against Labatt....

"A portion of these funds, I believe, was to accrue to Eagleson as criminal proceeds," the RCMP report states. "The evidence in support of my belief that Eagleson was aware of Conway's article is contained in a letter dated November 21, 1991, turned over to Swiss authorities by the Cambio Valoren Bank" — the fax Eagleson sent to his secretary and Marvin Goldblatt from Zurich, on Cambio Valoren stationery, referring to our mention of the Swiss bank account.

What Eagleson hoped to do in late 1991 and early 1992 was talk John Hudson into reissuing a backdated Labatt invoice, talk Volker Kosters of CWL into accepting a new, backdated agreement, and then bite the bullet. Rather than get caught with the end-board money, he'd get rid of it — by giving it back. And he almost pulled it off.

Kosters admitted that, at Eagleson's urging, he signed a new agreement — after our September report, and after the 1991 Canada Cup itself — back-dated to replace the one struck on December 10, 1990. The new agreement indicated that Labatt — not Hockey Canada — would receive $750,000 Canadian funds, plus 40 percent of the profits from CWL sales. The original agreement, of course, made clear that Hockey Canada would get that money. Kosters testified before a Swiss magistrate that Eagleson told him the change was being made for legal reasons, that Labatt owned a share of the 1991 Canada Cup.

In reality, Eagleson was attempting to cover up the fact that he had kept the end boards, and the proceeds from them, for All Canada Sports. If law-enforcement authorities began looking into his affairs, the Canada Cup bank account in Toronto, which he controlled, would become accessible, as would the records of All Canada Sports in Canada. His best hope was to destroy the original CWL agreement and replace it with one pre-dated to look as if it had been in force all along.

The new contract Kosters received was dated to read as if it had been agreed to on December 10, 1990. Eagleson was seeking to create the impression that CWL had been informed in 1990 that Labatt had been assigned 1991 Canada Cup rights and had received $750,000 from CWL. His motive was clearly to deceive Labatt and CWL — and, indirectly, Hockey Canada, the players, and the IIHF — and to confuse any investigation into the rink-board scheme.

Eagleson wrote to Kosters on January 20, 1992, advising him that $900,000 in Canadian funds plus interest would be returned to CWL so that CWL could pay the $900,000 to Labatt. He also wrote Werner Schwarz at the Cambio Valoren Bank, instructing him to return the $900,000 plus interest to CWL and to close out the Hockey Canada account. That same day, another account at the Cambio Valoren Bank was closed out: that of All Canada Sports.

Also that day, January 20, 1992, Eagleson wrote John Hudson of Labatt: "Pursuant to our meeting last week, I enclose the following material ... draft of letter from Labatt (J. Hudson) to Telesport A.G. and draft invoice (as per our discussion). I suggest that these be sent from your office no later than Tuesday, January 21st, so that payment of same will be prompt."

To execute the cover-up, Eagleson had also needed help from Hudson. He had asked Hudson to issue a false invoice; he wanted Hudson to imply that Labatt knew all along about the CWL agreement. But if Labatt had known of such an agreement, it would have known that CWL did not purchase end-board advertising for Team Canada games. In that case, why would end-board proceeds be going to the beer company?

The letter and invoice Eagleson drafted for Hudson were nearly identical to the letter and invoice Hudson sent to Kosters. The letter requested a $900,000 payment as per the enclosed invoice. Two Labatt executives, vice president James Emmerton and corporate lawyer Jim West, later agreed that the $374,500 payment to Labatt from Hockey Canada was odd. The Labatt invoice was not issued by the company's national office; it wasn't signed; there were no instructions for payment. Hudson himself, during an internal Labatt inquiry, was unable to explain why the payment had been made. He admitted that he had issued the $374,500 invoice after the 1991 Canada Cup tournament, on Eagleson's instructions.

A day after Hudson sent the letter and invoice to Volker Kosters, Werner Schwarz at the Zurich bank wrote Eagleson: "Everything is clear and I shall proceed as instructed." The next day, January 23, 1992, account number 289-576-253 in the name "R. Alan Eagleson...Sub All Canada Sports" was closed out, and $156,950.05 in Canadian funds was transferred to the account of Hockey Canada.

A day after that, on January 24, account number 289-576-261, in the name "R. Alan Eagleson ... Sub A/C Hockey Canada" showed a balance of $921,913.20, including the $156,950.05 transferred from the All Canada Sports account. That same day, Cambio Valoren Bank issued $921,884 to CWL Telesport, attention Volker Kosters. (The bank charged a $12.77 fee to close the account.) On January 31, 1992, CWL Telesport received the $921,884 Canadian payment from Cambio Valoren Bank. On February 3, the $900,000 payment was made by CWL to Labatt.

The backdated Labatt invoice to CWL Telesport was evidence, according to the RCMP, "that the invoice does not represent or reflect the actual business transaction that Labatt [thought it] had entered into with CWL (Telesport) around February 1991, whereby certain 1991 Canada Cup rights were sold to CWL (Telesport) through Eagleson for $725,000 U.S....

"There was no logical reason for CWL (Telesport) to backdate the

Agreement, and accept the $900,000 Cdn. (plus interest) back from the Cambio Valoren Bank, other than to accommodate Eagleson's desire to (falsely) document the fact that Labatt was identified as the assignee of 1991 Canada Cup Rights in the contract with CWL (Telesport)." The report concluded "that Eagleson initiated these actions in an effort to conceal his unlawful activities from U.S. and Canadian authorities.

"Eagleson, by mid-December, 1991, had isolated $430,963 Cdn., more or less, in criminal proceeds in Swiss bank accounts at the Cambio Valoren Bank. By returning the $900,000 Cdn. (plus interest) to CWL (Telesport) on January 24, 1992, and the $374,500 to Labatt (from Hockey Canada) Eagleson relinquished criminal profits, earned through the sale of end board advertising in the 1991 Canada Cup." The RCMP report noted, "He did this out of fear of being discovered by U.S. or Canadian authorities....

"Further," the report continued, "the $900,000 Cdn. invoice was designed to mask the fraud that Eagleson had committed against Labatt, by serving to (falsely) infer Labatt's (prior) knowledge of the existence of an Agreement between CWL (Telesport) and Canada Cup 1991....

"Hudson and Alan Eagleson acted together in creating a false $900,000 Cdn. Labatt invoice for the purpose of concealing Eagleson's fraudulent activities against Labatt," the RCMP report concluded. "In doing so, Hudson acted contrary to the interests of his employer, Labatt Brewing Company Limited."

According to the RCMP, Eagleson had other accomplices: "Irving Ungerman unlawfully assisted Eagleson by altering the business records of All Canada Sports in an effort to disguise or change the real nature of the business transactions relating to the disbursement of funds, by All Canada Sports, which were earned through the sale of rink-board advertising rights fraudulently obtained by Labatt. The motive...was to conceal Eagleson's fraudulent activities against Labatt."

The RCMP report said the evidence suggested that "Alan Eagleson, John Hudson, Irving Ungerman and All Canada Sports acted together in an attempt to obstruct justice."

There's no reason to think Eagleson invented his end-board scheme for the 1991 Canada Cup. Core Media sold end boards for All Canada Sports for the 1984 and 1987 tournaments, and before that Rich Bremner sold end-board advertising for long-time Eagleson friend and associate Arthur Harnett. In the 1970s and early 1980s, before All Canada Sports got involved in the Canada Cup, Harnett's companies — Arthur Harnett Enterprises, Harcom Consultants, and Harcom Stadium Advertising — helped broker millions of dollars in international hockey advertising. Marvin Goldblatt and Howard Ungerman were directors of Harcom Stadium Advertising.

As far back as the 1976 Canada Cup, Carling O'Keefe, the beer company, purchased $2.53 million in advertising from Harnett. Evan Hayter, Carling O'Keefe's marketing director at the time, told *Sports Illustrated* that even then, fifteen years before the 1991 end-board scheme, all agreements were made "directly with Eagleson."

14

THE WHEELS OF JUSTICE

"The indictment charges Eagleson with the commission of several crimes, including racketeering, mail fraud, embezzlement of labor organization assets, receipt of kickbacks affecting employee welfare plans, and obstruction of justice."

U.S. ATTORNEY'S OFFICE, DISTRICT OF MASSACHUSETTS

AFTER PUBLICATION OF THE *Eagle-Tribune* reports in September 1991, which precipitated Eagleson's end-board advertising cover-up attempt, we received scores of requests for copies of the newspaper. Among those who contacted us were the FBI, the Metropolitan Toronto Police, and a Toronto lawyer retained by the Law Society of Upper Canada, the regulatory body of the Ontario legal profession.

An FBI probe of Alan Eagleson had already been launched after the bureau reviewed complaints made by Bobby Orr and Brad Park. The results of the FBI investigation would determine whether a U.S. federal grand jury would be convened in Boston to determine if there was sufficient evidence to indict Eagleson. FBI Special Agent Tom Daly, whom I knew personally, asked if we'd turn over all our materials. He wanted my records and copies of the documents I used to put together our report. I said I'd have to discuss it with my editor, publisher, and the paper's lawyers. In the end, we decided not to provide the information freely. But if the material were subpoenaed, we indicated we would not challenge the order on constitutional grounds.

On November 19, a subpoena to testify before a U.S. grand jury at the United States District Courthouse in Boston was issued by U.S. Attorney

Wayne A. Budd. We were ordered to turn over "any and all records" in connection with our "Cracking the Ice" series, "except any records which would jeopardize the identity of confidential sources of the newspaper." By late December 1991, FBI Special Agent Bill McMullin confirmed that subpoenas requesting league records and documents were also being served on NHL president John Ziegler and on the owners of NHL clubs in the United States. The subpoenas directed the owners to turn over club and NHLPA records dealing with hockey insurance, pension funds, and other union-related activities.

I was happy to turn over our material for three reasons. First, it was clear the FBI was serious about Eagleson. Second, if anything happened to me, at least my records and documents would be in safe hands. Third, I cared about hockey and wanted to see justice done.

In the wake of our first reports, I also heard from Dennis Mills in Ottawa, the Liberal member of Parliament for Broadview-Greenwood, who had been talking to Carl Brewer. Mills was looking for Hockey Canada information. I later heard from two other Liberal MPs, David Dingwall (Cape Breton-East Richmond), the House Leader, and Bob Kilger (Stormont-Dundas), a former NHL referee. Dingwall said his request for detailed financials had also been rejected, even though Hockey Canada had received nearly $3 million in taxpayers' money since its inception in 1969. Would I be willing to turn over whatever information I had? I was taken aback. It was as if three U.S. Congressmen had phoned my home, asking for information about a government-subsidized agency.

"Canadian taxpayers helped support Hockey Canada, which ran the Canada Cup tournaments. It's a nonprofit organization. Why can't you see the financials?"

Dingwall said he'd been "stonewalled," so I agreed to write some questions that could be asked in Parliament. I faxed them to Ottawa in November 1992. Just before the holiday recess in December, during Question Period, he rose in the Commons.

"There are many, many questions — serious questions — which have been raised about the financial dealings of the nonprofit federal agency, Hockey Canada, and certain individuals," Dingwall said. "I ask the minister responsible: Will the government of Canada provide to this House a full financial disclosure, other than one-line item expenses and income reports for Hockey Canada since Hockey Canada has been incorporated?"

His question was fielded by Conservative justice minister and attorney general (and later, briefly, prime minister) Kim Campbell: "The government of Canada will offer no further information," she said, "until the RCMP has concluded its investigation."

A frustrated Dingwall later told CBC sportscaster Bruce Dowbiggin, "We've tried repeatedly through a number of different members of Parliament to seek this information. It's awfully interesting to note that approximately $1.5 million has been paid out in management fees. We have a right to receive this information. We have an obligation to ascertain where that money has gone."

Asked about Campbell's terse response, Dingwall said, "I would have thought the minister would have been much more descriptive and explanatory in her comments."

In the wake of Dingwall's question, RCMP constable Greg Peters told Canadian Press that the RCMP was "taking part in what's called the preliminary verification, assisting the FBI to see if there were any criminal acts committed in Canada."

I was dubious. The RCMP had been asked to look into Eagleson's business practices by Edmonton agent Rich Winter almost three years earlier, in January 1990. The RCMP had turned Winter's fifty-page complaint over to the Metro Toronto Police; it was directed to the Commercial Crime Section of the Fraud Squad, and there it sat. And sat. Retired Detective Bill Deconkey later explained that the Fraud Squad did not act because of the ongoing investigation into Eagleson by the Law Society of Upper Canada, to whom Winter had also complained. The idea that a Law Society investigation would supersede a potential criminal investigation I found bizarre. If a lawyer got caught stealing my car, would he not be charged until the Law Society had disciplined him?

Around Christmas, I spoke again with Tom Lockwood, the Toronto lawyer retained by the Law Society. Lockwood was planning a trip to Boston and wanted to review my documents. Knowing that the federal grand jury inquiry was underway, I spoke to the paper's lawyer, Peter Caruso. Although I had compiled the information as work product, it was now subject to the rules of grand jury evidence. By then, FBI Special Agent Daly was conducting an investigation and Assistant U.S. Attorney Paul V. Kelly was directing the grand jury proceedings in Boston. Caruso suggested that I could volunteer information and steer Lockwood in the right direction by answering his questions, but that I should stop short of giving him material because the grand jury proceedings were confidential.

Late in 1991, the FBI requested RCMP assistance on certain aspects of the investigation. The U.S. probe was seeking to determine whether Eagleson had violated U.S. Racketeering and Corrupt Organizations (RICO) laws. RICO convictions carry severe penalties, including lengthy prison terms. In addition, according to an RCMP affidavit, "other potential criminal and labour violations relative to Eagleson's role as the Executive Director of the NHLPA" were being investigated by U.S. authorities, including possible "insurance fraud, commingling of union funds and using them for personal gain, double dipping on the part of Eagleson."

RCMP Staff Sergeant Beer claimed in that sworn affidavit that the RCMP had assisted the FBI and U.S. Department of Justice in their investigation. Beer said he and RCMP Sergeant Hap Daley had "continued to evaluate the need" for the RCMP "to initiate a separate Canadian criminal investigation on the basis of information arising independent of the U.S. Grand Jury investigation." That process stalled, Beer said, when Daley was transferred and the RCMP was reorganized, resulting in "the reassignment of the Eagleson file."

In other words, while U.S. authorities did the legwork, the RCMP played the role of spectator. If the FBI and the U.S. Justice Department hadn't begun an investigation, I wondered, would the RCMP ever have entered the case? Or would the Eagleson file have remained buried at the Fraud Squad of the Metro Toronto Police?

In the summer of 1992, a source in Toronto told me where some Canada Cup tournament rink-board advertising records were stored. Evidently, the source gave the FBI the same information, because U.S. authorities asked the RCMP to execute two search warrants. The raids, at two Toronto locations, were meant to "seize the records of All Canada Sports Promotion

Limited relating to Canada Cup rink board advertising." In addition, the FBI requested that the RCMP seize the All Canada Sports bank records. These requests were made through a Canada-U.S. treaty called Mutual Legal Assistance in Criminal Matters (MLAT). Such requests are usually honored in short order; the U.S. and Canadian authorities had recently concluded an extensive joint drug investigation characterized by the highest degree of mutual regard and cooperation.

Following meetings between RCMP Staff Sergeant Beer, RCMP Corporal Glen Harloff, and officials of the Crown Law Office in the Ontario Attorney General's department, however, the U.S. request was denied. The Mounties, to the consternation of the U.S. authorities, refused to raid the buildings where the records were stored. "Execution of search warrants for All Canada Sports Promotion Limited records at that time would have impeded the parallel Canadian investigation," Beer said. Except that when the requests were made, the RCMP was supposedly assisting the FBI.

"Supplementary information as to U.S. jurisdiction over the rink board advertising allegations against Eagleson specified in the request would have to be provided," Beer wrote in the affidavit, "before any such request could be given future consideration." A second request was also denied, this time "because it did not contain sufficient information as to the criminal offences being investigated."

Beer cited "correspondence I received from RCMP Headquarters on November 16, 1992, which included a complaint to the Honourable A. Kim Campbell, Minister of Justice and Attorney General of Canada, by Dennis Mills, the Liberal member for the Broadview-Greenwood Riding, on behalf of retired Toronto Maple Leafs hockey player, Carl Brewer. Mills correspondence dated October 23, 1992, raised concerns about business practices of both Hockey Canada and Eagleson relative to, in part, the manner in which profits flowing to Hockey Canada from International Hockey Tournaments were disbursed...."

The affidavit was filed two years after the correspondence in question. Those two years of foot-dragging spoke volumes. Beer's affidavit also made clear that when Campbell told Dingwall that the RCMP was carrying on its own investigation, she was mistaken. As minister of justice and attorney general of Canada, Campbell was responsible for both law formation and law enforcement. She had responsibility for the RCMP and oversaw the force through the RCMP commissioner, Norman Inkster. According to the affidavit, the Mounties did not initiate their own investigation into Eagleson until January 28, 1993 — forty-eight days *after* Campbell said that Hockey Canada information could not be released because of the ongoing investigation.

When, in early 1993, I looked into the RCMP's handling of the Eagleson case, I was surprised to discover a familiar name — Timothy Lemay. Could this be the same Timothy Lemay who had worked for Eagleson's law firm and been part of the Canada Cup payroll? The same Timothy Lemay who was Eagleson's son's brother-in-law? The very one, as it turned out. He'd gone to work for the Department of Justice and had been loaned to the RCMP. And where, exactly, was he working? Out of the same Newmarket, Ontario, headquarters in which the RCMP was gathering information from U.S. authorities on Alan Eagleson.

A Toronto phone book dated April 1993 still listed Lemay's address as 37 Maitland Street, the Eagleson building. I contacted several of Lemay's relatives and friends with background questions before calling the RCMP and asking for Lemay himself. "Stunned" hardly describes his reaction when I identified myself. He had little to say when I asked about his work in the 1991 Canada Cup.

Exactly when Lemay went to work for the Canadian government was unclear. (Such information would be on the public record in the United States.) Lemay would not say, nor would Justice Department officials. "This is Canada," said Paul Evraire, director of the Canadian Justice Department's regional office in Toronto. "You American journalists are all the same. You're just a journalist. I don't have to give you any answers." Evraire did confirm that Lemay worked as an RCMP lawyer.

I contacted Assistant U.S. Attorney Kelly, and FBI Special Agent Daly, asking if they realized an Eagleson family member and former employee was working for the RCMP at the very time the RCMP was supposedly cooperating with them on the criminal investigation. They were both surprised and concerned.

That summer, in August 1993, David Merner, legal counsel for the deputy justice minister in the administration of then prime minister Kim Campbell, denied that Lemay had ever worked for the Justice Department or the RCMP. "Not now, not ever," he told Kathryn May of the *Ottawa Citizen*, in response to a question she asked on my behalf. "There's nobody by that name at RCMP legal services."

Two weeks later, Merner contacted the *Citizen*. This time he sang a different tune. He said that Lemay did indeed work for the RCMP. By then, Dennis Mills had confirmed that Lemay was on loan to the RCMP from the Justice Department, where he had been employed since March 1993, having previously worked for the attorney general's office in Nova Scotia. I got hold of RCMP Staff Sergeant Beer — who, despite being in charge of the RCMP investigation of Eagleson, had never contacted me — and asked him to confirm that Lemay was working with the RCMP. Beer said he was, but assured me Lemay had no involvement in the Eagleson probe.

ONCE IT BECAME CLEAR THAT the Justice Department had convened a federal grand jury in Boston to hear evidence, the RCMP was apparently troubled by the U.S. claim of jurisdiction over Eagleson, even though the vast majority of hockey players victimized by his actions were resident-aliens (and another 15 percent were U.S. citizens) working for U.S. corporations. "U.S. officials proceeded with this indictment," wrote Beer, "despite attempts by RCMP officials to settle, prior to indictment, outstanding jurisdictional issues related to alleged rink board advertising offences committed in Canada by Eagleson." Not only had the RCMP failed to execute the raids requested in 1992, but now they were fighting over jurisdiction. In the past, the two countries had routinely cooperated in bringing alleged criminals to justice. If Eagleson had been, say, a money launderer without political connections, there probably would have been little hesitation by Canadian officials to see the United States pursue its case.

In February 1994, I learned from the Bruins' Harry Sinden that an indictment by the federal grand jury in Boston was imminent. "I heard it in Lillehammer," Sinden told me. "It was from somebody who was close with

Eagleson in marketing Canada Cup tournaments. He said Eagleson was going to be indicted for false expenses and misuse of union funds."

By then, the *Boston Globe* was also suggesting that indictments were near. The newspaper reported that Eagleson's American lawyer, former federal prosecutor Jeremiah T. O'Sullivan, had been in Washington to meet with Justice Department officials about Eagleson. O'Sullivan had been a prosecutor when he led the federal organized crime strike force in Boston.

When Gary Bettman, the NHL commissioner who succeeded John Ziegler in late 1992, came to Boston as a guest speaker at a business function, I attended the press briefing. I was waiting to interview Bettman when I saw Boston Garden president Larry Moulter. We began chatting about the new arena under construction to replace the old Garden. Spotting Bruins owner Jeremy Jacobs, Moulter suggested I tell his boss how impressed I was that a new facility, after many failed initiatives, was finally being built. I'd met Jacobs several times over the years; Moulter re-introduced us.

Jacobs, in his early fifties, is a tall, balding fellow who ranks among the wealthiest men in America. Moulter mentioned that I was the one who'd written about Eagleson, NHL pensions, and past hockey business practices. He told Jacobs that Eagleson was on the verge of being indicted by a federal grand jury.

Jacobs glared at me, then snapped his fingers. "I know who you are now!" he said, and launched into a diatribe about how awful it was that Eagleson might face criminal charges. Jacobs went on to say how much Eagleson had done for hockey. People were out to get him and it would be a shame if he were charged. "He isn't a criminal," Jacobs said, adding that the investigation was a waste of taxpayers' money.

The U.S. Justice Department didn't share his view. The next day, at the U.S. Federal Courthouse in Boston, while a snowstorm raged outside, copies of a sixty-two–page, thirty-two–count indictment were passed out to reporters. The cover read: "United States of America vs. R. Alan Eagleson." The accompanying press release said, "A federal grand jury has indicted the former Executive Director of the National Hockey League Players' Association on charges of racketeering, fraud and embezzlement occurring during his tenure as the head of the players' union." His alleged violations included racketeering, mail fraud, obstruction of justice, receipt of kickbacks, and embezzlement of labor organization assets.

"He took $150,000 worth of Air Canada tickets?" somebody said. "Look at page 19. One trip was to Bombay, for God sakes!"

"Scouting for the Canada Cup," someone else deadpanned.

U.S. Attorney Donald K. Stern and FBI New England regional director Richard Swensen both spoke. Eagleson, about to turn sixty-one, was facing a possible twenty years in federal prison and $2 million in fines. "The heart of today's indictments," said Stern, "is that Mr. Eagleson breached his fiduciary responsibilities and obligations in the duty of providing honest services which he owed the members of the union."

"I wish it had been Canada versus Alan Eagleson," said Carl Brewer, who had flown in with Sue Foster. Why were the Canadian authorities seemingly reluctant to move against him? Apart from Eagleson's extensive political connections, Brewer believed, the union boss had the support of important people in the Canadian media, so the public outcry wasn't what it might have been. Some of the older reporters, Brewer thought, were "sycophants of Eagleson."

Red Fisher, the well-known Montreal hockey writer and sports editor, had been involved in Bobby Orr Enterprises. (At first I'd missed the connection in the documents I reviewed, since Fisher was referred to by his given name, Saul.) Fisher received $15,000 cash from Eagleson's pal and former Canada Cup advertising executive Arthur Harnett, in a buyout of Fisher's shares. According to Eagleson, in a 1979 letter to Bobby Orr's attorney, the shares "were worth substantially less than that amount. This purchase was arranged so that Mr. Fisher would suffer no loss and so that there could never be any complaint about his relationship as a shareholder of Bobby Orr Enterprises Limited."

On two occasions, I asked Fisher about the $15,000. He seemed startled that I knew about the deal and refused to talk. I wanted to ask him how a sports reporter can remain objective when he has financial ties to the people he's writing about. Fisher is a long-time supporter of Eagleson; his newspaper, the *Montreal Gazette*, had given remarkably little coverage to Eagleson's past practices and legal woes.

Jim Taylor, the Vancouver sportswriter whose friendship with Eagleson goes back to the early 1970s, wrote a column in late 1993 that pooh-poohed my findings and Bruce Dowbiggin's TV reports. The theme of the column was as simple as Taylor's thinking process: No matter what Eagleson did, they'd always be friends.

Eagleson's buddy Paul Godfrey was publisher and president of the *Toronto Sun* in February 1993 when the editorial-page cartoon depicted Eagleson on his back, tied to stakes, a vulture perched on his head, asking, "Are we having fun yet?" Poor Al. That same day, *Sun* sportswriter Steve Simmons did a puff piece. "Journalists are now winning awards digging deeper and deeper into Eagleson's past and it is difficult for those of us who have known him forever, for those who have dealt with him as a source, a confidant and an associate, to coldly separate years of a relationship with the police probes we read about from afar.

"It didn't matter to too many of us that Alan Eagleson may have broken laws, been involved with shady deals, or taken his autocracy to the extreme. It mattered more that we needed to find out what was really going on in Chicago or Detroit or New York and we knew we could trust his information."

George Gross, corporate sports editor of the *Sun*, besides having been the recipient of Wimbledon tickets, once received a $10,000, interest-free loan via Eagleson. The money came from one of Eagleson's player-clients at the time, Vaclav Nedomansky, who told me he'd been aware of the loan but not that it was interest-free.

Jim Proudfoot wrote in the *Toronto Star* that there was no excuse "for the preposterous rearrangement of history that's gone on. Eagleson did start the players' association in the 1960s. He did cause the Summit Series of 1972 to happen. He did think up and execute the Canada Cup. These worthy accomplishments wouldn't even begin to offset the abuses that are alleged to have grown out of them. But to maintain they didn't occur is either malicious or stupid."

Nobody was questioning Eagleson's many accomplishments. Of course, this was the same Jim Proudfoot who wrote in 1992 that Eagleson had sued my newspaper over our first report. Talk about a "preposterous rearrangement of history" — there was no lawsuit, just a notice from Edgar Sexton (who was also Brian Mulroney's lawyer), yet Proudfoot suggested to readers of the *Star* that our allegations were unfounded.

Not everyone in the media was so supportive. Many of the younger generation of sportswriters — Al Strachan, Bob McKenzie, Roy MacGregor, Randy Starkman, Mary Ormsby, Bert Raymond — and most of the French sports media in Quebec, saw through the bluster. Even the satirical *Frank* magazine delved into the Eagleson case, reporting news and gossip and raising issues that many conglomerate newspapers chose to ignore.

In the hockey world, the charges pleased many players and officials. The Los Angeles Kings were in Boston to play the Bruins the day of the indictment, and Eagleson was on everyone's lips that evening. NHL Commissioner Bettman tactfully said that the league and its teams had cooperated and would continue to "cooperate fully" with the FBI and the U.S. Attorney's office. Wayne Gretzky — who had sat on the fence during the 1989 uprising, not showing up at the Florida meetings — said he had been interviewed for five hours by U.S. federal investigators probing Eagleson's business practices. "It's too bad," he said of Eagleson, "but everybody gets their day in court."

"It's a sign of great progress for the whole league," said Gretzky's teammate and friend Marty McSorley. "It shows what went on in the league for twenty-four years won't be allowed now. There aren't many players who won't be happy about the decision to indict him."

Luc Robitaille, the prolific left-winger, also spoke his mind. "Things that he'd done, it had to come back at him. You knew it was going to come out like this some day. He used his power just too much. And us players, it was our fault for not paying attention to what he was doing."

ESPN hockey broadcaster and former Philadelphia Flyer Bill Clement said: "The way he spent players' money and operated the Canada Cup, he was telling players one thing and doing something else." Of the indictment, Clement cracked: "It couldn't have happened to a nicer guy. "

Bruins vice president Tom Johnson had long enjoyed Eagleson's company and considered him a friend. But even he, during his customary pregame, pressroom cribbage game, shook his head. "If he's proven guilty, he deserves to go to jail. Imagine charging players to get their own disability insurance. That's the part that really stinks."

Nor was Ken Linseman, who played fourteen seasons in the NHL, sorry to see Eagleson come to grief. "Everything in this world has a way of coming around. Now he has to deal with whatever he did."

AT THE INDICTMENT ANNOUNCEMENT, Assistant U.S. Attorney Kelly, U.S. Attorney Stern, and Richard Swenson, head of the New England regional FBI office, had said that Eagleson was expected to appear in Boston to be arraigned later in March. In other circumstances, the indictment might have been sealed until the accused had been arrested, but the U.S. authorities understood that Eagleson would appear voluntarily, thereby avoiding the ignominy of an arrest. O'Sullivan declared his client "innocent of all charges" and said he looked forward "to an opportunity to clear his name and have his day in court," but then a funny thing happened. The U.S. authorities got sand-bagged. Eagleson, who liked to brag that he never ran from a fight, ran from this one.

On March 3, the day the indictment was announced, he flew with Toronto Maple Leafs president and general manager Cliff Fletcher from Newark, New Jersey, to Toronto. Eagleson told Fletcher to expect to hear news of the indictment.

Shortly after takeoff, the captain announced that the plane was returning to Newark because of mechanical problems. A sick look came over Eagleson's face. He began sweating profusely. Perhaps there was no mechanical trouble. Perhaps the feds were turning the plane around so they could grab him.

As luck would have it, the mechanical problem was real. After a short time back on the ground at Newark, they were off again to Canada. And there Eagleson has remained.

Despite the detail of the indictment, O'Sullivan called it "remarkably vague and conclusory in its allegations." He said it contained "nothing more than a rehashing of stories which have circulated in the press for a number of years." Remarkably vague? The charges were quite specific. The indictment alleged that Eagleson had repeatedly lied to Players' Association members to conceal his illegal activities and to keep his job as executive director of the union. It alleged that he had fraudulently charged two former NHL players, Glen Sharpley and Bob Dailey, to process their career-ending disability insurance. It alleged that he had been paid more than $100,000 from insurance brokers and others in the form of gifts, fees, commissions, and kickbacks to give them disability insurance business for the NHL and the Players' Association, violating the U.S. Employee Retirement Income Security Act (ERISA). It alleged that he took more than $150,000 in airline tickets provided by Air Canada in exchange for rink-board advertising at Canada Cup tournaments, used them for personal trips to London, Zurich, Frankfurt, Bombay, and Tampa, and gave passes to family members, friends, and associates. It alleged that he had defrauded and stolen money from the NHL Players' Association in the five Canada Cups between 1976 and 1991. It also alleged that he "did knowingly intimidate, threaten, and corruptly persuade" a witness.

Later that month, in Toronto, Eagleson's Canadian lawyers — Brian Greenspan of Greenspan Humphrey and Edgar Sexton of Osler, Hoskin & Harcourt — announced that, despite their client's avowed eagerness to face charges against him, he was not going to show up for arraignment in Boston after all. And he would fight extradition to the United States. "We're not going to allow Mr. Eagleson to enter a trial by ambush," Greenspan told a press conference.

In Boston, the response was swift. "The U.S. Attorney's office looked forward to an expeditious discovery process and a prompt trial date," said U.S. Attorney Stern, "so that Mr. Eagleson would have a full and fair opportunity to answer." A warrant was issued for his arrest; he was now a fugitive from justice, and U.S. Customs officials were instructed to detain him if he attempted to cross the border into the United States.

Our fifth and final *Eagle-Tribune* report, published in March 1994, documented, among other things, more disability insurance cases. A few months later, Eagleson was hit with a superseding indictment, which reiterated the original but added two more racketeering charges. He was now also alleged to have "devised and intended to devise a scheme" to "defraud, to obtain money and property" from André Savard and Mike Gillis. He was accused of "compromising" Savard's disability insurance claim and billing the former player "even though Eagleson was obligated to supply such services to Savard as Executive Director of the NHLPA."

"This was a scheme to defraud, to obtain money by false and fraudulent pretenses, using the U.S. mail for the purpose of executing these matters," Assistant U.S. Attorney Kelly said of the new charges. "Today's action by the grand jury brings to a close the active portion of our investigation of Eagleson. Now that all charges versus Eagleson have been brought forward, the U.S. Attorney's office will focus its efforts on submitting a formal extradition to Canada to compel Eagleson to face the charges in the United States."

IN THE WAKE OF THE U.S. INDICTMENT, Ian McClelland, a Reform Party member of Parliament (Edmonton South-West), phoned me in Massachusetts. He was upset to learn that Hockey Canada had postponed its investigation and was stunned to realize that the RCMP had never contacted me for information. "That's insane. You've dug all this up, reported it, the U.S. authorities jump on it and issue charges. Where are our people? That's what I'd like to know."

On March 11, 1994, McClelland raised the issue in Parliament, as David Dingwall had done in 1992, asking Solicitor General Herb Gray about the RCMP investigation of Eagleson. Gray said the RCMP had been assisting the FBI but that "it would not be appropriate to comment further." When McClelland asked for full disclosure of Hockey Canada financials, Michel Dupuy, the heritage minister (responsible for amateur sports), offered a similar "it is inappropriate to comment" response. When McClelland sought assurance that the government would cooperate with the United States in extraditing Eagleson, Justice Minister Allan Rock replied that he did "not think it appropriate for me to comment, other than to assure the honorable member that I have every confidence the system will work as it should."

"The system is working, all right," McClelland said later. "For Eagleson. We're not getting any answers and he's out walking the streets."

McClelland wrote to Prime Minister Jean Chrétien. "The Eagleson Affair was first brought to light by an American investigative journalist, Mr. Russ Conway, Sports Editor of the *Eagle-Tribune*, a Massachusetts newspaper. There is far more to this story than the activities of Mr. Eagleson in isolation." McClelland told the prime minister that I was willing to meet with Canadian authorities but lacked "confidence in senior RCMP officials."

That was an understatement. Having seen the RCMP's disinterest in our findings, having discovered a former Eagleson employee working for the Mounties, and having gained some understanding of Eagleson's extensive political connections, I didn't trust the way the Canadian government was handling its investigation. I knew that Paul Palango was about to issue a book, *Above the Law*, with Rod Stamler, the former number two man in the RCMP; the book documents political interference in RCMP investigations of well-connected people. And Stevie Cameron, working on her exposé of government corruption during the Mulroney years, *On the Take*, warned me that there were two sets of laws in Canada, one for those with high-ranking political connections and one for everybody else.

Not long after McClelland's questions in the House, RCMP Commissioner Norman Inkster announced that he was planning to step down. He later became a partner in KPMG, a chartered accounting firm, where he heads forensic accounting investigations. Inkster's resignation was in no way linked to the Eagleson probe, so far as I knew, but I got a kick out of a quote attributed to him in the *Toronto Star* after he quit. Inkster said he would not be involved with fraud investigations at his new job. "Absolutely not. It's been so long since I headed a fraud investigation, I've forgotten how to."

McClelland's letter to Chrétien went unanswered for more than six months. Finally, Solicitor General Herb Gray replied: "The office of the Prime Minister of Canada brought to my attention your letter of March 21, 1994, concerning the investigation into the activities of Mr. Alan R. [sic] Eagleson. I have referred this matter to the Commissioner of the Royal Canadian Mounted Police (RCMP) who will ensure that your concerns are examined. Once this examination is completed, the RCMP will respond to you directly. I will also be advised of the results. I trust that this action is satisfactory."

Not long afterward, the new RCMP Commissioner, J.P.R. Murray, wrote McClelland: "As you are aware, a criminal investigation is being conducted by the Commercial Crime Section of the Royal Canadian Mounted Police (RCMP) in Newmarket, Ontario. A review of the financial transactions pertaining to the National Hockey League players' pensions and to the International Ice Hockey events is part of this criminal investigation. As I am sure you can appreciate, this matter has been made more complicated by decisions rendered in international jurisdictions."

More complicated? One could argue that, to the contrary, the matter had been considerably simplified by the Americans' involvement. After all, the U.S. authorities had done a great deal of investigative work and shared much of it with the Mounties. I wondered if the Mounties had perhaps been subject to political interference while Mulroney was still prime minister, then been embarrassed at being scooped when the indictments were announced in Boston. In any case, the "made more complicated" line didn't really wash with McClelland.

"With respect to your comments pertaining to Mr. Russ Conway," Commissioner Murray continued, "I am satisfied that the investigation in Canada is being handled as expeditiously and effectively as possible. Should Mr. Conway have any information to provide the RCMP investigators in this matter, I suggest that he contact Staff Sergeant J. Beer, of the RCMP's Newmarket Commercial Crime Section. The RCMP will assess any information that Mr. Conway wishes to provide."

The investigation was being handled as expeditiously and effectively as possible? It sure didn't look that way. It looked like the whole matter was playing right into Eagleson's hands. The longer it took, the better for him. Justice delayed is justice denied.

In reply to Commissioner Murray, McClelland wrote: "I am not the kind of person who tilts at windmills nor am I easily manipulated by those who would use my office to further their ends....There are both the reality and perception of two sets of rules. One set for the powerful and one for everyone else. Nothing I have seen since I became involved with this issue, almost a year ago, has convinced me otherwise....

"There are some obvious questions.

"1. Why did the RCMP sit on this for years?

"2. Why did the Law Society of Upper Canada sit on this for years?

"3. Why did Metro Toronto Police sit on this for years?

"4. Why did U.S. authorities bring down indictments in a relatively short time and the RCMP continues to dither?

"It is interesting, the Liberal Solicitor General, the Hon. Herb Gray has responded to questions in the House of Commons exactly as the previous Conservative Solicitor General responded to exactly the same questions: 'The case is under investigation by the RCMP.'

"I do not believe the RCMP has any intention of proceeding with a substantive investigation. Why else would the RCMP have done nothing for all these years?

"Why is the integrity of Canada's National Sport being protected by U.S. jurisprudence? The bulk of the alleged wrongdoing occurred in Canada to Canadians."

McClelland addressed the fact that Timothy Lemay had been found working for the RCMP. "Even the most charitable would consider the investigation compromised." He closed his letter by noting that "the cornerstone of our democracy is fair and equal treatment before the law for all citizens. There is much about this file that brings discredit to everyone involved. I will not be deflected away from an honest conclusion and ask that you pursue this case with a fresh vigor."

In the fall of 1994, McClelland again raised the issue in Parliament, demanding a progress report on the Eagleson investigation. This time his questions seemed to produce results. Staff Sergeant Beer now made a series of calls to my newsroom and my home — the first time he'd phoned me. I asked, jokingly, where he'd been for the past four years. Busy, he said, but it went both ways — why hadn't I called him? An experienced RCMP investigator knew that we had pertinent information, and we were supposed to call him? Tom Lockwood, the Law Society investigator, certainly didn't see it that way. By then he had traveled to Boston four times for lengthy meetings.

Eagleson, meanwhile, was circling his wagons. In early 1993 he'd put his Collingwood waterfront home on the market. In April 1994, I learned that his Manalapan villa, now in his wife's name, had also gone on the market. I called Assistant U.S. Attorney Kelly and asked if such a sale would be permissible, given Eagleson's fugitive status. The answer was swift. In May, Eagleson's personal property was attached by U.S. District Court Judge Nathaniel M. Gorton. The attachment orders prevented Eagleson from selling property he owned or controlled in the United States or England without permission from the U.S. authorities until he faced the charges. The property included the

Florida villa, a condominium he owned in Manhattan, and the flat his family business owned with Bernard Warren in London. In addition, Judge Gorton ordered $374,500 in 1991 Canada Cup tournament funds allegedly held by Labatt Brewing Company frozen until the U.S. criminal charges were resolved.

Eagleson's U.S. lawyer, O'Sullivan, appealed, hoping to get the court decision overturned, but Judge Gorton would have none of it. "Eagleson has refused to submit to this Court's jurisdiction or to abide by the consequences of its ultimate judgement," he wrote in his decision. "He is, therefore, considered a fugitive by this Court and will not be afforded the opportunity to challenge the subject."

In October 1994, at a luncheon honoring Metro Toronto Police Chief William McCormack (who was under pressure to step down for reasons unrelated to Eagleson), the chief's supporters turned out to rally behind him. Among those who showed up at the Variety Club in Toronto and gave McCormack a standing ovation were Ontario Chief Justice Charles Dubin, Ontario Chief Justice Roy McMurtry, and fugitive from justice R. Alan Eagleson.

Paul Godfrey, the *Toronto Sun* president, former Metro chairman, and long-time Eagleson friend, was a luncheon speaker. "When you have a man like Bill McCormack as your chief," Godfrey told the faithful, "you should be kissing the earth, the ground he walks on." Eagleson may well have concurred. McCormack was chief when Rich Winter first complained about Eagleson's alleged fraud and abuse of power.

From Eagleson's cocky demeanor and gruff affability at the luncheon, you would not have guessed he was about to come under even heavier siege. Finally, two years after the original FBI request, in November 1994, the RCMP raided two Toronto buildings in search of records and documents related to the Canada Cup and All Canada Sports. Just how much may have been missing from those records we'll never know.

A week after those raids, on November 11, 1994, the Law Society of Upper Canada issued a forty-four–charge complaint against him, alleging professional misconduct and conduct unbecoming a barrister and solicitor.

The complaint alleged, among other things, that Eagleson had loaned trust funds belonging to the NHLPA and the Canada Cup without the authorization of those clients; that he had failed to take precautions that the loans were adequately secured; and that he had authorized others to create documents to create the false impression that he had the authority to invest NHLPA funds. It alleged that Eagleson had failed "to conscientiously, diligently and effectively, serve the interests of his client, the NHLPA, or his former clients, the retired hockey players." It accused him of "acquiescing to the exemption of the National Hockey League Pension Society from the applicable Ontario pension legislation." It alleged that he had had the NHLPA pay his personal legal bills for a lawsuit against former player agent Bill Watters and the *Boston Globe*, and billed the union for his personal legal services, provided by Edgar Sexton of Osler, Hoskin & Harcourt. It alleged that he had failed to properly serve the interests of various clients including Bobby Orr, Jim Harrison, André Savard, Mike Gillis, Bob Dailey, and Glen Sharpley. It also alleged that he and others had wrongfully used Air Canada passes.

Once the Law Society investigation was reported in the Toronto papers, new sources came forward. One was John Earle, a Toronto businessman, who was steered my way by Bruce Dowbiggin. Earle told me that, in 1988, he'd had to relocate his manufacturing business. In southeast Toronto he found a 67,000-square-foot property with three buildings already up, a property he felt was "just perfect."

From earlier real estate dealings, Earle knew Norman Donaldson, Eagleson's former business partner (whose companies had received NHLPA loans). Earle, Donaldson, and Eagleson agreed to form a partnership to buy the property. Then, says Earle, problems developed. Eagleson and Donaldson, he said, refused to sign an agreement. "I'm the kind of guy who's detail-oriented," Earle recalled. "I wanted everything written down." Earle wanted to know how the money was being raised. He recalls Donaldson, in his Scots accent, getting huffy. "He said, 'Don't worry about it. It's coming from the bloody hockey players!'"

Earle began to feel uncomfortable with his new partners. So did his lawyer, Glen Solomon, who advised him to make the purchase on his own. But Donaldson swore out an affidavit, claiming there was already a partnership agreement and threatening to sue Earle. The title was tied up, preventing Earle from buying the property. The dispute ended up in court, where a Toronto master ruled against Earle. To go through with his purchase, Earle had to settle with Donaldson and Eagleson. He paid them $450,000, issuing the check to Osler, Hoskin & Harcourt.

If the money for the property deal was indeed coming from the NHLPA, as Earle had assumed, presumably at least part of the settlement should have gone to the union. None of the $450,000 ever showed up as income in the NHLPA financials.

IN THE UNITED STATES, the *Eagle-Tribune* won many accolades for our investigative pieces about Eagleson and the NHL — including awards from the New England Newspaper Publishers' Association, the New England Press Association, and the Associated Press — and was a finalist for a 1992 Pulitzer Prize. The story is viewed in some quarters as the biggest scandal to hit major professional sport since the Chicago White Sox threw the 1919 World Series.

Say it ain't so, Al.

In Canada, however, the media have been oddly restrained, and many of the older Canadian sportswriters have continued their bull-headed defense of Eagleson, treating the U.S. indictment as some groundless American plot to destroy a national treasure. "Frankly, I don't blame Alan Eagleson for not going to Boston to face the music," Jim Hunt wrote in the *Vancouver Province*. "For starters, the racketeering statute that he is being charged under was designed to nail members of the Mafia. Whatever the Eagle has done, he hardly deserves to be classed with the kingpins of organized crime."

Hunt made this interesting observation: "It would help his cause if the RCMP officers got off their horses long enough to finish their investigation. One thing you may have noticed about the Mounties is that though their motto is, 'we always get our man,' the truth is they do so when it suits them...."

A column by long-time Eagleson friend Doug Fisher in the *Toronto Sun* was equally forgiving. Fisher, a former member of Parliament, director of Hockey Canada from 1969 to 1979, and chairman for much of that time, drew parallels between the Eagleson indictment and a bogus complaint years earlier against former Liberal cabinet minister John Munro, which was later dismissed. Fisher praised Eagleson for getting the players' union started in 1967 and for effecting major changes in hockey economics. He concluded that the "charges don't square with the man with whom I worked over a decade."

Despite the widespread support of Eagleson in Canada, the wheels of justice continued their slow turn. In July 1995, the Law Society, understanding a formal extradition request to be imminent, agreed to adjourn its Eagleson hearing until November. In return, Eagleson agreed to cease practicing law, to wind up his practice, to open his books to the Law Society, to reconfigure the office space at 37 Maitland Street, to remove the signage from his building, and to strike the designations "barrister," "solicitor," "lawyer," "notary public," "commissioner of oaths," and "Q.C." from any letterhead or business stationery bearing his name. It must have been a humiliation, but Eagleson turned the sign removal into a media event, hamming it up for a TV cameraman.

As the noose tightened, Eagleson found himself with more and more legal bills and fewer and fewer friends. Over the summer of 1995 he wore his brave face on the courts at the Toronto Lawn Tennis Club, and he was his jovial old self at the party his family and friends threw for him in Collingwood, but the fact that no charges had been brought against people close to him suggested that they may have cooperated with the authorities in return for immunity.

As of late September, the Americans were "pursuing certain new information" while putting the finishing touches on their formal request for extradition and collecting affidavits from a wide range of people in the hockey world. Once the request is made, the Canadians will have sixty days in which to rule. If Eagleson is ordered to face the U.S. charges, he could appeal, delaying his appearance in Boston for as long as possible. He may try to cut a deal — to pay restitution and plead guilty to certain offenses if other charges are dropped — but the Americans, burned when he failed to show for his arraignment and feeling they have a strong case against him, are unlikely to bargain away the racketeering charge and its mandated incarceration.

All of which means Eagleson may prefer to take his chances in Canada, which does not have a racketeering statute. In his own country, his lawyers could delay a trial for as long as Canadian law permits before cutting a deal that would see him pay restitution and serve time in a "country club" prison of the sort Harold Ballard once called home.

The only problem with this scenario is that, north of the border, Alan Eagleson has been accused of no criminal wrongdoing. At this writing — nearly five years after Rich Winter's complaint, three years after David Dingwall raised the matter in the House of Commons, and eighteen months after the U.S. indictment — the RCMP has yet to lay charges.

EPILOGUE

"We continue to take the position that Mr. Eagleson was
not in any way engaged in any misconduct."
BRIAN GREENSPAN, SEPTEMBER 1995

P

ROFESSIONAL HOCKEY HAS undergone many changes
since Alan Eagleson, under intense pressure, stepped down as head of the
NHLPA in January 1992 and Gary Bettman became commissioner of the
NHL in early 1993.

In September 1994, when the NHL owners, at loggerheads with the
union over a new collective bargaining agreement, locked out the players
and precipitated a 103-day work stoppage, the Players' Association, now
led by Bob Goodenow, finally established itself as a formidable union that
effectively represents its members. The owners understand that it's
no longer business as usual — a wink here, a quiet word there. Goodenow has moved the union offices out of 37 Maitland Street, and the
NHLPA has tightened the rules governing agents, prohibiting them from
representing members of management at the same time that they represent players.

After Terry O'Reilly's health insurance problems came to light, the
Boston Bruins — thanks to Harry Sinden's efforts — offered to pay the
surcharge on O'Reilly's group health premium in return for personal-
service appearances on behalf of the team. O'Reilly's son, Evan, continues to

await a liver transplant. Meanwhile, Brad Park's son, Robbie, confined to a wheelchair, remains in relatively good health.

During Bettman's enlightened administration, Ed Kea, Jim Harrison, and Blair Chapman have all been helped by the NHL's emergency fund. The fund is financed partly by the league's disciplinary fines imposed on players during the season and used to aid former players and their families in distress. Chapman finally went to court over his career-ending disability case and, in early 1994 — thirteen years after suffering a ruptured disk — he settled with Lloyd's of London for an unspecified sum. The action cost him about $60,000 in legal fees.

Mike Gillis's lawsuit against Alan Eagleson, in which he seeks more than $500,000 in damages plus the $41,500 U.S. slice from his disability payout, is scheduled to be heard in April 1996. Jim Harrison and Glen Sharpley are among the other disabled former players now contemplating lawsuits against Eagleson.

The NHL's threatened suits against Bobby Orr, Gordie Howe, Billy Harris, and others, which grew out of comments attributed to them in newspaper stories about the NHL pension dispute, have been abandoned.

The retired players' suit against the NHL Pension Society, spearheaded by Carl Brewer and orchestrated by Mark Zigler, has finally borne fruit. The week of September 11, 1995, the first checks for additional pension funds were sent to retired players currently collecting pensions. The Canadian action took precedence over the U.S. class-action suit filed by Ed Ferren on behalf of Bob Dailey, Reggie Leach, and others. Had the retired players lost their case in Canada, they could have taken their battle to the U.S. courts. Ironically, the NHL may be fortunate to have lost the suit in Canada. Under U.S. law, millions of dollars in punitive damages could have been added to the award.

The NHL is proceeding with its suit against Baker & McKenzie, the Chicago law firm that advised the league about the pension surplus in the early 1980s.

Many NHL teams now display a very different attitude toward retired players. In September 1995, for example, the Bruins brought in a number of former NHL greats — including Frank Mahovlich, Johnny Bower, Phil

Esposito, Jean Béliveau, and Maurice Richard — to participate in a magnificent ceremony to mark the closing of the old Boston Garden. A few years ago, such a heartfelt expression of reconciliation would probably not have been made.

Another change in past pro hockey business practises occurred in early October 1995. In a joint announcement, Bettman, Goodenow, the International Ice Hockey Federation, and the Canadian Amateur Hockey Association (CAHA) unveiled an agreement allowing NHL players to play in the 1998 Olympics in Japan. They also announced a new World Cup tournament format to begin in late summer 1996, replacing what was once the Canada Cup. The NHL and NHLPA also agreed during early October that the new collective bargaining agreement would be honored for a full five-year period, guaranteeing no NHL labor interruptions through 1999.

In July 1995, the RCMP raided Alan Eagleson's office at 37 Maitland Street in Toronto. Among other things, the raid turned up documentation suggesting that in 1984 Eagleson used a rink-board advertising scheme similar to the 1991 scheme outlined in this book. In 1984, Eagleson directed some $470,000 to All Canada Sports, the company controlled by his friend Irving Ungerman. In total, the documents suggest, All Canada Sports earned $504,000 from rink-board sales in the 1984 tournament. Of that, $201,620 was paid to Kingsmar Holdings, another company associated with Eagleson. Arthur Harnett was once the president of Kingsmar; on November 15, 1984, his company, Harcom Stadium Inc., was paid a $75,000 "commission fee."

The RCMP raid also revealed that expenses paid by All Canada Sports included $5,000 campaign contributions to a number of prominent Ontario Conservative politicians, including Dennis Timbrell, Frank Miller, Larry Grossman, and Roy McMurtry. Other expenses included a $10,000 payment to former player Mike Walton, and a $2,000 repair bill for a Rolls-Royce shown as belonging to former Boston player Derek Sanderson. Sanderson, now a TV color commentator with the Bruins, told me he did not even have the car at the time. "I never knew about any two grand for repairs."

Alan Eagleson's winter home at La Coquille Club Villas in Manalapan, Florida, has been sold, and the proceeds — $224,622.04 U.S. — frozen by the U.S. government. Eagleson's waterfront home in Collingwood, Ontario, has also been sold.

In late summer of 1995, I was contacted by Chicago lawyer Martin Oberman, who is preparing a $370-million class-action collusion case against the NHL, John Ziegler, William Wirtz, and Alan Eagleson. In essence, the suit will argue that, during Eagleson's tenure as head of the NHLPA after the NHL-WHA merger, player salaries were artificially suppressed because of the collusion between labor and management.

Not long after word of the pending suit got around, Wirtz, owner of the Blackhawks, former chairman of the NHL board of governors, and a staunch Eagleson supporter, suffered a mild stroke.

In September 1995, I obtained an RCMP affidavit stating that various Eagleson associates had been interviewed by the RCMP. Irving Ungerman was one. The affidavit stated that Ungerman had struck a deal whereby any information he provided to them would not be used against him in any criminal proceeding.

Others who have spoken to the RCMP include Gordon Canning, secretary-treasurer of Monterra Properties, who was asked about Eagleson's real-estate dealings in the Collingwood area. Canning's information helped the RCMP conclude that the $500,000 NHLPA loan arranged through Howard Ungerman to his father's company, Irving Investments Ltd., went toward the purchase of land in which Eagleson and his family company had an ownership stake.

Chris Lang, recently retired as a twenty-five-year board member of Hockey Canada, told the RCMP that "Eagleson had never disclosed to him or other members of the board of directors" that $100,000 of Hockey Canada money had also been used in the Collingwood property deal in which Eagleson and his family had a stake.

Sam Simpson, the former NHLPA director of operations, was also interviewed. Among other things, Simpson told the RCMP that "he received his direction from Eagleson regarding mortgage investments," that "Eagleson did not disclose any related party transactions on any of the mortgage investments," and that Simpson was not aware of "any specific approval that was obtained from the Executive Board [of the NHLPA] by Eagleson allowing him to invest in any private mortgages." Simpson said that he was "sure that Eagleson did not disclose the fact that he had a financial interest in Monterra Properties Limited at the time of obtaining the [$500,000 Irving Investments] loan," and that, if Simpson had known, he "would have seriously questioned making the loan." Through his lawyer, Simpson also admitted altering loan documents following conversations with Howard Ungerman.

On September 26, 1995, Eagleson's lawyer, Brian Greenspan, told Mary Ormsby of the *Toronto Star*: "We continue to take the position that Mr. Eagleson was not in any way engaged in any misconduct [and he] broke no laws. We look forward to the conclusion of whatever criminal investigation is taking place in Canada and should law enforcement and prosecution choose to charge Mr. Eagleson in Canada, we look forward to vigorously defending any and all allegations of misconduct."

PHOTO CREDITS

The author acknowledges with gratitude the following sources.

Bruce Bennett/*Hockey News*: Photo section I: p. 5 bottom middle and right

Boston Herald: Photo section I: p. 1 bottom (photo by Ray Lussier)

Canada Wide: Photo section I: p. 3 top left; p. 4 bottom right; p. 7 top right; bottom left.
   Photo section II: p. 1 bottom right; p. 3 top left and right, bottom; p. 4 top left;
   p. 7 bottom left and right; p. 8 top left and right; bottom left

Canapress Photo Service: Photo section II: p. 7 top

CBC-TV: Photo section I: p. 7 bottom right

Debbie Cassidy: Photo section I: p. 8 top right

Crawley Warren 1987 Financial Report: Photo section I: p. 6 top left and bottom

Wayne Cuddington/*Ottawa Citizen*: Photo section I: p. 6 top right

Eagle-Tribune files: Photo section I: p. 5 middle left; p. 8 top left, middle right,
   bottom left. Photo section II: p. 1 bottom left and middle (courtesy of Compuware);
   p. 2 bottom left (courtesy of Toronto Maple Leafs); p. 6 top, bottom left

Ed Garvey: Photo section I: p. 2 top left

Mike Gillis: Photo section I: p. 5 middle right

Hockey News: Photo section II: p. 4 bottom left

John Major/*Ottawa Citizen*: Photo section II: p. 8 bottom right

Jerry Manco/*Inside Hockey*: Photo section I: p. 8 middle left

Tim McKenna/Canada Wide and Toronto *Sun*: Photo section II: p. 5 top

Al Ruelle: Photo section I: p. 1 top and middle; p. 2 top right, bottom left and right;
   p. 4 top left and right, middle left, bottom left; p. 5 top right, middle middle, bottom left.
   Photo section II: p. 1 top; p. 2 top; p. 4 top right, bottom right

Robert Shaver: Photo section I: p. 5 top left

Toronto *Sun*: Photo section I: p. 7 top left (Canadian Press/AP). Photo section II:
   p. 2 bottom right; p. 5 bottom

Rich Winter: Photo section I: p. 3 top right

Ken Yuszkus: Photo section I: p. 3 bottom

INDEX

Above the Law (Palango), 257

Ackroyd, John, 181

Adams, John, 15

Adams, George, Jr., 125

Adams, Weston, Jr., 115

Affleck, Don, 51

Agro, John, 18, 224

Ahern, Fred, 32

Air Canada, 101, 102, 103, 104, 105, 181, 200, 202, 203, 208, 232-33, 255, 261

Alan Candy's, 235

Alberta Labor Relations Board, 165-66

Allan, Bob, 187

All-Canada Sports Promotions, 188, 190, 211, 234-40, 241-42, 246-47, 260, 267

All-Star Game (1991), 31, 40, 112, 175

Alsemgeest, Marty, 231

American Airlines, 63, 203

American Arbitration Association, 20

American Football League, 136

American Specialty Insurance Group, 79

Angotti, Lou, 108, 115, 151, 156-57, 158-59

Arthur Harnett Enterprises, 242

Arthurs, H.W., 133-34

Assured Assistance Associates Inc., 100, 102, 104

Atlanta Flames, 75, 76

Awrey, Don, 3, 4, 6, 15, 16, 154

Aubut, Marcel, 79, 170-71

B

Backstrom, Ralph, 108, 162

Baikie, Roger, 144

Bailey, Ace, 2, 11-12

Baker, David, Sr., 194, 195-96, 197

Baker & McKenzie (law firm), 128, 266

Ballard, Harold, 173, 174, 264

Ballard, Yolanda (McMillan), 174

Baltimore Skipjacks, 65

Barber, Bill, 81

Barnett, Mike, 224

Barr, Dave, 36, 185

Barrett, Freddy, 163

Bartlett, Steve, 224

Batchelder, Vic, 88-89, 96, 99

Bathgate, Andy, 110, 113, 120, 162

Baun, Bobby, 136, 162

Beber, Monty, 191

Beer, John K., 238, 246, 247, 249, 258, 259

Béliveau, Jean, 15, 162, 267

Berenson, Red, 162

Betterley, Rick, 34

Bettman, Gary, 127-28, 250, 253, 265, 266

Bigione Management Services Ltd., 184

Bigione, Nick, 184

Blackhawks. *See* Chicago Blackhawks

Blady, Judi, 181

Blaney, Pasternak, Luck and Smela
(law firm), 136

Blue Mountain Resorts Ltd., 181, 188-89,
191-92

See also Monterra Properties Limited

Bobby Orr Enterprises Ltd., 137, 149, 221,
231, 251

Bobby Orr Sports Injury Clinic, 132, 133

Bond, Al, 196, 197

Boss Man, 235

Boston Braves, 27

Boston Bruins, 1, 2, 4, 5, 6, 8, 11, 12, 13,
16, 22, 27, 28, 29, 36, 43, 74, 76, 78,
80, 89, 115, 120, 121, 125, 129, 130,
136-47, 154, 169, 177, 185, 192, 205,
213, 222, 253, 265, 266, 267

Boston Globe, 250, 261

Boston Mutual Insurance Company, 89, 90

Bourne, Bob, 29

Bourque, Ray, 5-6, 16, 120, 163, 222-23

Bower, Johnny, 110, 266

Bradshaw, Robert, 75, 76, 77, 90, 93-96

Bremner, Rich, 235-242

Brewda, Erv, 190, 195, 196, 197

Brewer, Carl

and "Merry Christmas letter,"107, 109

pension (amount), 107

pension dispute, 24, 30-31, 40, 43, 56,
106-7, 109-10, 112, 113, 114, 118-19,
120, 127, 128, 136, 244, 247, 251, 266

response to Ziegler letter (1991), 123-24

Britz, Greg, 63, 203

Brown, Jeff, 175

Brubaker, Bill, 10

Bruins. *See* Boston Bruins

Bucyk, Johnny (the Chief), 8, 16, 107,
120, 128, 129, 131, 139

Budd, Wayne A., 244

Budzban, Edward, 52

Buffalo Bills, 209

Buffalo Sabres, 77, 78, 89, 163, 164,
172, 174

Bull, Charles, 46, 47-48, 49, 50, 53, 54,
69, 80-81, 132, 191

Bull, James, 191

Buss Marketing, 235

Butcher, Garth, 36, 118

Buyer's Guide to Travel Health Insurance
(McCartney), 103

Buynak, Gord, 156-58

Byers, Lyndon, 29, 120

C

CAHA. *See* Canadian Amateur Hockey
Association

Callen, Jack, 181

Cambio Valoren Bank (Zurich), 234, 236,
238-41

Cameron, Stevie, 257

Campbell, Kim, 245, 247-48, 249

Campbell Manufacturing Co. Ltd., 206, 218

Canada Cup, 7, 8, 9, 12-13, 20, 21, 24,
33, 95, 100, 109, 110, 174, 183, 188,
202, 209, 210-11, 213-28

financial statements (1976-91), 229-31

total profit (1981/84/87), 231

See also International hockey;
Team Canada

Canada-Soviet series. *See* Soviet Summit
Series (1972)

Canadian Bar Association, 23

Canadian Football League, 202

Canadian Amateur Hockey Association
(CAHA), 225-28

Can-Am Enterprises, 149

Canning, Gordon, 181, 189, 191

Canon, 235

Capitals. *See* Washington Capitals

Career-ending disability insurance.
See Insurance

Carleton, Wayne, 1, 43

Carling O'Keefe Breweries, 170, 171, 242

Carroll, Mike, 4-5

Carson, Jimmy, 13

Caruso, Peter, 246

Cashman, Wayne, 2, 16, 76, 108, 147

Chapman, Blair, 59-64, 90, 91, 93, 266

Chapman, John, 23

Checkoway, Allan, 79

Cheevers, Gerry, 2, 6, 8, 16, 120, 125

Cherniak, Earl, 123

Cherry, Don, 74, 147, 174

Cherry, Zena, 181

Chicago Blackhawks, 4, 19, 25, 34, 43-44, 47, 50, 52, 53-54, 55, 56, 83, 84, 140-48, 149, 151-53, 156, 169, 179, 208, 268

Chicago Cougars, 156

Chrétien, Jean, 256, 257

Christian, Dave, 29

Christopher Lang & Associates, 218

Chuvalo, George, 188

Clark, Gordie, 29

Clark, Graeme, 49, 54, 205, 206, 207

Clark, Joe, 137

Clarke, Bobby, 3, 71, 211

Clement, Bill, 253

Cleveland Barons, 10, 31, 192-94

Clune, Brenda, 181

Collective Bargaining Agreement(s) (CBA), 6-7, 10-11, 23, 24, 25, 63, 67, 68, 112, 116, 118, 121, 165, 166, 265

Collingwood land deal. See Monterra Properties Limited

Colorado Rockies, 69, 74, 80

Compaq, 235

Compuware, 168-69, 170, 171, 173, 174, 175, 176, 178, 179

"Confidential Report to NHLPA Players." See Garvey, Ed, report (1989)

Considine, Pat, 142

Continental Football League, 208

Continental Insurance Company, 53

Contracts. See Collective Bargaining Agreement(s); Free agency and compensation

Conway, Russ, 232, 256, 258

La Coquille Club Villas (Manalapan, Fl.), 207, 209, 210, 218, 267

Core Media, 235, 241-42

Costello, Murray, 225-27, 228

Courtnall, Geoff, 82

Courtnall, Russ, 82

"Cracking the Ice" series (Conway), 238, 244
    See also Eagle-Tribune

Crawley Warren Group, 53, 67, 68, 80, 83-84, 86, 89, 90, 96, 97, 98, 100-101, 102-4, 135

Cromartry, J. David, 208

Croteau, Gary, 73-75

Cruise, David, 135

Curran, Rick, 220-21, 222

CWL Telesport, 234, 235, 236, 238-41

CWL Werbung, 234

D

Dailey, Bob, 85-87, 91, 120-21, 255, 261, 266

Daley, Hap, 246

Daly, Tom, 243, 246, 248

Davis, Bill, 189

DeBartolo, Ed, 153

Deconkey, Bill, 245

Defense Never Rests, The (Dowbiggin), 106

Deford, Frank, 122, 124

Dempster, David, 18

Depenbrock, J.F., 38

Dermody, Bill, 18, 37, 186-87, 194, 197, 224

Detroit Junior Red Wings, 168, 179

Detroit Pistons, 71

Detroit Red Wings, 28, 29, 36, 74, 94, 115, 164, 168

Dettrey, Charles, 77

Dingwall, David, 244-45, 247, 256, 264

Dionne, Marcel, 183

Dipple, Ted, 79, 80, 82, 84, 99-100

Disability insurance. See Insurance

Donaldson, Marie, 182

Donaldson, Norman, 181-87, 189-90, 261-62

Doneagle Construction Ltd., 181

Doneagle Investments Inc., 189-90

Dorey, Jim, 203

Dovey, William C., 40-42, 203

Dowbiggin, Bruce, 106, 126, 152, 161, 162, 209, 245, 252, 261

Dryden, Ken, 124, 162, 194
Dubin, Charles, 260
Dupuy, Michel, 256

E

Eagleson, Alan
and conflicts of interest, 7, 8, 9, 10-11,
    18, 19, 21-22, 25, 48-49, 53, 54,
    78-79, 80-82, 85, 86, 92, 97-98,
    119-20, 151-53, 267
assessment of union leadership,
    (Garvey 1989), 18-23
assets frozen, 267
bonuses and benefits, 18-19, 20, 199,
    219
childhood and youth, 135
class-action suit against, 267
contract, 19-20, 37, 219-20
criminal investigations into, 243-64
indictment, 250, 254-55
reactions to: by media, 251-53, 262-63
    by players/officials, 253-54
violations, 250-51, 254-56
and demise of WHA, 7, 8-9, 10, 22, 24,
    25, 32, 267
education, 135, 136
expenses, 32-33, 39, 42, 95-96, 101,
    198-204, 210-11, 231-32
and disclosure of information, 12-13,
    19, 21. 22, 23, 30, 37, 112, 124,
    134-35, 177-78, 185, 193-94, 197,
    213-14, 223-24
fights extradition, 255
Hall of Famer, 56
and handling of clients' finances,
    132-34, 137, 204-7
and insurance fraud, 85, 86-87,
    254, 255
See also Insurance and international
    hockey, 20-21, 23, 33, 37, 99,
    165, 199, 214-28.
See also Canada Cup; Team Canada
    loans and land deals, 9-10, 13-14,
    36, 37, 88-89, 96-99, 101, 182-97,
    252, 261-62, 268

and free agency, 4, 25, 39, 165
management style, 7, 26-27, 92, 94,
    153-56, 158, 222
and "Merry Christmas letter" (to
    Brewer), 107, 109
and Mike Gillis lawsuit, 82-83, 266
and Monterra Properties Limited, 191,
    192, 268
pension, 20, 106, 199
and Pimlico Road apt. (London),
    88-89, 96-99, 101
and player pension dispute, 106-28
See also Pensions
and player perception of, 3-4, 7, 7-8,
    9, 10-11, 14, 15, 26, 55, 150, 153-54,
    156
and political connections, 32-33, 41-42,
    137, 189, 208, 257, 267
reveals confidential information,
    170-72, 174
and relationship with John Ziegler, 9,
    19, 20, 88, 101, 169, 176, 192
resigns, NHLPA, 265
and rink-board advertising scheme/
    coverup (1991), 100, 232-33, 234-42,
    243, 255; (1984), 267
salary, 37, 198-99
and Swiss banking connections, 222,
    233-34, 236, 238, 241
union leadership challenged, 7, 14,
    18-23, 110-11, 120, 253
Eagleson, Jill Anne (daughter, Alan), 190,
    191, 200, 206, 233
Eagleson, Nancy (wife, Alan), 206, 210, 233
Eagleson, Trevor Allen, (son, Alan), 190,
    217, 233, 235
Eagleson, Yasmine (wife, Trevor Allen), 233
Eagleson Family Trust, 39, 98
Eagleson Ungerman (law firm), 39, 82,
    200, 215, 216, 217, 236, 237
Eagle-Tribune (Lawrence, Mass.), 2
reports on Eagleson/NHL, 5, 26, 96,
    97, 138, 146, 174, 178, 185, 223,
    224, 225, 233, 243, 255, 256
finalist, Pulitzer Prize (1992), 262

Earle, John, 261-62

Edgeworth, Jim, Jr., 79, 80, 84

Edmonton Oilers, 6, 9, 11, 12, 13, 43, 50, 165, 171, 177, 180, 211

Eggleton, Art, 181

Elston, Murray, 119, 120, 126, 127

Emmerton, James, 240

Employee Retirement Income Security Act (ERISA), 107, 121, 255

ESPN, 253

Esposito, Phil, 2, 3, 8-9, 15-16, 138, 143, 177, 179, 266-67

Esposito, Tony, 3, 55, 153, 185

Estey, Willard, 202, 227-28

Evraire, Paul, 248

Ezekiel, David, 34-35

F

FBI (Eagleson investigation), 243-51, 254-56

Felter, Ken, 177

Ferren, Ed, 120-21, 266

Fieldhaus Ltd., 201

Financial Times of Canada, 189

FInancial World, 148

Fisher, Doug, 262-63

Fisher, Red, 251

Flaman, Ferny, 31, 108, 127

Flames. See Atlanta Flames

Fletcher, Cliff, 254

Flood, Curt, 4

Flynn, Michael, 63

Forbes, Dave, 37, 111-12, 113-14, 122-23, 160, 214

Forristall, John, 130

Foster, Dwight, 5

Foster, Sue, 106, 109, 110, 127, 251

Fox, Jimmy, 118

Francis, Emile, 57-58, 60, 61

Frank magazine, 253

Free agency and compensation, 4, 5, 6, 10, 11, 24, 25, 39, 163-66
in baseball, 4, 5, 24
in basketball, 24

Freyer, Steve, 68-69

Fuhr, Grant, 154

Full House Inc., 207, 208

Fulton, Davie, 137

G

Gale, George A., 208

Gans, Arthur M., 23

Garrett, John, 206

Garrick, James, 72

Gartner, Mike, 36, 117, 177, 185

Garvey, Ed, 24, 26, 27, 36, 37-40, 111, 113, 118, 120, 177, 194, 195, 198, 203
report (1989), 18-23

Gassoff, Bob, 58

Gaudet, Len, 190

Gelinas, Martin, 13

George, Patti, 220, 233, 238

Gilbert, Rod, 162

Gilden, Jerome, 61-62

Gillette, 235

Gillis, Mike, 80-83, 87, 101, 255, 261

Giovinazzo, Tony, 195

Globe and Mail, The, 129, 131, 181, 187

Goals (newsletter), 36, 38, 40, 56, 198

Godfrey, Paul, 181, 252, 260

Goldblatt, Marvin, 40, 69, 70, 78, 81, 82, 149, 155, 181, 187, 191, 192, 205, 215, 218-19, 221, 223, 232, 233, 238, 242

Goodenow, Bob, 114, 126, 169, 223, 232, 265

Goring, Butch, 206

Gorton, Nathaniel M., 259, 260

Goulet, Michel, 170, 171

Grant, Joe, 202

Gray, Herb, 256, 257, 258-59

Gray, Malcolm, 187-88, 197

Green, Rick, 159

Green, Teddy, 2

Greenspan, Brian, 255, 268-69

Greenspan Humphrey (law firm), 255

Gregory, Jim, 202

Gretzky, Wayne, 12-13, 117, 137, 138, 164, 171, 172, 188, 202, 212, 224, 253

Griffiths, Alison, 135

Griffiths, W. David, 208
Gross, Elizabeth, 202
Gross, George, 201-2, 252
Grossman, Larry, 267
Grosvenor Estate Restorations, 97, 98
Guttman, Robert M., 166

H

Hadfield, Vic, 123
Haggert, Bobby, 158-59
Haig, Alexander, 210
Hall, Glenn, 1
Harcom Consultants Limited, 183, 242
Harcom Stadium Advertising, 242, 267
Harloff, Glen, 247
Harnett, Arthur, 95, 181, 183, 222, 242,
    251, 267
Harnett Consultants, 181
Harris, Billy, 124, 136, 266
Harrison, Jim, 43-52, 53-56, 69, 70, 83,
    132, 266
Harrison, Liz, 46, 47, 49
Hartford Whalers, 9, 14, 16, 50, 62, 118,
    177, 178, 179
Harvey, Doug, 15, 108
Hayes, George, 108
Hayes, Judy, 108
Hayter, Evan, 242
Henderson, Paul, 206, 215
Herron, Denis, 31-32
Hextall, Rex, 154, 155
Hockey Canada, 20, 24, 32, 33, 112, 133,
    137, 191, 203, 204, 206, 209,
    213-28
    expenses, 215, 216-17, 218, 219, 220-
    21, 222, 225, 230, 232
    sued by CAHA, 227-28
    financial disclosure, 244-45
    See also Canada Cup; International
    hockey; Team Canada
"The Hockey Canada Trust," 228
Hockey Hall of Fame, 56
Hockey News, The, 216
"Hockey Night in Canada," 133
Hodge, Ken, 1, 2, 142, 143

Hodge, Ken, Jr., 29
Holland, Nancy, 207-8
Holland, Richard, 207-8
Holmes, Derek, 222, 233
Honderich, Beland, 209
Hood, Bruce, 31, 113
Horvath, Bronco, 139
Howe, Colleen, 107-8, 127
Howe, Gordie, 14-15, 110, 113, 114, 117-
    18, 120, 123, 124-25, 127, 128, 137,
    138, 162, 266
Howe, Mark, 36
Howland, William G.C., 208
Huber, Willie, 70-72
HUD Holdings, 191
Hudson, John, 234, 235, 238, 239-40, 241
Hull, Bobby, 106, 110, 112, 113, 118,
    120, 162
Hull, Brett, 112-13, 164
Hunt, Jim, 262

I

ICE (NHL-owned insurance co.), 29-30,
    31, 33-35, 91, 135
Ingle, Robin, 101-2
Ingraham, Rob, 66
Inkster, Norman, 248, 257
Insurance coverage, 27-30, 34
    career-ending disability, 34, 51, 52,
        53-55, 58-59, 62-87, 89-95, 99-100
    health, 34, 35, 59
    player disputes regarding, 43-87
    travel, 100, 101-5
International hockey, 20, 24, 33, 37, 165,
    213-28
    and player pension fund, 21, 109, 110,
        116-17, 124, 213-14, 223, 224, 230
    See also Canada Cup; Hockey Canada
International Ice Hockey Federation
    (IIHF), 99, 225, 226, 231, 234, 239
International Professional Hockey Alumni
    Association, 121
    See also National Alumni Association
Intra-Continental Ensurers Limited (ICE),
    34-35

Irving Investments Limited, 190, 191, 268
Irving Ungerman Limited, 18, 191, 197
Ivan, Tommy, 143

J

Jacobs, Jeremy, 12, 138, 141, 142, 147, 148, 250
Janney, Craig, 29
Jarvis, Kenneth, 208
Jialson Holdings, 83, 97, 98, 191, 200, 203
Jim Dorey Enterprises, 205
Johansen, Trevor, 47, 69-70, 89
John Ingle Travel Insurance, 101-2
Johnson, Dennis, 81, 90, 96, 97, 98
Johnson, Don, 226
Johnson, Ross, 144, 145, 146, 148, 208
Johnson, Tom, 10-11, 130, 138, 140, 213, 253
Johnston, Eddie, 2, 16, 48, 49, 56, 153
Jones, Janet, 13, 202
Jutan International Limited, 203

K

Kadwell, John, 191
Karn, Donald W., 189
Karnco Limited, 189
Kasper, Steve, 13-14, 36, 185
Kaminsky, Art, 73
Karmanos, Peter, 168-79
Kea, Ed, 57-61, 64, 66, 70, 90, 91, 93, 94, 266
Kea, Jennifer, 57-58, 60, 61
Keenan, Mike, 3, 55, 152, 153, 188
Kelly, Paul V., 246, 248, 254, 256, 259
Kelly, Red, 110
Kelly, Tom, 149
Keon, Dave, 33
Khawly, Ramez, 238
Kilger, Bob, 244
Kingsmar Holdings Limited, 81, 82, 83, 191, 267
Kisio, Kelly, 71
Knox, Seymour, 172
Kolb, Louis W., 43-45, 46, 47, 49, 50, 53
Korn, Jim, 36

Koskie & Minsky (law firm), 109
Kosters, Volker, 234, 238-39, 240
Kukulowicz, Aggie, 37, 200, 202, 208, 232-33
Kukulowicz, Shayne, 200

L

Labatt Brewing Company Ltd., 232, 234, 236, 237, 238-41, 260
Labor Management Reporting and Disclosure Act, 38
Labrosse, J.M., 208
Lamby, Dick, 32
Lang, Chris, 206, 218, 223, 224, 227-28, 234, 268
Lang, Helen, 209
Lang, Howard, 209
LaPorte, Helen A., 62, 65
Larouche, Pierre, 66-67
Latto, Larry, 19, 203
Laughlin, Jim, 204
Laughren, Floyd, 125-27
Law Society of Upper Canada, 23, 110-11, 208, 243, 245, 258, 259
    investigation (Eagleson), 260-61, 263
Leach, Reggie, 31, 120-21, 266
Leeson, John, 185-86, 195, 196, 197
Lemay, Timothy J., 217, 248-49, 257, 259
Lemelin, Reggie, 29, 120
Lemieux, Mario, 66, 137, 138, 153, 188
Licensing Corporation of America, 202
Lindros, Eric, 188
Lindsay, Ted, 24, 162
Linseman, Ken, 11, 26, 120, 254
Liut, Mike, 176, 185
Lloyd's of London, 59, 64, 67, 68, 69, 76, 81, 82, 84, 90-91, 94, 99, 101, 102, 104, 266
Lockwood, Tom, 110, 245-46, 259
Lorentz, Jim, 15, 16
Los Angeles Kings, 13, 56, 69, 72, 74, 76, 118, 140, 154, 164, 169, 171, 177, 223, 253
Ludwig, Lloyd R., 207-8
Lumley, Ed, 144

Lush Realtors, 190

Lynch, Jack, 55

M

McCann, D. Scott, 181

Maclean's magazine, 187

McClelland, Ian, 256, 257, 258-59

McCormack, William, 260

McCourt, Dale, 164-65, 167

McCreary, Keith, 123

Macdonald, H. Ian, 132-33, 219

McGuire, George, 72, 73

McCartney, James I., 103, 104, 105

MacGregor, Roy, 253

McKenzie, Bob, 253

MacInnis, Lyman, 148

McKeam, Tom, 135-36

McKenzie, Johnny, 1, 8, 16, 127

Mackenzie, Michael, 101

McCrimmon, Brad, 5

MacMillan, Robert, 104

McMullen, John, 172

McMullin, Bill, 244

McMurtry, Roy, 101, 201, 202, 260, 267

McNall, Bruce, 13

McSorley, Marty, 120, 177, 253

Magnuson, Keith, 55-56, 153

Mahoney, Lorraine, 186, 228

Mahovlich, Frank, 110, 128, 162

Maitland House, 22, 97, 199, 203-4, 216, 265, 267

Manalapan property. *See* La Cocquille Club Villas

Manufacturers Life (Manulife), 108, 110, 17, 121, 122

Maksymiw, Roman, 184

Maple Leafs. *See* Toronto Maple Leafs

Marcotte, Don, 33, 107, 120, 127

Marotte, Gil, 143

Martin, Pit, 143

Marty's (clothing), 149

May, Kathryn, 227, 249

Merner, David, 249

Microsoft, 235

Middleton, Rick, 33, 56, 117, 142, 155, 158, 205-7, 218, 228

Milbury, Mike, 7-8, 29, 92, 99-100, 185

Miller, Frank, 267

Miller, Kelly, 40

Mills, Dennis, 244, 247, 249

Minnesota North Stars, 84

Mohns, Doug, 56, 162

Monterra Properties Limited, 191, 192, 268

Montreal Canadiens, 15, 31, 66, 72, 77, 159, 169, 194

Montreal Gazette, 251

Montreal Trust, 228

Moog, Andy, 5, 6, 16, 29, 37, 112, 125, 161-62, 176, 185, 213

Mooney, Paul, 4, 139, 141, 142, 145, 147-48, 192

Morris, Paul, 196

Moulter, Larry, 250

Mulcahy, Charlie, 141

Mulroney, Brian, 41-42, 101, 137, 253, 257, 258

Muni, Craig, 165, 166

Munro, John, 263

Munson, Lester, 122-23, 124

Murphy, Hugh, 207

Murphy, Ron, 16, 31

Murray, Bob, 224

Murray, J.P.R., 257-58

Mutual Legal Assistance on Criminal Matters (MLAT), 247

N

Namath, Joe, 136

Nangill Investments, 206, 207, 218

Natale, Cam, 232

Natale, Gene, 232

Natale's Clothiers, 231, 232

National, The (newspaper), 122, 124

National Alumni Association, 121

National Basketball Association (NBA), 24, 71, 79

National Football League (NFL), 79, 142, 161, 209

National Hockey League (NHL) antitrust action (1973), 164, 167 compensation rules, 25

contracts, 25

See also Free agency and compensation

emergency fund, 266

and entry draft, 26

and expansion, 38, 115, 175, 178-79

and insurance coverage, 27-30, 34, 53-55, 58-59, 60, 62-87, 90-95

and labor law scrutiny, 165-67

negotiating pattern, 24

owned insurance co., 29-30, 31, 33-35, 36, 91

owner lockout (1994), 265

pension plan:

surplus monies from, 14, 24, 33, 107, 116, 109-19, 120, 121-23, 266

ruling on, 125, 127-28

changes to, 113, 115, 116

and player exemption, 119-20, 125-27, 151, 261

See also Pensions

player tenure in, 5, 25

serves legal notice to players, (1991), 124, 266

tampering rule, 141, 142, 143-44

See also NHL-WHA merger National Hockey League Pension Society, 24, 30, 56, 107, 108, 109, 110, 114-19, 121-24, 125-28, 261

player exemption, 115-17, 119-20, 125-27, 151, 162

post-Eagleson, 265

National Hockey League Players' Association (NHLPA)

audit report (1987/88/89), 40-41

and conflict-of-interest rules, 265

dues, 199

expenses, 19-20, 22, 37, 41-42, 95-96, 97, 101, 175, 198-204, 211, 220-21, 231-32

payments made to Eagleson firms, 200-1

formed, 24

insurance:

career-ending disability, 51, 52, 53-55, 58-59, 62-87, 89-95, 99-100

health, 35, 59

travel, 100, 101-5

and labor laws, 37-38, 160-61, 165-67

loans and real estate investments, 9-10, 13-14, 36, 37, 88-89, 96-99, 101, 182-97, 192-94

negotiating pattern, 25

player perception of, 7-8

and product endorsements, 158-59

Nedomansky, Vaclav, 252

Neely, Cam, 29, 120, 154

Net Worth (Cruise/Griffiths), 135

New England Newspaper Publishers' Association, 262

New England Press Association, 262

New Jersey Devils, 163, 172

New Leaf Florists Limited, 182, 183, 184, 185, 186, 187, 197

New York Islanders, 29, 125, 171-72, 176, 193

New York Jets, 136

New York Rangers, 16, 28, 58, 66, 71, 138, 142, 156, 172, 177, 205, 207

NHL-WHA merger (1979), 7, 8-9, 10, 24, 25, 50, 65, 267

player participation in, 32

Norris family, 94

Norris, Jack, 143

Norris Trophy, 5, 137

North American Claims Facilities, 52, 62, 63, 65, 67, 68, 80, 81-82

O

Oberman, Martin, 267

O'Connell, Mike, 185

O'Neill, Brian, 49

Ontario Health Insurance Plan (OHIP), 103, 104

Ontario Hockey Association (OHA), 26

Ontario Hockey League (OHL), 136, 168

Ontario Pension Commission. *See* Pension Commission of Ontario

Ontario Progressive Conservative Association, 137, 183

On The Take (Cameron), 257

Oppenheim, Lou, 224-25

O'Reilly, Evan, 27, 28, 31, 265-66

O'Reilly, Terry, 6-7, 11, 22, 27, 29-30, 31, 89, 91, 120, 124, 127, 193, 265

Ormsby, Mary, 253

Ornest, Harry, 60-61

Orr, Bobby, 1-2, 4, 5, 9, 10, 12, 25, 27, 29, 31, 46, 47, 55, 76, 107, 110, 113, 118, 122-25, 127, 129-35, 143-45, 151-52, 160, 183, 202, 209, 243, 261, 266
   early relationship with Eagleson, 136-37
   financial problems, 132, 134, 148-49
   named vice pres./NHL, 137
   ownership offer (Bruins), 146-48
   severs ties with Eagleson, 134, 149, 153, 205
   and sports clinic (York) pledge, 129, 131-34
   traded to Chicago, 136-42, 209

Orr, Brent, 149

Orr, Darren, 149

Orr, Doug, 136

Orr, Peggy, 142, 148, 149

Orr-Walton Sports Camp (Orillia), 10, 31, 147, 149, 220, 221

Osler, Hoskin & Harcourt (law firm), 255, 261, 262

O'Sullivan, Jeremiah T., 250, 254, 260

Ottawa Citizen, 227, 249

Owchar, Dennis, 113

P

Paiement, Rosaire, 9-10, 32, 156, 192

Paiement, Wilf, 9-10, 31, 33, 192-93

Palango, Paul, 257

Papanek, John, 10

Paquette, Dennis, 166, 167

Park, Brad, 7-8, 19, 28-29, 35, 91, 107, 114, 116, 120, 124, 162, 193, 214, 243, 266

Park, Gerri, 28

Park, Robbie, 28, 29, 266

Pash, Jeff, 127

Patey, Larry, 58

Patrick, Dick, 172

Patrick, Lynn, 136

Patterson, Arnie, 188

Pattison, Jim, 180

Pension Commission of Ontario, 110, 114, 117, 119, 122, 123

Pensions, 3, 4, 8, 10-11, 20, 21, 23-24, 30-31, 33,
   contributions to: owners, 114, 115, 123, 128;
      players, 109, 114, 115
      executives/officials, 31, 108
   labor laws concerning:
   Canada, 113, 119
   U.S., 107
   retired players, 11, 14-15, 30-33, 38, 40, 110, 112-13, 118, 121-22, 125, 127-28
   amounts, 107-8
   and dispute, 106-28
   resolution of, 266

Peplinski, Jim, 185

Percy, Ted, 72

Peters, Greg, 245

Philadelphia Flyers, 31, 70, 71, 76, 77, 81, 154, 155, 156, 172, 211, 253

Pickett, John, 171-72

Pickett, Robin, 171

Pittsburgh Penguins, 9, 61, 66, 77, 83, 153, 178

Players Voice (newsletter), 38

Pocklington, Peter, 12, 171, 172, 177, 180, 202

Polin, Abe, 172

Pony Sporting Goods, 206, 207, 218

Porter, Anna, 181

Porter, Julian, 181

Potvin, Denis, 117

Poulin, Dave, 29

Power Play (Eagleson), 40, 179, 181, 194

Prentice, Dean, 56

Price Waterhouse, 40, 203

Progressive Conservative Party, 41-42, 101, 137

Proudfoot, Jim, 252, 253

Pulford, Bob, 3, 44-47, 49, 51, 54, 55, 56, 84, 135, 136, 151-52, 153
Putnam, Bill, 116

Q

Quebec Nordiques, 9, 50, 78, 170-71
Quinn, Jack, 175
Quinn, Jim, 161
Quinn, Pat, 75-77

R

Rae, Bob, 125
Rae-Con Consultants Limited, 78, 79, 80, 81, 82, 83, 181, 200, 201, 219
R. Alan Eagleson Sports Medicine Clinic, 134, 219
Ralston-Purina, 58, 60-61
Ramsay, Craig, 163
Ratelle, Jean, 107, 120, 162
Rauch, Larry, 35, 36
Raymond, Bert, 253
RCMP
    interviews (Eagleson associates), 268
    investigate Eagleson, 237, 238, 240-41, 245-49, 256-60, 262, 264
    raid (Eagleson's office, July1995), 267
Reagan, Ronald, 210
Red Wings. See Detroit Red Wings
Regan, Gerry, 227
Regan, Larry, 121, 122
Registrar of Insurance Companies (Bermuda), 33, 35
Reid, Robert F., 208
Reise, Leo, 120
Renwick, Gordon, 226-27
Revenue Canada, 122, 148, 205
Richard, Maurice, 108, 128, 267
Rickaby, Peter, 208
Rick Middleton Enterprises, 205-6
Rink-board advertising, 100, 188, 190, 232-33, 234-42, 246-47, 249, 255, 267
Robert Bradshaw and Associates, 65
Robert, Rene, 113
Roberts, Gord, 117
Roberts, Ron, 65-66, 70, 75, 159-60

Robichaud, Louis, 32-33, 41-42
Robison, Ron, 20, 225, 228
Robitaille, Luc, 154, 156, 253
Rock, Allan, 256
Rowley, Ernie, 190, 236
Royal Canadian Mounted Police. See RCMP
Rutherford, Jim, 169, 170, 173, 174-75, 176
Rutherford, Robert C., 208

S

Sabres. See Buffalo Sabres
St. Louis Blues, 1, 32, 57-59, 60-64, 90, 156-58, 163-64, 170, 172, 174-75
St. Paul Fire and Marine Insurance Company, 53, 94
Salazar, Jose, 45
Salcer, Ron, 13, 18, 111, 223
Salt Lake Eagles, 57, 59, 61, 62
Sanderson, Derek, 8, 16, 267
Sandhill Construction, 190, 236, 237
San Jose Sharks, 177
Sather, Glen, 13, 50, 51, 180, 211
Sator, Ted, 29
Saunders, Jack, 124
Savard, André, 77-80, 81, 101, 255, 261
Sawchuk, Terry, 58
Sawyer, Ken, 113, 118, 119, 125
Schmidt, Milt, 108, 120, 127, 143
Schwarz, Werner, 234, 239, 240
Scott, Charles, 82-83
Secord, Al, 5
Seiling, Ric, 89-90
Semenkod, Dave, 9
Senecal, Louise Helene, 232
Sexton, Edgar, 252-53, 255, 261
Shack, Eddie, 110, 120, 124, 128, 162
Shaheen, Bill, 107
Shanahan, Brendan, 163-64, 165
Shanahan, Mike, 174
Shanley, Paul, 149
Sharpley, Glen, 84-85, 87, 91, 255, 261, 266
Shea Gardner (law firm), 203
Sheffer, Murray, 188
Shenkarow, Barry, 172

Sheppard, Greg, 9

Simmons, Steve, 252

Simpson, Sam, 29, 40, 41, 54, 59, 68, 71, 72, 75, 154, 183-84, 185, 191, 192, 201, 215, 218, 219, 223-24, 268

Sinden, Harry, 3, 4, 28, 29-30, 33, 74, 139, 140-41, 142, 146-47, 162, 178, 214, 223, 249, 265

Sittler, Darryl, 181

Skalbania, Nelson, 190

Sleigher, Louis, 68-69

Sloan, Ted, 108

Smith, Bobby, 161

Smith, Brian, 164, 165, 167

Smith, Dallas, 1, 2, 3, 4-5, 6, 25, 107, 162, 163

Smith, Rick, 15, 159-60

Solomon, Glen, 261

Solomon, Sid, Jr., 147

Solurush, John M., 126

Songin, Tom, 31

Sony, 235

Sopinka, John, 202-3

Soviet Summit Series (1972), 116, 137, 215, 252

Speer, Billy, 1

Sports Illustrated, 10, 20, 63, 134, 221, 242

Sports Management Consultants, 205

Sports Management Limited, 55, 74, 86, 147, 173, 175, 193, 200, 205, 215, 220-21

Sports Representatives Ltd., 158

Squadron Insurance, 53

Stamler, Rod, 257

Standard Brands, 144, 148, 149, 208

Stanfield, Fred, 15, 16, 143

Stanley, Allan, 110, 113, 120, 124, 128, 162

Starkman, Randy, 253

Stastny, Peter, 170, 171

Stedman, Judy, 210-11

Stedman, Kim, 211-12

Stein, Gil, 78, 82, 177, 230

Stern, Donald, K., 251, 253, 255

Stevens, Scott, 163, 164

Storer Broadcasting, 141, 146

Strachan, Al, 253

Stratton, Bert, 90, 96

Strosberg, Harvey, 144

Superintendant of Financial Institutions, 101

Sutton, William, 35, 60, 65, 68, 69, 89, 90, 92, 93, 95, 96, 202

Swados, Bob, 172

Sweeney, Bob, 29

Sweeney, Don, 29

Swensen, Richard, 251, 254

T

Taglianetti, Peter, 185

Talafous, Dean, 45, 49, 53

Tallon, Dale, 54-55, 83-84, 87, 101

Tauber, Martin, 188, 197

Taylor, Jim, 252

Team Canada, 3, 6, 13, 33, 55, 69, 232
   expenses: (1976), 229, 230
   (1981/84/87), 231
   See also Canada Cup

Team USA
   expenses: (1976), 229, 230
   (1981/84/87), 231

Teledyne Canada, 181, 209-210

Teledyne Inc., 210

Teperman, Marvin, 195, 196-97

Tesher, Ellie, 134

Tesson Developments, 182-87, 197

Thayer, Skip, 44, 46

Thompson, Rollie, 224

Tierney, Robert, 89, 90-92

Tikkanen, Esa, 165, 166

Tim Horton Donuts, 235

Timbrell, Dennis, 267

Tkaczuk, Walt, 162

Toronto Maple Leafs, 24, 43, 56, 65, 69, 70, 75, 106, 115, 121, 136, 169, 173, 174, 181, 205, 247, 254

Toronto Rifles, 208

Toronto Star, 121, 134, 209, 252-53, 257, 268

Toronto Sun, 124, 181, 201, 252, 260, 262

Toronto Sun Publishing Company, 124

Toronto Transit Commission, 181

Travel insurance. *See* Insurance
Trottier, Bryan, 37-38, 40, 112, 161, 176
Trudeau, Pierre, 144
Tuele, Bill, 215
Turco, Anthony, 155
Turnbull, Ian, 65-66

U

Ullman, Norm, 115, 162
Ungerman, Howard, 181, 184-85, 190,
    191, 194-95, 217, 233, 234, 242, 268
Ungerman, Irving, 149, 188, 190, 195, 196,
    211, 234, 241, 267, 268
U.S. Department of Justice, 166, 167, 210,
    246, 250
U.S. Department of Labor, 38, 166, 167
U.S. Internal Revenue Service (IRS),
    122, 148
U.S. National Labor Relations Board, 160
U.S. Racketeering, Influence and Corrupt
    Organizations (RICO) laws, 246
USA Today, 39

V

Vachon, Rogie, 164
Vancouver Blazers, 180
Vancouver Canucks, 75, 76, 83, 118, 154,
    172
Vancouver Province, 262
Vedatsky, Robert J., 76-77
Veitch, Darren, 84
Verbeek, Pat, 36, 41, 117, 120, 161, 177,
    185
Voyageur Insurance Company of Canada,
    202
Voyageur Travel Insurance, 100, 101-5

W

Walter, Ryan, 36, 117, 185
Walton, Mike, 206, 267
Warren, Bernard J., 80, 81, 83-84, 85-87,
    89, 90, 92, 95, 97-98, 99, 100-101,
    102-3, 105, 135, 201, 202, 260
Washington Capitals, 55, 84, 163, 172, 192
Watson, Harry, 108

Watters, Bill, 10, 69-70, 74, 94, 147, 153,
    157, 193, 220-21, 261
Weider, George, 189, 191
Wells, Dalton C., 208
Wells, Tom, 181, 201, 202
Wendling, Flora, 190
Wesley, Glen, 29, 120
West, Jim, 240
Western Broadcasting, 172
Westfall, Eddie, 16, 125, 127, 162, 193
Westin Harbour Castle Hotel, 235
White, Bill, 54, 55
Wieder, Jozo, 189
Wilson, Doug, 177
William J. Sutton & Company, 65, 80,
    89, 96
Wilson, Doug, 176
Wilson, Murrary, 72-73
Wilson, Ralph, 209
Wilson, William, 182
Windsor Spitfires, 168, 173
Winnipeg Jets, 9, 50, 172
Winter, Rich, 13, 18, 110-11, 154-56, 165,
    166, 223, 245, 260, 264
Wirtz, Bill, 19, 25, 34, 46, 52, 56, 83, 84,
    106, 142, 143, 144, 145, 148, 151-52,
    153, 169, 170, 175, 176, 179, 208,
    209, 267
Wirtz Corporation, 52, 151
Wirtz Insurance Agency Inc., 52
World Hockey Association (WHA), 8, 9,
    25, 26, 32, 50, 156, 164, 180-81
    See also NHL-WHA merger World
    Hockey Association Players'
    Association, 65, 70, 159, 229
Worsley, Gump, 128

Y

York, Marty, 129, 132
York University (sports injury clinic), 129,
    132-34, 219

Z

Zarins, Bert, 69
Ziegler, John, 35, 38, 46, 65, 127, 128,

170, 172, 178, 179, 202
class-action suit against, 267
and Hockey Hall of Fame selection
   com., 56
 and insurance coverage, position on,
   29, 59, 61, 63, 93, 94-94
and internatinal hockey, 21, 214, 230
letter to players (1991), 123, 160
response to, 124
 and "Merry Christmas letter " (to
   Brewer), 107, 109
and pension surplus, position on, 30,
   113-14, 116, 120-21
and Pimlico Road (London) apartment,
   97-99
player perception of, 63, 106, 123, 125
and relationship with Alan Eagleson, 9,
   19, 20, 88, 101, 169, 176, 192
rules on Jim Harrison dispute, 47
subpoenaed by FBI, 244
Zigler, Mark, 30-31, 109-10, 111, 120,
   126, 127,266

This book was designed and typeset by
James Ireland Design Inc., Toronto, Canada.

The text is set in 10 point Méridien with 6 point
leading to a measure of 26 1/2 picas. Méridien is
a classically influenced serif typeface developed
by the Swiss designer, Adrian Frutiger, in 1955.
The headline type, Univers Ultra Condensed,
was also designed by Frutiger and first appeared
in the year 1957.